# Extravagant Expectations

## BOOKS BY PAUL HOLLANDER

The Only Super Power

Political Violence (editor)

The End of Commitment

From the Gulag to the Killing Fields (editor)

Understanding Anti-Americanism (editor)

Discontents: Postmodern and Postcommunist

Political Will and Personal Belief

Anti-Americanism

Decline and Discontent

The Survival of the Adversary Culture

The Many Faces of Socialism

Political Pilgrims

Soviet and American Society

American and Soviet Society (editor)

# Extravagant Expectations

*New Ways to Find Romantic Love in America*

Paul Hollander

**IVAN R. DEE**
Chicago

Published by Ivan R. Dee
A wholly owned subsidiary of The Rowman & Littlefield Publishing Group, Inc.
4501 Forbes Boulevard, Suite 200, Lanham, Maryland 20706
http://www.rowmanlittlefield.com

Estover Road, Plymouth PL6 7PY, United Kingdom

Distributed by National Book Network

www.ivanrdee.com

Library of Congress Cataloging-in-Publication Data:

Hollander, Paul, 1932–
   Extravagant expectations : new ways to find romantic love in America / Paul
Hollander.
      p. cm.
   Includes index.
   ISBN 978-1-56663-777-0 (cloth : alk. paper) — ISBN 978-1-56663-934-7 (electronic)
   1. Man-woman relationships—United States. 2. Mate selection—United States. 3.
Love—United States. 4. Personals—United States. I. Title.
   HQ801.H7155 2011
   306.73'40973—dc22                                                2010048051

# Contents

# Preface

In light of the differences between this book and others I have written, an explanation is in order to account for my change of direction. Unlike my other books, which involved political themes and messages, the subject of this volume has none, and it does not seek to confirm any predisposition.

During most of my career as a political sociologist, I was a student of Communist systems and later a sociologist of ideas, becoming eventually what may be described as a sociologically inclined intellectual historian. I have written extensively about Western, especially American, intellectuals, their political attitudes and beliefs, and their critiques of Western societies and of American society in particular. My background—I am a native of Hungary and left there in my early twenties—readily explains these preoccupations. Personal experiences find their way to scholarly interests. While growing up in Hungary, my experiences included World War II, Nazism, Soviet-style Communism, and finally the Revolution of 1956.

Throughout my life and scholarly career I have been interested in— indeed morbidly fascinated by—the conflict between illusion and reality, the apparent and the real. Not surprisingly, this interest has also been linked to the phenomenon of deception and self-deception, both at the individual and the collective (or institutional) levels. While living in Hungary I had prolonged (and apparently indelible) experiences of political propaganda as the major institutional source and conveyor of illusions; later in the United States I found commercial advertising playing a similar role. Both phenomena were highly intrusive and impossible to ignore.

My interest in these matters found expression in writing about the political illusions and self-deception of many Western intellectuals who persuaded themselves of the admirable qualities of Communist systems. I have also written about political propaganda and commercial advertising. The apolitical celebrity cult in American society also belongs to such phenomena, since those addicted to it are beholden to the illusion that they are admiring overpowering greatness of some kind when in fact there is little of it in the objects of these fleeting devotions.

Both political propaganda and commercial advertising misrepresent, distort, or at best stretch reality. Both attempt to conceal or obfuscate the difference between the way things are as opposed to the way they ought to be, or could be, as seen and desired by the propagandist or advertiser. Here I part company with my postmodernist academic colleagues who question the existence of objective reality altogether. Without a belief in objective reality, one could not propose that propaganda and advertising misrepresent and distort reality, one could merely note with apparent detachment that each has its own ways to present and represent "reality."

Unlike postmodernists—we might as well call them relativists—I continue to believe that while *perceptions* and *interpretations* of social, political, economic, and other realities vary, the realities exist regardless of how they are perceived. For example, and contrary to the message of innumerable advertisements, human happiness and fulfillment cannot be attained by the prudent purchase and use of certain types of shampoo, deodorant, or laxative; and the possession of a powerful and shiny car will not make us more youthful.

Both propaganda and advertising deliberately and determinedly misrepresent the world but in somewhat different ways and with different purposes. Understanding the persistence of these deceptions, both the commercial and political varieties, and the willingness to devote huge resources to their propagation, despite their obvious untruths, remains a challenge for social scientists.

My doctoral dissertation was the first written expression of my interests in propaganda and the illusions it seeks to create. It dealt with Soviet socialist realist literature[1] and its presentation of both virtuous and evil human beings (called the positive and negative heroes). These deliberate, politically inspired misrepresentations and the associated idealization of socio-political reality were, of course, a form of political propaganda. There was hardly any connection between the literary representation of these archetypes and actual Soviet people, nor between the social environment and institutions depicted in these novels and the nature of Soviet society and its existing institutions.

It is a long way from these preoccupations to a study of the pursuit of romantic personal relationships, but there are some elusive connections. One link has been my long-standing interest in classical romantic (as well as nonromantic) literature, which portrays the goals and expectations of men and women who are involved in romantic relationships and who personify romantic values. Romantic love involves illusions and idealization as well as high and unrealistic expectations about human beings and relationships. Regrettably enough, reality rarely supports a belief in enduring romantic attitudes and involvements.

More specifically, my interest in writing this book can be traced to the "personals" published over a long period of time in the New York Review of Books. I have found these notices implausible and puzzling, defying common sense and credibility. I kept asking myself: Do such people (those who describe themselves in the personals) really exist, and if they do, why would they need to advertise their overpowering, self-evident attractions? These self-presentations, most of them by women, seem to embody illusions and illusory self-conceptions, to say the least. They are also highly patterned and surprisingly standardized. I found the phenomenon interesting enough to write an article about it some years ago.[2] Later I came upon a book that was an anthology of such advertisements culled from the London Review of Books, a British publication quite similar to the New York Review and seemingly modeled on it. This book was not a study of the phenomenon but a humorous compilation of such advertisements with a brief introduction.[3] It occurred to me that there might be room for a serious study of the phenomenon, including its increasingly popular electronic version. My publisher, Ivan Dee, agreed and encouraged the undertaking.

An additional motive for embarking on this project is my interest in the society where I have spent most of my adult life—its customs, institutions, and problems. This ethnographic curiosity reinforces the classical sociological interest in the relationship between the social and personal realms of life. How, and to what degree, do social forces, institutions, and cultural trends shape or influence personal lives and attitudes, including their most intimate aspects which involve emotional and sexual connections with other human beings?[4]

Despite having spent most of my adult life in the United States—half a century, to be precise—I have never taken for granted many characteristics of American society. The customs of this country have remained to me matters of great curiosity, including American ways of looking for a romantic partner. This investigation has allowed me to combine my interest in romanticism, illusion, and reality, and the empirical question of how people in present-day America try to establish important and intimate relationships and what expectations and values they bring to this quest. These matters, needless to say, are linked to the much-discussed phenomenon of loneliness or social isolation in modern American society and its connection with the pursuit of romantic love. Romantic relationships promise the dramatic alleviation of loneliness while gratifying the individualistic desire for self-fulfillment.

It is important to make clear that in this study I have not attempted to find out how successful are the present-day attempts—mostly online and in printed messages—to initiate romantic and long-term relationships. Nor have I tried to speculate about their success rates in comparison with older, more conventional ways that are still with us: face-to-face meetings in various settings and introductions, planned or by chance. Even more difficult, if not altogether impossible, would have been to compare the durability of long-term nonmarital relationships based on these different ways of meeting. Another book could be written about the experiences of people who take different paths to the same goal, about their respective accomplishments and failures. Instead in this study I try to bring together new information about the beliefs and preferences that shape the love life and emotional aspirations of Americans, their connection to larger sociocultural forces, and the difficulties they experience at the intersection of personal wants and cultural pressures.

I am grateful to the Bradley Foundation for a research grant that enabled me to hire research assistants and cover other research expenses. Teresa Kenyon, who was at Smith College when she worked with me, ably assisted with the quantitative data collection and analysis; Emily Huesman, also of Smith, helped with library research and the solution of computer problems. Both were thorough and dependable.

I discussed the subject of this book with several friends and colleagues, including some who have sought to find partners online with different degrees of success. Some of them read the manuscript and offered helpful comments. David Popenoe and Barbara Dafoe Whitehead, well-known specialists in the study of the family and contemporary personal relationships in America, encouraged my undertaking and read the manuscript. Their comments and critiques have made this a better book than it would otherwise have been.

Martin Whyte at Harvard University, an expert on the comparative study of the family, made many excellent suggestions and helped restrain my generalizations about tradition and modernity. Several friends and former colleagues at the University of Massachusetts, Amherst, also read the manuscript and provided a wide variety of helpful and thoughtful comments—Jay Demerath, Christopher Hurn, Michael Lewis, and Sue Model, all sociologists. Daphne Patai, also of the University of Massachusetts, Amherst, a student of literature and American culture, was another reader who shared with me her keen observations. I further benefited from the comments of a nonacademic friend, Anthony Daniels, a British psychiatrist and wide-ranging social critic.

Paul Hollander
Northampton, Massachusetts
September 2010

# Extravagant Expectations

# CHAPTER ONE

# Introduction: From Arranged Marriage to Social Isolation

For most of history it was inconceivable that people would choose their mates on the basis of something as fragile and irrational as love.

Stephanie Coontz[1]

We are confronted by the spectacle of innumerable individuals seeking to escape from the very processes of individualism and impersonality which nineteenth-century rationalists hailed as the very condition of progress. . . . There is a growing appeal of pseudo-intimacy with others, a . . . pathetic dependence on the superficial symbols of friendship and association.

Robert Nisbet[2]

This book is an attempt to shed light on three major questions. The first one concerns the influence of romantic ideals and ideas on personal relationships and, more generally, the extent to which stereotypical romantic ideals have survived in modern American society. Are Americans in search of durable, intimate relationships still motivated by expectations of romantic fulfillment, and if they are, how similar or different are these ideals and expectations from corresponding ideals of the past?

Secondly, how do people go about looking for partners in present-day American society, and in what ways do these methods and approaches differ from the conventional ones?

Thirdly, I was most interested in what kind of human qualities or attributes are most highly valued in prospective partners and how these preferences find expression in printed "personals," Internet dating messages, and "relationship books" or self-help literature that seek to advise readers about the most desirable human qualities essential for long-term, fulfilling relationships.

Chapter 1 seeks to sketch the broad social-historical background of the differences in the processes of mate selection in traditional as opposed to modern societies, with special reference to the problems associated with modernity and the rise and growing domination of individualism. Chapter 2 examines the major attributes of the romantic worldview and mindset as originally formulated and expressed in European and American novels of the nineteenth and twentieth century. Chapter 3 delineates what I call the popular romanticism that emerged in twentieth-century American society, with special reference to popular culture and advertising. Chapter 4 offers a substantial sampling of the self-help literature and the advice it offers about the methods and goals of finding fulfilling personal relationships. Chapter 5 examines a sampling of printed messages in various publications designed to initiate romantic relationships. Chapters 6, 7, and 8 present regional Internet samplings of a major dating site and the attitudes and values these communications reflect. Chapter 9 summarizes the findings of the book, emphasizing the impact of individualism and modernity on romantic ideals and intimate personal relationships.

Loneliness is a modern idea and state of mind. I have been well aware that there are many lonely people in America, along with a bewildering array of efforts devised, or improvised, to alleviate loneliness. It was far from evident why this should be the case in a society that began as one dedicated to maximizing individual happiness, and that still provides unusual opportunities to improve one's live. Moreover, it continues to attract millions of people from every corner of the world. Clearly, idealistic and benign socio-political intentions and arrangements have been compatible with a great deal of individual unhappiness. This paradox was thought-provoking and among the stimulants for undertaking this study. More specifically, it led me to ponder the quality and survival of romantic love in America, especially in comparison with earlier incarnations of the romantic mindset that found literary expression in classical European novels.

I also hoped to shed light on the apparent combination of a widespread—if diluted—romanticism prevalent in American society (portrayed and promoted by popular culture) with the practical, pragmatic, and hardnosed attributes of individual Americans. I was curious to learn what today's Americans expect from romantic relationships, how they go about finding them, and, most important, what kinds of human qualities they value most highly and look for in potential long-term partners. I had a particular interest in the relationship between American-style individualism and the romantic outlook, and I assumed that the former helps to explain the latter.

As a dutiful sociologist, I also wished to learn more about the sociocultural influences that play a part in the pursuit of romantic relationships and find expression in the huge volume of self-help, advisory literature ("relationship books") and electronic communications provided by self-styled experts.

I had one rather unoriginal preconception about the love life of Americans: that it is troubled, that high expectations are common and often unmet, and that it is marked by an increasing amount of confusion and conflicting desires and preferences. I also sensed that individualism, in combination with identity problems, simultaneously promotes and undermines durable romantic relationships, if indeed there is such a thing as durable romance.

## Making Connections

Making enduring connections with other human beings is a universal and quintessential requirement of our existence. It is not only a matter of perpetuating the species; human relationships are essential for our physical and psychic survival and well-being. To say that humans are social animals suggests the importance of belonging to a group but does not express the need for one-on-one connections and relationships, especially between men and women. While these needs are universal, the ways in which they are gratified, or the attempts to gratify them, vary greatly by time and place.

The needs themselves diverge—that is, what human beings seek in one another varies over time and place, notwithstanding certain basic similarities. Probably the major differences between these needs can be found between traditional and modern societies, but there are also innumerable cultural differences *within* different traditional and modern societies. At the same time our shared biological heritage imposes certain uniformities and limitations on such variability. A study by David M. Buss of "international preferences in selecting mates" in thirty-seven cultures finds that "despite . . . cultural and sexual variations there were strong similarities among cultures and between sexes on the preference ordering of mate characteristics. This implies a degree of psychological unity, or species-typicality, of humans that transcends geographical, racial, political, ethnic, and sexual diversity."[3]

For example, it is difficult to find a predominantly cultural explanation of the fact that tallness in men is an important attraction for women and that

"tall men tend to have a higher status in nearly all cultures." Nor are conceptions of beauty as culturally variable as one might think, despite the wide
range of social and historical differences in clothing and self-decoration.
Again, Buss writes, "Many people hold . . . that standards of beauty are
arbitrary . . . that cultures differ dramatically in the importance they place
on appearance, and that Western standards stem from brainwashing by the
media, parents, culture, or other agents of socialization. But standards of attractiveness are not arbitrary—they reflect cues to youth and health . . . to
reproductive value."[4]

Methods of mate selection have parallels even in the animal kingdom:
"Just as weaver-birds display their nests and scorpion flies their nuptial gifts,
men and women must advertise their wares on the mating market."[5]

Highly patterned similarities often transcend cultural or temporal differences in the priorities of men and women in different cultures. Thus, "More
than females, males prefer mates who are physically attractive. More than
males, females prefer mates who show ambition, industriousness, and other
signs of earning potential. These differences appear to be the most robust
psychological sex differences of any kind to be documented across cultures."[6]

Highly patterned preferences based on sex have also been found in a study
limited to the United States:

> Men are more willing than women to engage in sexual relations in the absence
> of emotional involvement and marital potential, and are more likely to seek
> sexual relations with a number of partners for the sake of variety. Men are
> more readily aroused sexually than women by visual stimuli. When choosing
> partners for sex or marriage, men place more emphasis than women on physical
> attractiveness and women place more emphasis than men on socioeconomic
> status. . . .
>
> The present findings are consistent with an evolutionary view of sex differ-
> ences in sexuality and mate selection. Men are motivated to seek sexual rela-
> tions with physically attractive women, whereas women are motivated to seek
> high levels of investment [i.e., commitment].[7]

Evidence of this divergent emotional disposition of men and women has
also been documented in the most comprehensive national survey of sexual
practices undertaken in the United States. It indicates that "48% of women
have intercourse for the first time out of 'affection for their partner,' compared to only 25% of men."[8] Further data supporting these gender differences
has been reported by Helen Fisher: "American men who place courtship
ads in newspapers and magazine are three times more likely than women to

mention that they seek beauty in a partner"—a finding that has been interpreted as a subconscious reference for "reproductive payoffs."[9] The different priorities of women have in turn been captured by a survey of eight hundred printed advertisements, which finds that "American women sought partners who offered financial security twice as frequently as men did."[10] Another study of such newspaper advertisements reaches similar conclusions: "Overall the results indicate that gender-stereotypic behavior persists as evidenced by exchange of physical characteristics, attractiveness, financial security and the age desired in a partner. . . . Men were more likely to seek younger women, whereas women were more likely to seek older men."[11]

A longitudinal study of Americans from 1939 to 1996 concludes that

> for both men and women there appeared to be an overall increase . . . in the value of mutual attraction and love, education and intelligence, sociability and good looks. In contrast there appeared to be a general decrease in the valuation of refinement, neatness and chastity for both men and women. . . . Men placed a higher premium than did women on good health, being a good cook and housekeeper, and good looks. In contrast, women placed a higher premium on . . . ambition and industriousness, similar educational background and financial prospects.[12]

The importance of physical attractiveness in women is also reflected in the 2003 finding that "the fastest-growing segment of the cosmetic surgery market is women in their 20s and 30s. . . . There is competition in the mating market. . . . Both young men and women today place a much higher value on physical attractiveness and sexiness in a mate than in years past."[13]

If indeed the preoccupation with women's physical attractiveness has increased—notwithstanding the ground gained by feminism that seeks to deemphasize it—it may be attributed to several factors. Most important may be our egalitarian ethos that pervades popular culture and advertising and conveys the message that everyone can be beautiful, that beauty can be acquired by diligence and effort, and that we all are endlessly perfectible in every respect. The American belief in the solubility of all problems supports this ethos. Another factor is the greater participation of women in the workforce and their consequent higher discretionary income that allows them to invest in improving their looks by cosmetics, clothing, or plastic surgery.

Popular culture supports beautification by endlessly disseminating images of beauty and physical attractiveness and thereby providing models to emulate. Advertising directly encourages preoccupation with looks and offers an endless supply of products that supposedly will beautify their users.

The apparent increase of sexual activity among the young that is devoid of emotional involvement (i.e., "hooking up") further enhances the importance of looks, which are bound to play a greater part in the initiation of such encounters.

The other major explanation of the preoccupation with physical attractiveness is the growth and spread of individualism. Individualism involves focusing and placing high value on oneself; it also entails the wish and the imperative to feel good about oneself. Self-esteem is an essential part of contemporary American individualism and encourages a concern with self-improvement that has a psychic as well as a physical dimension.

The centrality of physical attraction and attractiveness remains one of the links between different approaches to mate selection across different cultures and periods of history.

## Rules versus Choices

The most obvious difference between past and present practices that promote or lead to durable relationships (mainly marriage) between men and women is that until quite recently these pursuits used to be meticulously regulated by a vast range of rules and rituals, and by the opinions and beliefs of the groups or communities to which the individuals seeking or embarking on such relationships belonged. For example, in Africa, according to Max Gluckman, a large "number of special customs and taboos . . . attach to the relations between spouses. . . . African domestic life . . . seems to be full of special observances and ceremonies. . . . There is a whole series of rules to regularize relations within the family." Kinship ties outside marriage remain of great importance "so that emotional bonds in marriage do not outweigh other ties."[14] Among the Nuer of the Sudan, as reported by E. E. Evans-Pritchard,

> Displays of spearmanship and dueling with the club are major ways to impress the females. It is further required that a young man "be profuse and tireless in pouring out compliments to the girl whose favor he solicits, and he often sits opposite her with a stick in his hand to make lines on the ground to mark each new compliment." The possession of cattle by the man is a precondition of marriage.[15]

The aboriginal inhabitants of the Arnhem Land in Australia allow only "after preliminary betrothal arrangements have been made by parents and relatives, the two prospective spouses . . . [to] be shown to each other." Quali-ties sought by women in prospective spouses among these groups include

> their capacity to work . . . being a good hunter or fisherman . . . ability to in-dulge in fairly frequent coitus . . . (penis size is important here) . . . attractive physique and features. . . .
> [Men were looking for women] . . . with a good physically fit body, not too thin, with firm breasts, not lazy, a good domestic worker, industrious food gath-erer . . . capable of bearing children, sexually ardent but modest before other men and not promiscuous; obedient and dutiful to near kin, good tempered.

In Tikopia, a small isolated island in the Western Pacific, arranged mar-riages are preceded by "a trial period of courtship, and experimentation as lovers." There is also a "distinct predilection for taking their spouses from locations close at hand."

Among the Papago Indians of southern Arizona, "marriage had nothing to do with romance. . . . The couple in their early teens might never have seen each other until . . . the nuptial night." The bride's parents would look for "a family with a son of the right age who was industrious and brave, a good farmer, a good hunter, or both if possible. Good looks and charm were not considered." Relatives would also be consulted. Of the female, it was required that she be "industrious, help her mother-in-law and obey her husband . . . and submit to all he asked."

In Tibet in the past, horoscopes of the candidates for marriage were pre-pared, house calls were made by the parents of the bridegroom at the home of the bride, and presents were given to her parents. "All relatives on both sides take part in this ritual." In traditional families in India, three major rules are observed for marriage: that it take place early in life, preferably before the puberty of the female; that it be within the same caste group; and that it be arranged by elders and "not a result of mutual selection by the boy and girl concerned."

In the traditional Japanese family, marriages have been arranged by families with the help of go-betweens. Before the bride and groom meet, and to ensure the success of the union, "both families discussed the matter thoroughly and quietly investigated each other through friends and, in some cases, a number of private detectives."[16]

According to a more recent study of Japanese marriage before World War II, "most marriages were . . . arranged in the literal sense of the word. Partners were selected by the parents in consultation with relatives or friends of their own generation." Family interests played a major part in the prominence of parental influence since "marriage indexed the family's social standing. . . . Matches tended to follow lines of class and occupational status closely. . . . But the larger significance of parental control over marriage lay . . . in its congruence with prewar values stressing the subordination of the individual to the larger group."[17]

Similar patterns used to prevail in Korea, and some of them have survived to recent times. A 1982 book "describes marriage through an arranged meeting as more 'rational' behavior than simply falling in love because the candidates for romance and matrimony have already been carefully scrutinized by parents and matchmakers." In preindustrial Korea, "marriage was once exclusively a family matter determined by those who regarded a potential bride as a source of labor. . . . A Korean wife's abilities as a hard worker and frugal manager were recognized as a measure of the prosperity, harmony, and reputation of her household." In the 1950s in the capital city of Seoul, arrangements were sometimes made for the potential groom and his parents to view covertly the intended spouse: "a meeting would be arranged at the woman's house, where she would be told to fetch some water or perform some task so that the groom and his parents could observe her attitude, bearing, and speech."[18]

Such utilitarian attitudes toward marriage were not confined to the non-Western world. Marriage in fifteenth-century Florence, for example, was not about love. It involved money, property, class, political affiliation, and family prestige.[19]

None of this is to suggest that practical considerations are absent today, but they are no longer primary, nor fully respectable, and not readily acknowledged. This is reflected in the criteria for good relationships stipulated in the printed and online messages examined later.

Clearly, in traditional societies people did not select each other as a matter of personal preference. In these societies "it was generally agreed that young people of marriageable age were too inexperienced to have sound judgment in such an important undertaking."[20] Until the rise of modernity and its associated individualism, mate selection was not a matter of individual attraction and choice. As explained by William Fielding,

> The feelings of young people were not consulted or considered. The girls were usually betrothed and married so young that they were settled in the rigors of domestic life before they had an opportunity to develop romantic inclinations. Marriages were planned to strengthen the family position, to increase its economic importance . . . there was little courtship or wooing. . . . Romantic courtship did not exist—that is, the pre-marital love of one individual for another of his choice.

The custom of betrothing unborn children was the most striking mani-festation of such indifference to the feelings of those who would become couples: "In New Caledonia girls were betrothed at birth. In the Fiji islands it was the custom until recently . . . to marry the children when the infant bride and groom are only three or four years old."[21]

While in traditional societies the criteria for mate selection were pre-dominantly utilitarian, in modern societies far more elusive and intangible emotional considerations play a large part. Moreover there used to be far greater consensus about the desirable attributes of spouses than there now is. Stephanie Coontz, a historian of marriage, has noted, "Until the late eighteenth century, most societies around the world saw marriage as far too vital an economic and political institution to be left entirely to the free choice of two individuals, especially if they were going to base their decision on something as unreasoning and transitory as love."[22] And, "The modern Western ideal of marriage as both romantic and companionate is an anomaly and gamble. As soon as people in any culture start selecting spouses based on emotion, the rates of broken marriages shoot up."[23]

What used to be the prevalence of a double standard for male and female sexuality is another telling difference between traditional and modern social norms. As recently as 1971 the author of a best-selling book, the psychia-trist David Reuben, could write that "*sexual fulfillment* is officially denied to every adult female who is single, widowed or divorced. . . . Before a modern woman is allowed to use the equipment she was born with, she must, in ef-fect, find a man to sponsor her, obtain a copulation permit—diplomatically known as a marriage license—and officially file her intention to have sexual intercourse."[24]

Even today the highly individualistic and emotionally determined ap-proach to mate selection is limited to Western societies. And even in those societies, the anthropologist Suzanne Frayser has observed, "Marriage is not usually a transaction confined to the bride and groom. It extends beyond them, to include members of their families or kin groups. In most societies, the families of the bride and groom (52% of 58 societies) or the kin groups of both (35% of 58 societies) play an important role in the initiation of marriage."[25] Even in Western societies there remain (or have reemerged) pockets of tradition—as in the growing Muslim communities of Western Europe—and arranged marriages are by no means a thing of the distant past.[26] Sometimes modern methods are used to perpetuate traditional cus-toms, as in newspaper advertisements in Saudi Arabia posted by "parents seeking husbands for their daughters."[27] In South Korea, according to the

*New York Times*, the matchmaking tradition is sustained by Internet match-making services and more than a thousand dating agencies:

> Even now marriage is widely viewed as a contract between two families, and parents often take charge. They check the candidates' looks, education, income and horoscope. On weekends young men and women might face each other awkwardly in a hotel restaurant after being dragged there by their parents for a matchmaking session.[28]

In contemporary India the blending of traditional and Western ideas finds expression in the wider acceptance of divorce and the existence of marriage bureaus that advertise in Sunday papers. Still, "for the most part relatives come to sign up their kin, as older brothers and fathers and aunts would in the case of a traditional first marriage." The marriage bureaus remain very much concerned with "old-fashioned details: caste, income, whether vegetarian—and the exact time of birth for astrological purposes."[29] Even in the United States, in a remarkable combination of modernity and tradition, marriages are sometimes arranged with the help of websites by Indian parents seeking husbands for their offspring or by placing notices in immigrant newspapers. A young Indian American woman explains, "Indians of my mother's generation . . . like to say of arranged marriage, 'It's not that there isn't love. It's just that it comes after marriage.'"[30]

Another important difference between traditional and modern mate selection is that in traditional societies older people did not marry or remarry, or seek to establish long-term romantic and sexual relationships outside marriage. By contrast, in modern societies, especially in America, people enter into and experiment with new relationships and marriages well into their advanced years. A woman aged sixty-seven chronicled her relationships based on advertisements in the *New York Review of Books*.[31] The popular writer Gail Sheehy claims (rather implausibly) that a "Romantic renaissance" is taking place, with older single women "seeking romance again, declaring their right to sexual satisfaction and dreaming new dreams. . . . Long-married women . . . [are] also waking up to the possibilities of postmenopausal sensuality."[32] Such experimentation is an essential part of individualism, indeed a major expression of it, and illustrates the dream of self-realization, or self-fulfillment, the open-ended, self-conscious pursuit of happiness through intimate personal relationships.

Although tenaciously resisted, aging, even in present-day American society, casts a shadow on these pursuits. As Christopher Lasch points out, "In a society that dreads old age and death, aging holds a special terror for those who fear dependence and whose self-esteem requires the admiration usually reserved for youth, beauty, celebrity, or charm."[33] These apprehensions are accurately reflected in the tone and content of the "personals" in which people advertise their availability, their needs, and what they purport to offer. The latter includes attributes not typical of the middle aged and elderly: inexhaustible energy, an endless supply of good cheer, zest, spontaneity, and exuberance.

To sum up, durable relationships in the modern world are not limited to marriage and are initiated and established by the participants, not their relatives or their community. Far more mechanisms or methods are now available for choosing partners—for either short- or long-term relationships, including marriage—than used to be the case. Introductions by friends or relatives remain popular and involve an element of preselection or screening by third parties.

More typical of the modern ways of making contact with strangers are the opportunities created by proximity. Men and women study or work together and participate jointly in various recreational, cultural, religious, or political activities that also serve the purpose of socializing and mate selection. Total strangers can get acquainted in public places—in bars, museums, libraries, at sporting events, even on the street—without being disgraced. This approach, the pickup, is not governed by established and internalized rules but is improvised and random, stimulated by appearance—by the physical aspects of the parties involved.

## Contemporary Arrangements

The absence of a compelling or self-evident method of mate selection in modern societies accounts for the proliferation of organizations, businesses, and services that specialize in bringing strangers together. These include dating services, websites, printed publications, importers of mail-order brides from abroad, modern matchmakers, and "relationship experts" who dispense advice and guidance in writing and on the air. Today a vast number of connections can be made with ease, especially with the help of the Internet, which has both "expanded people's options and allowed them to be far more direct in expressing their desires."[34] A novel aspect of these methods is that they prompt the individuals using them to consider and specify their needs and expectations for intimate, romantic relationships. They are also expected to provide credible information of their own personalities—their strengths and perhaps their weaknesses as well. The new organizations and services that cater to these needs, and especially the online sites and services, represent collectively a new response to mate selection that is no longer met by conventional social arrangements and institutions.[35]

The sheer size and configuration of modern urban societies foster impersonality and isolation and magnify the demand for these new services. Urban settings are marked by a sharp contrast between the vast numbers of strangers one has little chance to meet—people seen on the street, on buses, in the subway, in shops and other public places—and the greatly circumscribed access to potential partners among these throngs of people. Many of them, it is easy to imagine, could gratify pressing social, emotional, and sexual needs. The wide variety of personals, both print and online, reach out to these otherwise largely unapproachable strangers.

David Brooks is among those who have recognized the problems created by the new ways of replacing the old pursuit of romantic partners:

> Once upon a time . . . courtship was governed by a set of guardrails. Potential partners generally met within the context of larger social institutions: neighborhoods, schools, workplaces and families. There were certain accepted social scripts. . . . Over the past decades these social scripts became obsolete. . . . Suitors now contact each other . . . separate from larger social institutions and commitments.
>
> People are thrown back on themselves. They are free agents in a competitive arena. . . . People once lived within a pattern. . . . The accumulated wisdom of the community steered couples.[36]

Perhaps to compensate for these new difficulties, even in present-day American society there remain matchmaking agencies which seek to combine traditional and modern methods by using large databases and attempting to apply social-psychological criteria to establish the compatibility of potential mates. Often these new matchmakers take a traditional approach. They believe, Melanie Thernstrom writes, that people "should marry within their tribes." They have "a deep distrust of romance . . . [and] believe that people should stop their agonized search for soul mates. . . . They have a finely honed ability to . . . classify people anthropologically and according to socioeconomic type and pair them off accordingly." Matchmakers often cater to high-income clients, chiefly men willing to pay $20,000 initiation fees or a minimum $10,000 for twelve dates with beautiful women. In effect these matchmakers are substitutes for relatives seeking to arrange marriages for clients who "like having their romantic lives managed by individuals of apparent expertise and authority."[37]

Another new development that partakes of traditional elements is the emergence of the paid dating coach (called by some a "love life manager"), who advises and trains would-be daters. Like the matchmaker, this individual too is an authority figure whose advice and instructions are expected to carry weight with clients. "Unlike matchmakers," reports the *New York Times*, "[they] do not arrange dates. Instead they act as cheerleaders and advisers, pointing out less than helpful behavior." One of them declares, "I treat it like a job hunt." Sometimes the coach offers "an image makeover" at $125 per session (or hour) and may spend an entire weekend with a client for $5,000 to $10,000.[38]

Resembling high-class prostitution, an online service (SeekingArrange ment.com) provides contacts between attractive young women and wealthy older (often married) men willing to pay large amounts for a regular, long-term relationship that combines sex with intimacy.[39]

Dating services have in common with printed personals and Internet dating sites a reliance on explicit specifications of what is being offered and what is sought. They employ impartial intermediaries who make judgments about the presumed compatibility of the interested parties based on the information they present. In theory such services could be successful if they benefited from psychological theories and findings about the sources of human compatibility—assuming that such theories and findings are available.

It is difficult even to speculate about the contribution these new methods make to the establishment of durable romantic relationships. On one hand, online communications and modern matchmakers with large databases can help gratify very specific needs and could, in theory, create better matches, reducing the trial-and-error aspects of the process. On the other hand, the seeming abundance of potential partners creates new problems: people are tempted to look for marginal advantages, never knowing for sure if those selected are the optimal choice in what appears to be an endless supply of prospects.

The summary self-presentations of individuals, whether in printed form or on the Internet, may encourage their authors to present a fantasy self. In other words, these forms of communication provide limitless opportunities and temptations for misrepresentation, for presenting an idealized self-conception with modest roots in reality. Consider some recent examples (by no means exceptional), such as the following:

> Adorable smile, sophisticated good looks and sly wit. Deeply curious, successful . . . fun-loving. Sometimes daringly funny, sometimes naughty, always congenial with irresistible appeal and informed interest in the world. . . . Slender, yoga-toned, affectionate, and very real. Prolific reader. . . . Aesthetically attuned, stylish yet uncomplicated. Adventurous, outgoing . . .

A radiant beauty, intellectually curious, tall, thin, blue-eyed. Adventurous with a touch of idealism, a girl-next-door approachability and genuineness of character. Expressive, affectionate. . . . Laughs a lot, thinks deeply. . . . Likes skiing, hiking, sipping coffee in Paris, theater in London, trekking in Nepal.

Sparkling eyes—smart, slender, very very attractive and refreshingly authentic with lots of heart and an athletic passion for outdoors. Loves taking on challenges, both intellectual and outdoors . . . spontaneous and easygoing. . . . Curious with wonderful smile, lively humor, and a touch of mischief. . . . Romantic at heart.[40]

Such self-presentations, while highly informative about present-day ego ideals, raise obvious questions: If such people actually exist, why are they compelled to advertise their remarkable attractions? Is their social life so barren that it affords no opportunities to meet compatible people who would appreciate them?

If such notices lead to meetings, the participants will be in a position to compare the written self-presentations to the real thing—with what results we do not know and cannot guess. Nor do we know what proportion of misrepresentations are instantly recognized, or how many others require more time to reveal themselves. Are contacts rapidly aborted when they rest on misrepresentations, or at any rate on questionable self-conceptions?

Both printed personals and Internet dating services are emblematic of modern consumer society: they offer a bewildering abundance and variety of choice, raise questions about the truthfulness of claims made on behalf of the "products" or "services" offered, and stoke the expectations of potential consumers.

While the differences between past and current mate selection are striking and obvious, even in modern societies, though individual preferences dominate the process, these preferences are to a considerable degree standardized and influenced by prevailing cultural values. There are, in addition, "deeply ingrained, evolved psychological mechanisms that drive our mating decisions," as David Buss has noted. "Men desire youth and attractiveness in a mate" while "women desire status and economic security." Moreover, despite the apparently prevailing individualistic and romantic orientation, economic considerations continue to play an important part in mate selection, and socioeconomic compatibility is rarely overlooked. The earning power or economic security that men are expected to provide remains an important consideration for women: "Evidence from dozens of studies documents that modern American women indeed value economic resources in mates . . .

[and] women still value good financial prospects in a mate roughly twice as much as men do."[41] These findings are not incompatible with the far greater earning power and career orientation of women in contemporary American society.

Because colonial America never had a system of arranged marriage, the ideal of free, individual choice is more deeply rooted in American society than in many other modern cultures. This is not to suggest that marital choices have been random and motivated purely by emotional considerations. In America as elsewhere, marital partners tend to resemble one another in regard to race, religion, ethnicity, education, and socioeconomic status. An early study of printed personals supports the hypothesis that "people seek to establish relationships with partners whose level of social desirability closely approximates their own."[42] Further evidence suggests that spouses tend to resemble each other in level of intelligence, in values, and in attitudes.[43] Socioeconomic considerations also enter into dating practices since, as a rule, people separated by substantial class differentials rarely have the opportunity to encounter one another, let alone establish lasting relationships.

All these circumstances suggest that, notwithstanding the conscious wishes and preferences of individuals, even in modern, individualistic societies such as the American, the gratification of romantic impulses faces obstacles. Social and cultural pressures impinge on individual needs and predilections.

## Modernity, Individualism, and Social Isolation

The rise and domination of personal preference in relationships that may lead to marriage is connected to broader social and historical trends and transformations—the eclipse of traditional societies. These transformations can be traced to the Enlightenment and its rejection of traditional authorities and beliefs, which were replaced by a high valuation of the power of reason supposedly possessed by the individual.

Traditional societies were past-oriented and resistant to change; those who lived in them took for granted that one's life would closely resemble that of one's parents, grandparents, and more distant ancestors. Such unquestioned continuity was a source of considerable social and personal stability.

The decline of traditional societies is inseparable from the decline of community and the rise of individualism. Local communities declined because of geographic and social mobility, technological and economic change, and the shifting outlook of individuals. The growth of individualism played an important part in new and growing uncertainties about finding a satisfactory place in society and finding a partner for a long-term relationship based on individual preference rather than tradition. As Robert Nisbet has written, "The modern release of the individual from traditional ties of class, religion, and kinship has made him free; but . . . this freedom is accompanied not by the sense of creative release, but by the sense of disenchantment and alienation."[44] This alienation has led to growing demands on personal relationships, which are expected to compensate for the larger deficits of social bonds and communal gratifications.

In the discussion to follow, I concentrate not on the political manifestations of this alienation but on the difficulties created by a liberating individualism in establishing and maintaining committed personal relationships and, paradoxically, in developing and maintaining a satisfactory sense of identity. As it has turned out, the glorification of individual autonomy, self-sufficiency, and uniqueness has made the establishment and especially the maintenance of close and durable personal relationships more difficult and the sense of self more brittle.[45]

The most obvious consequence of the decline of traditional society has been the diminution of spheres of life governed by custom, or internalized social norms, and the corresponding decline of the types of behavior and aspirations that could be taken for granted. In traditional society it was assumed that men and women would marry at a certain age, provided they met some basic requirements, and that their unions would be arranged by parents and other relatives. The entire process was governed by clear, well-established rules. The subsequent life of the couple would likewise be guided by well-established norms regarding division of labor and distinct social roles.

Under these circumstances there were few individual choices to be made. Women did not have to agonize over choosing between family and career or how to meet suitable husbands; at what age they should marry and to what type of person; to have or not to have children, when, and how many. Neither men nor women questioned the validity of the sex roles assigned to them by their society or culture, or entertained ideas about selecting a more satisfactory sexual identity. The modern Western notion that emerged in the second half of the twentieth century, that sex roles are "socially constructed," would have elicited genuine and profound astonishment and incomprehension in any traditional society. All such matters were taken for granted and appeared to be part of a long chain of generational continuity. Alternatives to these sanctioned ways of life were neither available nor conceivable. It was an implicit assumption that the individual was not qualified to make such major decisions and choices without the assistance and initiative of his group and the prevalent, seemingly timeless values and beliefs upheld by that group.

Traditional societies, the historian David Potter writes, "tended to produce a high proportion of men and women who attained their identity by adopting, quite readily, the roles which the society expected of them"—whereas in recent times "society was losing its capacity to assign roles, by which people can achieve identities." Not surprisingly, when people experience identity problems—that is, are unsure of who they are—there will be "an even more insuperable barrier to effective interpersonal relationships."[46]

Before the rise of individualism, the historian Jacob Burckhardt writes, "Man was conscious of himself only as a member of a race, people, party, family, or corporation—only through some general category."[47] The modern sensibility is diametrically opposed to such a disposition. The essence of individualism, and especially of its American variant, is the conviction that every individual is unique. This uniqueness is the principal foundation of his or her self-esteem and sense of identity, which cannot and should not be reduced to a social role. It is "the idea that somewhere, beneath the surface . . . there lies a stable and unadulterated self . . . something essential."[48]

The rise of individualism produced unforeseen consequences that are still with us. It is Robert Nisbet's contention that the demise of traditional society—which includes the weakening of the bonds of family, local community, and church—and the related psychic dislocations and deprivations created a new sense of anxiety and insecurity and an intensified pursuit of a compensatory intimacy in personal relationships and in the small, nuclear family. The new pursuit of intimacy was also connected to the sheer size of modern urban mass society. Growing social isolation placed a great burden of expectations on marriage and the family, made heavier still by the reduction of its economic and educational functions. It is a truism among social scientists that the extraordinarily high rates of divorce and separation in modern societies reflect these high expectations, which have proved to be difficult if not impossible to meet. James Q. Wilson has suggested an adverse relationship between the degree of individual emancipation and durable marriages.[49] Nisbet, in addition, discerned a connection between a cheapened and widened romanticism (a carrier of high expectations) and commerce:

> The fantastic romanticism that now surrounds courtship and marriage in our culture is drawn in part . . . from larger contexts of romanticism in modern history and is efficiently supported by the discovery . . . that . . . romance is good for sales. . . . The diminution in the functional significance of the family has been attended by efforts to compensate in the affectional realms of intensified romance. Probably no other age in history has so completely identified (confused, some might say) marriage and romance as has our own.[50]

It has been widely held in Western societies, and especially in the United States, that the individual is endowed with a virtually limitless capacity for growth and change (always for the better, it is understood). Expanding and changing personal needs fuel and reflect this growth, or so we are led to believe by advertising, popular psychology, self-help books, and celebrity gurus advising about ways to achieve a life of contentment and success. Materially comfortable Americans take pride in their personal needs and consumption patterns, including diet, which increasingly seem to define their sense of identity, their uniqueness as individuals.

David Popenoe has summed up the impact of individualism on American cultural values and social practices:

> "Secular individualism" . . . features the gradual abandonment of religious attendance and beliefs, a strong leaning toward "expressive values" that are preoccupied with personal autonomy and self-fulfillment . . . and tolerance of diverse life-styles. . . . The greater the dominance of secular individualism in a culture, the more fragmented the families. . . . The higher the educational and income levels of a population . . . the greater the degree of secular individualism. . . . The new religious strains that have emerged in recent decades, so-called New Age religions, have been profoundly individualistic.[51]

This more recent variety of individualism has been called by some social scientists "expressive individualism." In the words of Andrew Cherlin, "It is a view of life that emphasizes the development of one's sense of self, the pursuit of emotional satisfaction and the expression of one's feelings. . . . This kind of expressive individualism has flourished as prosperity has given more Americans the time and money to develop their sense of self—to cultivate their own emotional gardens as it were."[52]

Family instability has been a major outcome of individualism as it has replaced the traditional collectivism of the past.[53] Traditional societies demanded loyalty to time-honored, prescribed social roles and social bonds, a sense of duty, and absence of concern with "self-fulfillment." By contrast, modern society is characterized by "the primacy of the personal over social goals, emotional detachment from the group, and an emphasis on self-reliance, personal autonomy, and competitiveness."[54] Affluence directly contributes to individualism since materially comfortable individuals and families depend far less on group support.

Popenoe believes (as I do) that the United States is the most individualistic society in the world today. The most telling symptoms include the growth of the number of people living alone, the declining percentage of those who are married, and the reduced numbers of people who belong to voluntary associations and even the decline of informal visits with others.[55] The connection between individualism and the present-day pursuit of romantic love will be made clear in the chapters to follow.

## Individualism and Identity

Apparently the much-sought-after unique sense of identity, or selfhood, is not easily attained, and the self-conceptions of individualistic Americans are far from stable or invariably positive. Americans regularly experience identity crises, that is to say, at times they are not sure who they are, astonishing as this may sound to those who did not grow up in this society. When in my late twenties I arrived in this country and encountered references to this phenomenon, I could not quite grasp the idea of an "identity crisis" or a problematic sense of identity. What could it possibly mean, I wondered, that people do not know who they are? It seemed to me that all of us belong to certain self-evident categories that describe and define us: our sex, age, marital status, nationality, ethnicity, religious affiliation, education, occupation, and so forth. Admittedly, belonging to these shared categories and having identical social roles makes it more difficult to insist on our uniqueness.

A major source of Americans' identity problems may be historical. In so far as the individual's sense of identity is linked to and partially based on belonging to various groups or categories of people, possessing a sense of national identity makes an important contribution to the individual's sense of identity. But the American sense of national identity is somewhat abstract and obscure, not a self-evident source of knowing who one is or where one belongs.

The American national identity is unlike many others for two obvious reasons: it has been limited in time (this being a relatively young nation), and it has many ethnic components. For this reason the American national identity is not as self-evident as, say, the Chinese or Russian or Spanish. People who came to America spoke different languages, came from different countries, and had little in common other than the desire to improve their life; those of European ancestry shared an attenuated Christian or Jewish background. The American national identity was a political artifact, the creation of the Founding Fathers that did not benefit from self-evident, longstanding continuity and social bonds.

While the United States developed remarkable coherence as a nation and society, the limitations of the sense of national identity may have cast a persistent shadow on the individual's sense of identity.

People undergoing an identity crisis, or searching for a more gratifying self-conception, look for something that will distinguish them from their fellow human beings. It could be an unusual accomplishment; an artistic talent, endeavor, or interest; some evidence of creativity; unique experiences, rare traits of character, or an unusual personal affiliation or relationship; even an unusual hobby.[56] People in pursuit of a more satisfying sense of identity may climb mountains, take arduous trips to remote corners of the world, join radical political movements, take drugs, adopt a new diet, divorce and remarry, enroll in creative-writing classes, change their occupation or appearance or style of clothing. They may move from one part of the country to another, and in the most extreme cases they may alter their sexual identity by surgical means. Contemporary American society seems to be in the forefront of such efforts and aspirations.

In the wake of the 1960s, writes Eva Moskowitz, "a highly psychologized vision of liberation" and a more vigorous pursuit of a more gratifying sense of identity became widespread: "the me generation . . . waged a campaign against all that prevented emotional candor, intimacy, and self-awareness. Expressing feelings was akin to godliness. Salvation lay in openness and communication."[57] Some reasons for this trend are clearly historical. Generations of immigrants came to America in search of new opportunities (economic, religious, and political)—that is, with heightened expectations. Most of them found such opportunities. Improved living standards, higher educational achievements, and a greater sense of security led to more expansive notions of opportunity, to ever-increasing aspirations, and to an interest in new, more flattering self-conceptions. While aspirations and expectations grew, social and geographic mobility also increased, thus weakening communities or making their establishment more difficult. Personal isolation inadvertently became another stimulant to individualism—the isolated individual aspired to and often achieved greater self-sufficiency.

The value placed on solitude had been an entrenched feature of European romanticism, well before the American emphasis on the virtues of "rugged individualism," which often also involved a high tolerance for solitude. The "outsider" came to be romanticized in America even when his lawless or criminal behavior made him one. Often a very thin line existed between commendable nonconformity and the violent criminal behavior of the proud outlaw.[58]

Living in a competitive capitalist society has been another stimulant of the pursuit of personal distinction (individualism), involving both material gain and social recognition. Since America is a democratic *and* an egalitarian society, the pursuit of a distinctive personality has become widespread.

The accomplishment of uniqueness has become an ideal for vast numbers of people who in the more elitist past (or in other contemporary societies) would not have entertained such aspirations. The disjunction between the pursuit of uniqueness and American egalitarianism has been somewhat mitigated by the widely held cultural belief that *all* are entitled to and capable of this pursuit.

Thus everyone in American society nowadays is credited with a variety of talents, with great potential for personal growth and a capacity for original thinking. Making qualitative distinctions among people, on the other hand, has become suspect, that is to say, politically incorrect. Since the 1960s, egalitarian trends have intensified and found institutional expression, for example, in "open admissions" at colleges. If students did poorly in school it was not because they were intellectually limited, unmotivated, or disorganized but because their teachers failed to stimulate and motivate them, or because their home environment was not conducive to learning, or because their condition of poverty diverted them from higher aspirations.[59] Increasingly, American schools and colleges have encouraged these trends: children of widely divergent aspirations, work habits, and ability have been placed in the same classes to avoid "elitist" practices; ranking and competition have been discouraged and shunned. Grades are sometimes abolished altogether, and pass/fail (usually meaning pass/pass) is substituted, partly in response to a growing sense of entitlement among students.[60] Strangely enough, in present-day American society it is perfectly legitimate and even admirable for popular entertainers, football players, or bond traders to earn tens of millions of dollars a year while in schools and colleges teachers hold forth against the evils of inequality, competitiveness, and elitism.

The self-conscious embrace of individualism and the emphasis on uniqueness (on what the individual does *not* have in common with others) has yet another source. David Potter has suggested, "Our historic distrust of groups, our attribution of corruption to society and of innocence to man alone has run through our national thought. . . . A man alone . . . and all the folklore of man on his own against the universe."[61] The rugged individual is different and superior.

In the same spirit, advertisers urge millions of potential consumers to buy their products or services in order to distinguish themselves from the "herd" or "crowd." By making the correct choice, the savvy consumer asserts his wisdom and individuality—in the company of millions of similarly enlightened consumers.[62]

American individualism has often been portrayed as "narcissistic," that is to say, characterized by self-indulgence, self-absorption, and an unappeasable thirst for attention and acclaim. These traits are often reflected in current efforts to find romantic partners, as some of the personals quoted earlier indicate. According to David Popenoe, "A new form of individualism has emerged in advanced industrial societies . . . that is devoted to self-aggrandizement. . . . [It is] narcissistic, hedonistic, and self-oriented."[63] Such self-centeredness and craving for approval (sometimes called "support") interferes with the creation of relationships of depth and substance. As Christopher Lasch has also observed, narcissists "experience intense feelings of emptiness and inauthenticity," have no curiosity about others, yet "depend on others for constant infusions of approval and admiration." They are "chronically bored, restlessly in search of instantaneous intimacy—of emotional titillation without involvement and dependence."

Again, advertising doubtless contributes to these attitudes by stimulating "an unappeasable appetite not only for goods, but for new experiences and personal fulfillment."[64] It suggests that elaborate and supposedly tasteful and carefully considered forms of consumption will help define and refine the self. Consumption thus becomes a cherished form of self-expression.

As we shall see, narcissism leaves its imprint on current approaches to and techniques of mate selection, especially among the well educated. The personals of the *New York Review of Books* testify to the centrality of consumption, of a more rarefied hedonism, in self-definition associated with leisure-time activities and hobbies.

A relentless self-centeredness also finds expression in the fear of aging and the preoccupation with one's body and health. Lasch writes, "For those who have withdrawn interest from the outside world, except insofar as it remains a source of gratification and frustration, the state of their health becomes an all-absorbing concern."[65]

Lasch also draws attention to the inescapable competitive pressures permeating American society and their corrosive influence on intimate personal relationships, and especially marriage: "As business, politics, and diplomacy grow more savage and warlike, men seek a haven in private life, in personal relations, above all in the family—the last refuge of love and decency. . . . The overthrow of arranged marriage took place in the name of romantic love and a new conception of the family as a refuge from the highly competitive and often brutal world of commerce and industry."[66]

But the modern family has not been able to fulfill these expectations. Marriage, the hoped-for refuge, has failed to become this durable haven. Judith Wallerstein has found additional circumstances threatening the stability and durability of contemporary marriage:

For the first time in history, the decision to stay married is purely voluntary. . . . One in two American marriages ends in divorce. . . . Feelings of intense anxiety about marriage permeate the consciousness of all young men and women. . . . The confusion over roles and the indifference of the community to long-term conjugal relationships are there. . . . Our great unacknowledged fear is that these potent outside forces will overwhelm the human commitment that marriage demands.

Paradoxically, Wallerstein also notes, "In every study in which Americans are asked what they value most in assessing the quality of their lives, marriage comes first, ahead of friends, jobs, and money."[67]

Dating, the major path to marriage or at any rate to long-term relationships, is similarly competitive and anxiety producing. It is hardly surprising that the "dating culture" is also marked by the "rise of individualistic and consumption- and market-oriented philosophies," providing "underpinnings for new modes of recreational romance and 'playing the field,'" as Martin Whyte puts it. He refers to this phenomenon as the "marketplace learning scenario": people date a large number and variety of others to acquire experience that will enable them, it is hoped, to make prudent choices.[68]

American-style dating thus incorporates two not entirely consonant goals: the pursuit of romance and intense emotional involvement on the one hand, and on the other a deliberate, self-conscious, rational, trial-and-error procedure of sampling potentially available partners.

Of late the institution of dating is becoming less and less governed by "widely understood norms and expectations," as was found in a 2001 study of American college women. The authors reported that "no term for interactions between college women and men holds more ambiguity and reflects more confusion than the word 'dating.' . . . Our . . . respondents often expressed confusion and frustration at the lack of clarity surrounding mating and dating at their schools."[69]

More specifically, another recent study has pointed to the conflicting expectations surrounding marriage: "There are two powerful forces at war in America, a historic belief in marriage grounded in our religious heritage on the one hand, and a foundational principle of individual freedom and a post-modern sense of the right to self-fulfillment on the other."[70] These conflicted attitudes toward marriage continue to be reflected in high divorce rates *and* the high value placed on marriage and the large numbers who remarry. The study of dating among female college students finds that "marriage is a major life goal for the majority of today's college women. . . . 83% . . . in the national survey agreed that 'Being married is a very important goal for me,' and

63% agreed that 'I would like to meet my future husband in college.' . . . Most (96%) of the national survey respondents want and expect their marriages to last for life." Ninety-nine percent were optimistic about finding the right person to marry.[71] These positive expectations conflict with actual conditions on the campuses, including the imbalance between men and women (there being considerably more women) and the new importance of a career for women that inclines them to postpone marriage.

I sketched in this chapter the most obvious differences between mate selection in traditional and modern societies and the growth of individualism in the modern ones. Individualism had numerous unanticipated consequences, including increased social isolation.

The rise of romanticism, discussed in the next two chapters, has been an integral part of modernity and individualism. It continues to influence present-day attitudes toward mate selection and the conceptions of desirable human qualities.

❧

# CHAPTER TWO

# Modernity, Romantic Love, and the Rise of Expectations

Falling in love is not so much a fall as a grand leap of faith, a leap for unity and meaningfulness.

Michael Vincent Miller[1]

In four days he gave me a lifetime, a universe, and made the separate parts of me into a whole.

Francesca, in Robert James Waller, *The Bridges of Madison County*[2]

## The Historical Context of Romanticism

It is the reigning truism of the social sciences that individual behavior is influenced, if not determined, by larger social forces and cultural currents. Even in the most individualistic of all societies of all times—the American—personal choices and decisions reflect these larger forces and currents, and these choices show discernible patterns. Correspondingly, long-standing, widely held romantic beliefs and values color many of the attitudes, expectations, and preferences discussed in this book and as such deserve a closer look.

The core conviction of the romantics is that uniquely meaningful and satisfying relationships between a man and a woman can be established under unspecified conditions, based on the revelation of profound mutual attraction and some essential compatibility. Or, as Kenneth Gergen, an American psychologist, says, "It is a perspective that lays central stress on unseen, even

sacred forces that dwell deep within the person, forces that give life and relationships their significance."[3] These mysterious emotional affinities transcend
social class, education, ethnicity—any extraneous sociological or cultural
factors or criteria—and enable individuals to fully understand each other.
This heightened need for understanding is another integral part of individualism, tied to the belief that the individual in question is extremely complex
and prone to be misunderstood or insufficiently appreciated. The need to be
understood is closely linked to the pursuit of intimacy, which in turn is an apparent response to the threat of social isolation. As Christopher Lasch writes,
"The cult of intimacy conceals a growing despair of finding it. Personal relations crumble under the emotional weight with which they are burdened."[4]

Isaiah Berlin considered the romantic movement and the change in outlook it ushered in "a great break in European consciousness," introducing
new ideals and attaching "the highest importance to such values as integrity,
sincerity . . . wholeheartedness . . . purity of soul, the ability and readiness
to dedicate yourself to your ideal, no matter what it was." He regarded romanticism as a key component of the modern view of the world: "whatever
else may be said about romanticism . . . it did put its finger . . . upon these
unconscious dark forces . . . [and] it succeeded in transforming certain of our
values to a very profound degree."

The preoccupation with sincerity was especially prominent in this transformation, introducing the idea that motives or intentions are more important than the consequences of one's behavior. This disposition had a great
impact not only on personal relationships but on political behavior as well.
As Berlin put it, "The romantic movement . . . preached the importance of
character . . . of purpose over consequence, over efficiency . . . over success
and position in the world."

The upsurge of interest in nature, in "the remote in time and remote in
place," was part of a broad romantic rejection of the social order and the
man-made environment newly disfigured by "the horrors of the Industrial
Revolution." The romantics yearned to recover "control over the spiritual
element, which had become petrified as a result of human degeneration and
the wicked work of unimaginative killers of the human spirit"[5]—a sentiment
also widely held in recent times, especially during the 1960s.

The themes of romantic love are deeply embedded and find strong support in Western individualism, though they precede it chronologically. Denis de Rougemont traces these themes, somewhat improbably, all the way
back to twelfth-century Europe, and from there to contemporary America,
proposing that the West was different from all other cultures because of "its
invention of passionate love."[6] A student of romanticism, and especially of
"the glorification of passion" at its core, Rougemont writes of conditions in

twentieth-century Western societies: "everything within and about us glorifies passion. Hence the prospect of a passionate experience has come to seem the promise that we are about to live more fully and more intensely." He emphasizes the connection between passion and intensity, on the one hand, and those obstacles that interfere with the realization of passionate attractions:

> Unless the course of love is being hindered there is no "romance"; and it is romance we revel in—that is to say, the self-consciousness, intensity, variations, and delays of passion. . . . Between joy and its external cause there is invariably some gap, some obstruction—society, sin, virtue.[7]

Rougemont understands that fantasy, or idealization, looms large in romantic attachments. Lovers do not love each other as they really are; they love the imaginary other, or at best a blend of the real and the imagined. Freud suggests that romantic love amounts to "aim-inhibited sexuality"—that is, a sublimated expression of sexual frustration that stimulates the imagination. In the words of a more recent writer, "Love . . . burns itself out with the attainment of its goal, the possession of the loved one."[8] In turn, Bertrand Russell notes that "social barriers . . . were an essential part of the stimulus" in the love life of Shelley, an exemplar of the romantic disposition.[9]

A good deal of romantic love amounts to fantasies projected upon the object of love, a process that may be called idealization and is totally foreign to traditional or premodern societies. As Russell puts it, "In romantic love the beloved object is not seen accurately but through a glamorous mist."[10] As to why this "glamorous mist" arises in the first place, Alain de Botton suggests that "we fall in love because we long to escape from ourselves with someone as ideal as we are corrupt." In other words, romantic infatuation has a compensatory aspect—it bolsters our sense of identity: "Perhaps it is true that we do not really exist until there is someone there to see us existing. . . . To feel whole we need people . . . who know us. . . . Is it not comforting to be able to find refuge from the danger of invisibility in the arms of someone who has our identity firmly in mind?"[11]

More typically it is men who engage in such projection, exaggerating the positive attributes of women to whom they are attracted. Arguably, women tend to be more realistic about the attractions and attributes of men.

Rougemont also notes that these attitudes have trickled down from the upper classes to "the masses." Writing half a century ago, he anticipated what has become a massive phenomenon of our times: the purveying of diluted but nevertheless still potent versions of romanticism by popular culture and advertising. These new versions differ from the old by seeking to connect passion and happiness, or passion and contentment, and in doing so create unanticipated problems:

> Your happiness, it is being asserted from the pulpit of magazines, depends on this or on that . . . something that must be *acquired*. The consequence of this propaganda is that we are obsessed by the notion of a facile happiness and at the same time rendered incapable of being happy. For everything thus suggested introduces us to a world of comparisons. . . . Every wish to experience happiness, to have it at one's beck and call—instead of being in a *state* of happiness as though by grace—must instantly produce an intolerable sense of want.[12]

The phenomenon Rougemont describes is especially pronounced in American society, permeated by both high expectations and a belief in the availability of methods with which to achieve them, whether they are material, spiritual, or emotional.

Rougemont draws attention to the difficulty comparisons create: in a modern, competitive, socially mobile society such as the American, opportunities for comparisons are particularly compelling and produce a sense of relative deprivation. This is the feeling of being deprived *in comparison to* other people, or in light of certain ideals or ideas about what might be accomplished or possessed. Of late such comparisons are also stimulated by the vast offerings of the dating sites on the Internet, their large volume making it difficult to decide when to stop scrutinizing available options and alternatives.

The romantic, Rougemont points out, is "unable to take the other as he or she is because that would mean being first of all content with oneself. . . . A man or woman now sees on every side nothing but things to be coveted, qualities that he or she feels the want of, and grounds for comparisons." He is well aware of the connection between the pursuit of romantic passion and modernity: "romanticism set out to recover a primitive mysticism. . . . The moderns, men and women, expect irresistible love to produce some revelation either regarding themselves or about life at large. This is a last vestige of the primitive mysticism."[13]

How is romanticism linked to modernity? Is there a recurring pattern in the process of idealization, in the attributes projected upon the beloved or the person one expects to love? How in our times can such a largely unrealistic disposition be combined with the practicality and pragmatism that pervades modern American society?

There can be little doubt about the importance of romantic values and attitudes in American society. As early as 1929 Bertrand Russell wrote, "In

America . . . the romantic view of marriage has been taken more seriously than anywhere else."[14] Only in America has it been seriously proposed that romance can be extended indefinitely, including lifelong marriages. As Andrew Cherlin has argued, "Compared to our Western European counterparts, Americans are far more credulous about marriage." Surveys show that far fewer Americans consider marriage "an outdated institution than citizens of any other Western country."[15]

Russell, no admirer of romanticism, sees it "as a revolt against received ethical and aesthetic standards," and points out, "The romantic movement, in its essence, aimed at liberating human personality from the fetters of social convention and social morality." He identifies among its key components "a proneness to emotion . . . [which] must be direct and violent and quite uninformed by thoughts. . . . The romantic outlook . . . prefers passion to calculation [and] has a vehement contempt for commerce and finance." Central to this discussion, Russell notes the romantics' "contempt for the trammels of convention—first in dress and manners . . . then in art and love, and at last over the whole sphere of traditional morals."

Russell's observations suggest parallels with the prevalent attitudes of the 1960s:

> By the time of Rousseau, many people had grown tired of safety and had begun to crave excitement. . . . The romantics did not aim at peace and quiet, but at vigorous and passionate individual life. They had no sympathy with industrialism because it was ugly, because money-grubbing seemed to them unworthy of an immortal soul, and because the growth of modern economic organizations interfered with individual liberty. . . . The romantic movement is characterized as a whole by the substitution of aesthetic for utilitarian standards.

Russell identifies the reverence for spontaneity and authenticity as key romantic virtues: "They admire strong passions, of no matter what kind, and whatever their social consequences." He also emphasizes the connection between romanticism and individualism: "Revolt of solitary instincts against social bonds is the key to the philosophy, the politics, and the sentiments of . . . the romantic movement. . . . Self-development was proclaimed as the fundamental principle of ethics."[16]

## Literary Sources and Reflections of the Romantic Worldview

Since the ideals of romantic love have exerted a strong and lasting influence in American society, it is of interest to trace them to their European roots.

The European origins of romanticism are most clearly reflected in certain classical literary works. Goethe's *The Sorrows of Young Werther* and Chateau-briand's *Atala and Rene* are paradigmatic texts of German and French romanticism. They were exceedingly popular when first published because they expressed the growing and widespread sentiments of the period. These writings reveal a continuity between eighteenth- and early nineteenth-century European ideas and ideals and those which continue to permeate American popular culture. A third novel, Flaubert's *Madame Bovary*, deserves attention both as a detached and critical presentation of romantic passion and a meticulous inventory of its components and consequences.

There are good reasons for taking seriously works of fiction as sources of information about matters of interest for sociologists and social historians. As one observer has put it, "a great writer is like a great scientist: through his work something vital becomes known that wasn't known before."[17] Writers often are self-appointed social historians capable of connecting the uniquely personal with broader, sometimes universal human phenomena. Fiction is particularly informative in revealing details of social existence that elude other observers, including social scientists. Novels can grasp and depict the quality of human interactions, relationships, and expectations governed by elusive, informal norms, customs, or conventions. They can also capture the social determinants of personal problems and predicaments.

Goethe's *The Sorrows of Young Werther*, published in 1774, may be regarded as the first major literary statement codifying romantic attitudes. It made a huge impact throughout Europe.[18] Reportedly the book even prompted numerous imitations of the behavior of the main character, who at the end of the story commits suicide.[19]

The tale is a simple one: Werther, a young, educated German with a private income and much free time on his hands, falls in love with a woman who is already engaged and has no interest in breaking her engagement. Convinced that he can never feel the same toward any other woman, and without other sustaining interests or obligations, Werther kills himself. As the story unfolds, the reader is offered a detailed portrait of the romantic mind-set that Werther embodies.

The major claim of the romantic hero, such as Werther, is that certain personal attachments and relationships cannot be replicated or duplicated, that objects of love are not interchangeable (in sharp contrast to modern, pragmatic American beliefs), that those linked to each other in true love have been predestined for such an attachment. These singular attractions are based on the unique inner essence of the individuals involved and defy classification, labeling, or even rational analysis. While true romantics focus on this indefinable inner essence or quality, and on a correspondingly singular compatibility or "harmony of spirits," they are far from indifferent to physical attributes. They believe that these visible characteristics somehow mirror core qualities, that beauty—especially in women—is associated with warmth, kindness, sensitivity, and generosity. Other, more tangible attributes are seen in quite a different light. Werther considers social class, status, occupation, education, income, and rank to be ephemeral and unimportant. They are attributes that place people in categories, diverting attention from what is truly important—their personality and quintessential personal qualities. In short, romanticism and individualism are inseparable.

The romantic worldview thus has both egalitarian and elitist components and implications: it rejects conventional hierarchies based on rank, income, or power, but embraces with a vengeance distinctions based on other, far more intangible, obscure, or esoteric differences or personal qualities. Simple, poor, and powerless people are highly valued because they are perceived as uncorrupted—here lies the egalitarian dimension. Werther and his many successors admire "simple people" (less exotic incarnations of the "noble savage"), who are seen as unburdened by the pretense, formality, or moral corruption of the upper classes. Werther believes that "Love, loyalty, and passion . . . live and can be found in all purity among a class of people we like to call uncultured and crude." He writes, "The simple folk here already know me and seem to be fond of me, especially the children," whereas "persons of rank tend to keep their cold distance from the common man." The "simple folk" he refers to are peasants in the rural area he has moved to. Children, he declares, "are our equals and . . . we should use [them] as models."[20] (Such views were, of course, widespread in the 1960s.)

The emphasis on uniqueness explains the romantics' preoccupation with being properly understood[21]—a concern very much with us today. It finds expression in broken relationships that began with high expectations and were followed by bitter disappointments. Werther believes that "to be misunderstood is the miserable destiny of people like myself."[22] This fear of being misunderstood, needless to say, implies a flattering self-conception of great depth and complexity.

The sharp distinctions that romantics make among people are based on the presence or absence of qualities such as sincerity, sensitivity, compassion, and capacity for intense and authentic feeling as well as physical appearances that somehow mirror these attributes. In the past, as in recent times, romantics have despised and rejected rules and conventions, anything that diverts attention from the uniqueness of the individual and inhibits a deep connection with another human being and with nature. As Werther notes in his diary, "Rules and regulations ruin our true appreciation of nature and our powers to express it."[23] The chief objection to rules is that they are depersonalizing because they are external to the individual; they cannot accommodate individual variability. The intense hostility to bureaucracy that occurred during the 1960s was based precisely on such sentiments.

Werther proposes that "all exceptional people who created something great . . . have to be decried as drunkards or madmen. And I find it intolerable . . . to hear it said of almost everyone who manages to do something that is free, noble, and unexpected: He is a drunkard, he is a fool."[24] Here Werther alludes to the creative artist, supposedly misunderstood and mislabeled, who deserves to be liberated from the norms of sensible, conventional behavior. Not incidentally, in the subplot of the novel Werther is ostracized by members of established, aristocratic families who consider him socially inferior—that is, middle class.

In addition to a capacity for strong and pure feeling, authenticity is the most cherished value of the romantics. It further explains why they so often rail against pretense and hypocrisy. The preoccupation with authenticity has two dimensions. The more obvious is the imperative of congruence between professed belief and actual behavior, regardless of the consequences. Feelings must not be compromised by actions that fail to reflect them. The other dimension of authenticity is the notion "to be true to oneself"—a somewhat murky proposition since it is not clear what the "true self" is or what aspect of it must be revered. The belief that there is an attribute of great value in every human being, to be cherished as an infallible guide to one's conduct, is also integral to individualism.

Romantics like Werther often feel and act socially isolated and lonely, as a matter of choice and because they do not "fit in" and are poorly understood. They often seek solitude—preferably in an attractive natural setting—because they believe that isolation is purifying and promotes reflection and self-understanding. Such withdrawal also signals the rejection of existing society with its conventions and institutions, and may also find expression in travel to remote or exotic places.

Given his veneration of feeling, passion, and the capacity for experiencing an irresistible attraction to another human being (at the expense of rational cognition or calculation), Werther holds in contempt those who are incapable of such feelings: "Oh, you sensible people! . . . Passion. Inebriation. Madness. You respectable ones stand there so calmly, without any sense of participation. . . . I have been drunk more than once, and my passion often borders on madness, and I regret neither."[25] A contemporary writer, Christina Nehring, testifying to the persistence of romantic notions, takes a similarly dim view of "sensible people": "Sensible people are not inspired people. Sensible people . . . are often shortsighted people. They cannot penetrate into the secrets of the universe."[26]

Werther characteristically rejects an offer of books from a friend: "I beg you—don't [send books]. I have no wish to be influenced, encouraged, or inspired any more. My heart surges wildly enough without any outside influence. . . . I coddle my heart . . . and give in to its every whim."[27]

This capacity for strong feelings finds further expression in the shedding of tears. It is quite remarkable that in societies characterized by rigid sex role differentiation, and a belief in the fundamentally different character of men and women, men are often portrayed as equally ready to shed tears as women. Werther finds tears "refreshing," and he has often "begged God to give me tears, as a plowman begs for rain when the sky is leaden above him and his parched earth."[28] Easily moved to tears, he is certainly in touch with his feelings (as today's Americans would say) and strongly disapproves of any restraint on their expression.

The intensity of romantic emotions seems to stem from quasi-religious attitudes, in which the love object acquires a religious aura, stimulating the kind of veneration earlier reserved for God.[29] Werther writes of his beloved:

I longed to throw myself at her feet, as one throws oneself down before a prophet who has just washed his people clean of sin. . . . How wildly my blood courses through my veins when, by chance, my hand touches hers. . . . I start away as if from a fire, a mysterious power draws me back and I become dizzy. . . . When . . . the heavenly breath from her lips touches mine . . . then I feel I must sink to the ground as if struck by lightning. . . . She is sacred to me. All lust is stilled in her presence.[30]

Such sentiments are far from congruent with modern romanticism. The lust of modern romantics is hardly "stilled" in each other's presence. Nevertheless the quasi-religious imagery helps explain the evolution of the romantic mind-set and especially the intensity of emotions brought to these attachments. Christopher Lasch observes that in contemporary American society, "people demand from personal relations the richness and intensity of a religious experience."[31]

The capacity for unrestrained veneration (even of objects belonging to or touched by the beloved[32]); the attribution of perfection; love as the ultimate and complete source of security and fulfillment—these attitudes suggest a redirection of emotional energies that had earlier been reserved for the religious sphere. By the same token, religious devotion is sometimes felt to be an alternative to romantic love, as in the reflections of Rene, hero of the Chateaubriand story examined later:

> [R]eligion beguiles a gentle soul. For the most violent love, religion substitutes a kind of burning chastity in which lover and virgin find fulfillment. It purifies our sighs and transforms into an eternal flame what was perishable. It blends its divine calm and innocence with the remains of anguish and voluptuousness in a heart which seeks rest and a life which seeks apartness.[33]

It bears repeating that the intensity of romantic attraction is stimulated by the obstacles that surround and frustrate wish fulfillment, such as the fact that Werther desires a woman already engaged. She correctly poses the question: "Why me of all people who already belongs to another? . . . I fear that it is just the impossibility of possessing me that makes your desire so fascinating."[34] At this juncture the romanticism of the past parts company with the more recent variety since contemporary seekers of passionate fulfillment are, or believe themselves to be, capable of intensity without stimulation by obstacles. The far easier access to sexual gratification in our times is among the factors that have changed the quality of romantic longing.

Another important part of the romantic disposition illustrated by *Young Werther* was (and remains) the veneration of nature. In addition to nature's usefulness as a setting for contemplative seclusion and spiritual uplift, the worship of nature is best understood as a counterpart of the rejection of (or alienation from) human society and the physical environment that has been disfigured by human beings. Social critics past and present have found in the apparent perfection, beauty, and harmony of nature a foil that highlights the sordidness or folly of social arrangements and misguided human aspirations. When Werther learns that some walnut trees that have always "delighted" him have been cut down, he is so outraged that he "could murder the dog that drove in the first ax"—sentiments that present-day environmentalists would appreciate. On another occasion he has tears in his eyes while contemplating the freshness of the countryside after a thunderstorm.[35]

Veneration of nature merges with his fondness for the simple, traditional ways of life he finds in the small village where he is staying: "Nothing can fill me with such true, serene emotion as any features of ancient, primitive life like this. . . . My heart can feel the simple, harmless joys of the man who brings to the table a head of cabbage he has grown himself." Similar feelings may readily be found among today's suburban gardeners or members of rural communes of the 1960s and 1970s. Like other romantics, Werther projects onto the past the authenticity and beauty he fails to find in the present. Traditional ways of life are superior to what he sees in rising modernity; travel allows him (and us) to revisit the past, or what is left of it. He finds new houses and "all other innovations" "repulsive." He believes that his "glorious ancestors" were happy, "their feelings and poetry childlike." "Childlike" is tantamount to pure and authentic. Children are more "natural," guileless, uncorrupted by social norms and arrangements and false human aspirations; they are "true to themselves" in an effortless way. Doubtless Werther also appreciates children for their spontaneity. He believes that "those people are happiest who live for the moment."[36]

Contemporary romantics would find it easy to resonate to virtually all the feelings Werther personifies and expresses, with the important exception of his pessimism and the tragic outlook that convinces him there are no alternatives to an unavailable woman.

*Atala and Rene*, written by François-Auguste-René de Chateaubriand and first published in 1802, is another major romantic text that was an instant success. In his foreword to the 1961 edition, Walter T. Cobb observes:

> Rene is to France what Werther was to Germany. . . . There have been few books in the history of French literature which, upon first publication, have appealed so universally and instantaneously as did *Atala*. There have been few books which have so refreshingly responded to the needs of their time. . . . Within months of its publication, new editions, translations, fraudulent imitations followed one another in rapid succession.[37]

*Atala and Rene* shares with *Werther* the tragic dimension of unfulfilled love that culminates in suicide. Here, however, the obstacle to fulfillment is of a different nature. In these stories what may be called religious romanticism is the major determinant of the protagonists' behavior.

In understanding the appeal of *Atala and Rene*, it helps to bear in mind that it reflects a reaction against the cerebral rationality and somewhat shallow optimism of the French Enlightenment. It questions and rejects rationality and modernity—a rejection inherent in the romantic worldview, including its manifestations in recent times. In *Atala and Rene* the romantic rejection of modernity finds expression in the worship of nature, the idealization of the Noble Savage (the uncorrupted native), the presentation of romantic virtues, and, more unusually from the contemporary perspective, in the embrace of religion (Catholicism).

The countercultural beliefs of more recent times, notably those of the 1960s, have similarly entailed the rejection of rationality, impersonality, the elaborate division of labor, urbanization, industrialization, and other components of modernity. Moreover the 1960s spawned not only political activism but religious quests and revivals. Central to this sensibility has been the injunction to get in touch with one's feelings—a durable romantic imperative.

The separate stories of Atala and Rene take place, for the most part, in colonial America, which the author visited in the late eighteenth century. This visit provided him with literary raw material and personal experience to convert into fiction. In *Atala*, Chactas, an American Indian, is captured by another tribe and is freed by the Indian woman Atala, who joins him in the escape and subsequent wanderings through the wilderness. It is a complicated story with many obstacles to the fulfillment of their love, foremost among them Atala's earlier conversion to Christianity and her vow of chastity. She commits suicide because of the insoluble conflict between her love of Chactas and her religious beliefs ("feeling between you and me an invincible barrier!").

These stories make clear that Chateaubriand's five months' visit to America did not provide him with realistic information about American Indians; instead it stimulated him to project upon them a wide range of romantic attributes they were unlikely to possess. The Muskogee and Seminole Indians, he writes, were "all gaiety, affection and contentment," the tribal chiefs exhibited "joyous simplicity." Atala "was beautiful with even features. On her face one could detect a certain virtuous, passionate air, the charm of which was impossible to resist. . . . Extreme sensitivity and profound melancholy shone through her eyes; her smile was from heaven." Chactas readily admits of his obsessive infatuation with Atala: "I had become indifferent to all which did not concern Atala! Without strength to reason like a man, of a sudden I had regressed to a kind of childishness."

Chactas personifies another key attribute of the romantic: a free-floating need for an all-embracing attachment, which precedes meeting the specific individual who could become the object of such feelings. As Rene (in the other story) puts it, "My soul, which no passion had yet consumed, looked for an object on which it could lavish affection."

Another characteristic that these protagonists share with those in *Werther* is a readiness to burst into tears and shed them copiously—an unlikely attribute of American Indians. Interestingly enough, there are no sex distinctions here either: in both books men cry as readily as women.

Given these noble savages' supposed life in harmony with nature, there is a convergence between the nobility of nature and the feelings of the protagonists. As Chactas explains, "Great passions are solitary, and when you take them into the wilderness, you bring them to their natural home." Unlike human society, the nature depicted here is majestic, authentic, harmonious, and kind: "All was calm and magnificent in the wilderness . . . a large number of animals, placed by the hand of the Creator . . . add enchantment and life." A thunderstorm is at once "frightening" and "magnificent," and in its aftermath "the Great Spirit covered the mountains with heavy clouds of darkness." Two hundred years ago, as in recent times, idealized nature is the counterpoint to the folly and evil perpetuated by human beings. Chactas has "a strong distaste for city life" developed during his stay in St. Augustine, Florida, where he was "wasting away."

The tragic element is more pronounced in *Atala and Rene* than in *Werther*. While Goethe's unhappy love story culminates in suicide, the world as a whole is not portrayed as a valley of tears in which only religion offers solace. In *Atala and Rene*, a hermit (the third important figure) gives voice to a somber religious view of the world in which human beings vainly seek happiness and all human attachments are futile:

> I have yet to meet the man who has not been betrayed by his phantom dreams of happiness, nor the heart which has not hidden a secret wound. . . . You lose little in losing this world. . . . Whether he lives in a cave or a palace, everyone suffers, everyone bewails his lot. Queens have been seen to weep like simple women, and you would be astonished at the quantity of tears stored in the eyes of kings!

At the end of the story Chactas, as an old man, reaches a similarly melancholy conclusion at the graves of Atala and the hermit: "Thus passes on this earth all that is good, virtuous, and sensitive! Man, you are but a hasty dream, a vision of sorrow; you exist only as misery; you are something only by the sadness of your soul and the eternal melancholy of your thought!"

Chateaubriand's gloomy romanticism is colored by his reaction to the French Revolution and its aftermath, which he associated with an overall decline. Whereas as a child he saw the end of a "splendid century," the eighteenth, "it was no more when I returned home. Never has a more astonishing or more sudden change taken place in a people. From the height of genius, from respect to religion, from perfection of manners, everything suddenly degenerated to . . . godlessness and corruption."

Melancholy and the influence of religion are especially prominent in the story of Rene. He is the son of a French aristocrat whose mother died while giving birth to him and whose father was remote and without parental warmth. He is close only to his sister Amelia, who ends up in a cloister. Rene possesses numerous prototypical romantic traits. He is inclined to loneliness and feels unable to fit in or to feel part of any group or community. He is unstable, impulsive, moody, and consumed by vague, insatiable desires. Unbeknownst to him, he teeters on the brink of an incestuous relationship with his sister, who on her deathbed confesses her "guilty passion" for him.

Chactas, echoing these feelings, knows that "By nature I was impetuous and erratic. Sometimes disturbed and joyful, silent and sad, I gathered around me young companions. Then suddenly I would leave them and go sit by myself to gaze at the fleeting clouds or to listen to the falling rain in the foliage. . . . I found ease and contentment only with my sister." Nature is a refuge from his sorrows: "Melancholy led him to the depths of the woods." Elsewhere Chateaubriand writes, "Solitude, the spectacle of nature, soon plunged me into a mood almost impossible to describe. . . . Sometimes I cried for no reason. . . . I lacked something that could fill the emptiness of my existence. . . . I tried everything, and everything failed."

A missionary, the foster father of Rene, offers a refreshingly down-to-earth diagnosis of the *weltschmerz* of Rene and the associated romantic worldview:

> I see a young man intoxicated with his illusions, displeased with everything, withdrawn from the burdens of society, given to idle dreams. One is not . . . a superior man because he sees the world in shadow. . . . What do you do all alone in the forests where you waste your days, neglecting all your duties?

These observations contain in a nutshell some of the preconditions of the extreme romantic melancholy that consume Rene: an abundance of free time, freedom from work, a life unstructured by compelling external demands, and an attendant sense of emptiness that needs to be filled—but it is not clear by what or whom.

Rene's alienation from his familiar environment and society leads him to travel: "Full of enthusiasm, I set out alone on the tempestuous ocean." But the ruins of ancient Rome and Greece fail to cheer him and prompt further gloomy reflections about the "strength of nature and weakness of men." He "wanted to see if living civilizations offered more goodness and less suffering than those which had vanished." In North America he finds "happy savages" and sadly asks, "Why can I not enjoy the same peace that always goes with you? . . . Needs dictate your motives, and you reach better than I the goal of wisdom, like children between games and sleep."[38]

An aspect of Rene's story to which the modern American reader can readily relate is the hopeful belief that it is possible to escape personal problems, grief, or frustration by removing oneself to an unfamiliar social and physical setting. Rene relocates from France to North America, expecting to be revitalized—as do millions of Americans who move not merely to find better jobs or climate but because they hope and expect a wide range of psychic benefits, nothing less than a rejuvenation in sunnier settings.

A third and most remarkable literary portrayal of romantic infatuation and its dire consequences is presented by Gustave Flaubert in *Madame Bovary*, first published in 1857. The important difference between this story and those of Goethe and Chateaubriand is that it is infused with a critical, clinical sensibility. Flaubert presents romantic infatuation as misguided, delusional, and destructive. The romantic relationships of Madame Bovary are adulterous and ruin her emotionally, socially, and financially; her life ends in suicide, as do Werther's and Atala's, but her motives and circumstances are more squalid and are entangled with deception and self-deception.

The story of Madame Bovary and those of Werther, Atala, and Rene have in common the theme of passion intensified by obstacles. Madame Bovary is a married woman, a mother and housewife living in a small rural French town in which traditional beliefs and customs hold sway. Adulterous affairs and divorce are uncommon and ostracized. From an early age, Emma (Madame Bovary) is imbued with romantic longings and aspirations that her marriage to a dull, self-effacing, and all-too-ordinary doctor cannot satisfy. Her affairs require elaborate and secretive arrangements and subterfuges; the obstacles she must overcome intensify the passions involved. An adulterous affair in this time and place cannot be routinized; it is forbidden and dangerous, and for all these reasons exciting.

Early in life, while in a Catholic convent, Emma tries to learn from her readings "what was really meant in life by the words 'happiness,' 'passion,' and 'intoxication'—words that had seemed so beautiful to her in books." Later, after marrying, she continues to fantasize that she might "give herself up to love. In the moonlight of the garden she would recite all the passionate poetry she knew by heart and would sing melancholy adagios" to her husband. But these performances have little impact on either of them. Her notion of love certainly is not realized in her marriage: "Love, she believed, should arrive at once with thunder and lightning—a whirlwind from the skies that affects life . . . and plunges the entire heart into an abyss." Emma adores "stories that . . . frighten you. I hate everyday heroes and restrained emotions like the ones in real life." Leon, her interlocutor and kindred spirit (with whom she later has an affair), adds, "Of course those works that don't affect the emotions miss the real goal of art. With all the disillusionments of life, it is good to be able to identify . . . with noble characters, pure affections, and portrayals of happiness. As for myself, living here far from the world, it's my one distraction. Yonville has so little to offer!"[39] This conversation alerts the reader to the part played by boredom in the generation of romantic fantasies.

Leon has his own fantasies of glamorous life in Paris: "He arranged his occupations in advance, he furnished his rooms in his imagination. He would lead the life of an artist: take guitar lessons; own a dressing gown, a beret, blue velvet slippers!" In the nineteenth century as in more recent times, many people intended to make a statement about their beliefs and values by their clothing. Madame Bovary and Leon also share the romantic view of nature as a setting that inspires or validates authentic feelings:

> "I find nothing as inspired as sunsets," she said, "but especially at the seashore."
> "I adore the sea," Monsieur Leon said. "And don't you agree," Madame Bovary
> continued, "that your spirit soars more freely over that limitless expanse? That
> just looking at it elevates your soul . . . ?" "Mountain landscapes do the same,"
> Leon said. "I have a cousin who traveled through Switzerland . . . and he told
> me that you can't imagine the poetry of the lakes, the charm of the waterfalls,
> the gigantic effect of the glaciers. . . . Sights such as these overwhelm you,
> dispose you toward prayer and ecstasy!"

A modern touch is the repeated authorial suggestion that Madame Bovary's longings are stimulated and supported by the popular culture of the time. She subscribes to and voraciously reads various magazines published in Paris: "She knew the latest fashions, the addresses of good tailors. . . . She studied descriptions of furniture in Eugene Sue's books; she read Balzac and George Sand, searching in their writings for vicarious gratification of her own desires."

Flaubert even anticipated the connection—so apparent in our times— between shallow romantic fantasies and their accessories in the realm of consumption. Emma tries to make her life more meaningful by acquiring expensive clothing and furnishings to fill what she considers the emptiness of her life. While she feels trapped "in the mediocrity of existence," she believes that somewhere

> the immense world of happiness and passion extended itself as far as the eye
> could see. In her yearnings she confused the sensualities of luxury with the joys
> of the heart. . . . Didn't love, like the Indian plants, need a cultivated land, a
> special temperature? Sighs in the moonlight, long embraces, tears . . . all the

fevers of the flesh and languors of tenderness did not separate themselves from
the balcony of the great castle . . . of boudoirs with silken shades, thick rugs,
filled flower stands, and a bed mounted on a platform, nor from . . . precious
stones and the lace ornaments of livery.

Also thoroughly modern is Emma's belief that "certain places on the earth
must produce happiness. . . . Why couldn't she be leaning her elbow on the
balcony of a Swiss chalet or indulging her moods in a Scottish cottage with a
husband dressed in a black velvet suit . . . soft boots . . . and elegant cuffs!" This
is the notion of an "in" place that in our times is thought of—if not exactly as
producing happiness—as conducive to a sense of self-importance, satisfaction,
and status, a place where important and fashionable people congregate.

Emma's fantasies about the places where she might escape with her lover
would be appreciated by producers of present-day American television commercials:

[A] new land from which she and Rodolphe would never return. . . . Often
from atop a mountain they would see some splendid city with domes . . . forests
of lemon trees. . . . There would be bouquets of flowers . . . offered by women in
red bodices. They could hear the bells ringing and mules braying, the murmur
of guitars and fountains. . . . Then they would arrive in a fishing village one
evening where brown fishnets were drying . . . in front of the huts. There they
would settle. . . . They would float off in a gondola, swing in a hammock; and
their existence would be as relaxed and easy as their silk clothes, as warm and
starry as the gentle nights they would contemplate.

Her first lover, Rodolphe, is a hard-nosed cynic, well acquainted with
romantic boilerplate. He advises her:

Our duty is to discern the great and cherish the beautiful and not to accept all
those conventions of society with the ignominies it imposes on us. . . . Why
argue against the passions? Aren't they the only beautiful things on earth, the
inspiration for heroism, enthusiasm, poetry, music, art, for everything? . . .
There are two moralities . . . the petty, conventional morality, the morality of
men . . . [and] the other, the eternal morality . . . all around and above us . . .
like the blue sky that sends down its light.

Rodolphe makes good use of the romantic critique of conventional morality in his campaign of seduction:

Doesn't this conspiracy of society revolt you? Is there one ounce of feeling
that it does not condemn? The most noble instincts, the purest emotions, are

persecuted and slandered, and if two poor souls finally meet, everything is organized so that they cannot unite. But they will keep trying . . . because destiny demands it and they were born for each other.

After succumbing to Rodolphe, Emma experiences an unsustainable romantic fervor:

> She kept telling herself, "I have a lover!" . . . she was finally going to possess those joys of love, that fever of happiness. . . . She was entering into something marvelous where all would be passion, ecstasy, delirium. . . . Ordinary existence seemed to be in the distance, down below in the shadows. . . . She remembered the heroines in the books she had read, and the lyrical legion of these adulterous women began to sing in her memory with sisterly voices. . . . She was realizing the long dream of her adolescence, seeing herself as one of those amorous women she had so long envied.

Assured of the imperishability of her fantasies, she urges Rodolphe to escape with her and embark on a new life of unobstructed fulfillment: "There is no desert, no precipice, no ocean that I wouldn't cross with you. Each day that we live together will be like a tighter, more complete embrace. We'll have nothing to bother us, no worries, nothing in our way. We'll be alone, all to ourselves, forever." But Rodolphe is a realist who knows that the endless togetherness that Emma envisions will sooner or later sour into boredom and constraint. He informs her in a letter that he has called off their plans and left town.

Emma's nervous breakdown follows, and later a new affair with Leon; huge debts accumulate in pursuit of her avid consumption of luxuries, and Leon too grows tired of her and both become sated with the relationship. Unhappily she "was finding in adultery all the banalities of marriage."[40] To escape the scandal attendant upon ruining her husband financially, as well as what has become a meaningless, desolate life, she poisons herself.

*Madame Bovary* is, and was intended to be, a morality tale. Flaubert had nothing but contempt for the excesses and delusions of romanticism. The novel makes clear that he was similarly skeptical about organized religion and the shallow, cheerful secularism bequeathed by the Enlightenment.

We need not return to the nineteenth century to find popular literary depictions of romantic relationships and beliefs—the best-selling romantic novel *Love Story* (also made into a movie), by Erich Segal, was published in the

United States in 1970.[41] It sold twenty-one million copies and was translated into thirty-three languages. The book is the source of the well-known tagline "Love means never having to say you're sorry," which probably means that misunderstandings or fights between lovers need not be taken seriously, that the profound emotional bonds between them should make any conflict insignificant.

The 1960s was a time not only of political protest and utopian hopes but also of a resurgent belief in the power of love. "Make Love Not War" was one of the slogans of the period, reflecting the belief of many young middle-class people that scarcities of love were just as easy to overcome as material shortages—both equally unrealistic beliefs held with great fervor.

It is not easy today to grasp the appeals of *Love Story*, which was for the most part a highly conventional tale suffused with intimations of the spirit of the 1960s. This spirit is reflected mainly in the generational conflict between the hero, Oliver, and his wealthy, well-established father. Oliver's nonconformist impulses are limited, as he chooses a well-paid job with a prestigious law firm instead of becoming an advocate of the poor. His objections to his father are personal and emotional rather than ideological or political. He resents his father's apparent lack of affection and warmth; he finds him unexpressive and faults his style of communication. He refers to his father as "Old Stonyface," an uptight WASP of traditional beliefs and attitudes—a counterpoint to the emerging countercultural beliefs and attitudes of the times.

The young lovers, Oliver and Jennifer, are separated by deep ethnic and class cleavages as well as different personalities and interests: the hero is an achievement-oriented, competitive, upper-class "jock"; the heroine is a talented, socially mobile, assertive, independent woman devoted to classical music. She is from a lower-class Italian family, or, as she puts it, "a social zero vs. a preppie millionaire." They meet in the privileged enclave of Harvard University and rapidly fall in love, effortlessly scaling the barriers of class and personality. A somewhat unusual aspect of their relationship is a preference for a semi-articulate, tough, and sarcastic conversational style (mostly on her part) that is supposed to conceal strong feelings and steers clear of overt tenderness. "Goddamn" and "bullshit" are favored adjectives; he often calls her a "bitch"; she calls him a "preppie" or "bastard."

While profoundly alienated from his family, especially his father, Oliver is far from being the typical isolated, reflective, or brooding romantic figure. He is a popular and successful ice hockey player, acts much of the time as an inarticulate, uncouth jock, but works hard and gets good grades, has many friends, and has been accepted by Harvard Law School. A mildly sexist womanizer, he has taken numerous young women to bed but is smitten by Jennifer and is not sure how to proceed with her in the sex department. It is she who initiates sex before they marry. He marries her despite parental disapproval of a socially inappropriate bride and the punitive cessation of financial support that follows. They live happily in romantic poverty while he goes to law school and she works to make ends meet. After finishing school he is inundated with job offers and accepts a very well-paid position with a prestigious New York City law firm. They embark on a blissful, comfortable wedded life, prepared to have a baby. When Jennifer cannot get pregnant, tests reveal that she has terminal leukemia. She dies at age twenty-four. Upon her death Oliver reconciles with his father, crying in his arms.

Without Jennifer's unexpected death at an early age, this would not be a tragic, romantic love story. Had both young people lived, it is quite possible, even likely, that their romance would have foundered: differences in class, ethnicity, upbringing, and cultural interests might have emerged to erode their bond. Had they lived together longer there might also have developed a conflict between her wishing to have a musical career and his preference for her to remain a traditional mother-housewife. She might have become a militant feminist. They were very different individuals—and not only on account of their socioeconomic background—but in the short run love overcame the mundane obstructions. Her death preserved the purity and intensity of this love.

In the wake of the 1960s, the success of *Love Story* might have been partly due to a renewed public receptivity for old-fashioned romance at a time of great social and political conflict and change.[42]

Robert James Waller's *The Bridges of Madison County* is another best-seller of recent times (also made into a movie) that demonstrates a remarkable continuity of the essential attributes of the romantic worldview and disposition. The great popularity of this short novel is perhaps even more puzzling than that of *Love Story*, unless we simply ascribe it to the timeless appeal of the tragic and impassioned story of love. It concerns an exceptionally torrid love affair that lasts only four days, yet—the reader is supposed to believe—it profoundly alters and gives new meaning to the lives of the protagonists forever. The affair originates in a seemingly accidental encounter when Robert, the hero, asks Francesca, the heroine, for directions along a remote rural road in Iowa. As the author intimates, and as the lovers come to believe, they are in some mysterious way predestined for each other. Following their brief meeting, Robert writes to Francesca:

It is clear to me now that I have been moving toward you and you toward me for a long time. Though neither of us was aware of the other before we met, there was a kind of mindless certainty . . . that ensured that we would come together. Like two solitary birds flying . . . by celestial reckoning, all of these years and lifetimes we have been moving toward one another. . . . In retrospect, it seems inevitable—it could not have been any other way.

The romantic tension and brief duration of their affair is determined by a crucial impediment: Francesca is married, a mother of two, and, though sorely tempted, will not abandon her family. These lovers are also worlds apart spatially in their ways of life, and in their personal dispositions. He lives in Seattle, she in Iowa; he moves around the world restlessly, she stays put as a dutiful housewife, leading a highly routinized, circumscribed, and predictable life (at least until they meet). Francesca is married to a good-natured but emotionally limited farmer; Robert is a loner, adventurer, and nature-loving world traveler, a nature photographer by profession without a family or close friends. He is alienated from the modern world, calling himself "the last cowboy." Like other true romantics, he is not merely a person capable of strong and authentic feelings who yearns for self-realization in a fulfilling relationship; he is also an outsider, a critic of society with its conventions and falsehoods. His critique of modernity and of modern American society reflects the sensibility of the 1960s and is integral to his romanticism. As he puts it:

There is a certain breed of man that is obsolete. . . . The world is getting organized, way too organized for me. . . . Rules and regulations and laws and social conventions. Hierarchies of authority, spans of control. . . . Corporate power. . . . A world of wrinkled suits and stick-on name tags. . . . In older worlds there were things we could do . . . that nobody or no machine could do. We run fast, are strong and quick. . . . We can throw spears long distances and fight in hand-to-hand combat.

Eventually, computers and robots will run things . . . men are outliving their usefulness. All you need are sperm banks to keep the species going. . . . Most men are rotten lovers, women say, so there is not much loss in replacing sex with science. . . . I am one of the last cowboys. My job gives me free range of a sort. As much as you can find nowadays.

Like most romantic heroes, Robert is also an aspiring artist and a critic of the debasement of art by mass culture:

I don't just take things as given. . . . I try to find poetry in the image. . . . That's the problem in earning a living through an art form. You are always dealing with markets . . . mass markets . . . designed to suit average tastes. . . . The market kills more artistic passion than anything else. . . . Profit and subscriptions . . . dominate art. We are all getting lashed to the great wheel of uniformity.

Robert's musings recall both the sensibility of the 1960s and that of D. H. Lawrence: "Analysis destroys wholes. Some things, magic things, are meant to stay whole. If you look at their pieces, they go away."

Robert is the archetypical romantic, the modern incarnation of the noble savage, perceived by Francesca as "a half-man, half-something-else creature" and possessed of "a peculiar, animal-like grace." His physique is as impressive as his personality: he "looked as if he ate nothing but fruit and nuts and vegetables," which is in fact the case. During their impassioned lovemaking she conceives of him as a "leopard [sweeping] over her, again and again, like a long prairie wind." He was an animal: a "graceful, hard, male animal who did nothing overtly to dominate her yet dominated her completely." In a posthumous letter to her children, she feels obliged to confess and explain her life-changing love affair:

> In a way he was not of this earth. . . . I have always thought of him as a leopard-like creature. . . . He somehow coupled enormous intensity with warmth and kindness, and there was a vague sense of tragedy about him. . . . He was like an arrow in his intensity. . . . He was all of those things—a stranger, a foreigner . . . a wanderer. . . . Robert believed the world had become too rational, had stopped trusting in magic as much as it should. . . . We remained bound together as tightly as it is possible for two people to be bound. . . . We had ceased being separate beings.

The sensual and the spiritual elements of their bond were inextricably intertwined:

> The night went on and the great spiral dance continued. Robert Kincaid discarded all sense of anything linear and moved to a part of himself that dealt only with shape and sound and shadow. . . . He heard the words he whispered to her, as if a voice other than his own were saying them. . . . Deep inside her, Robert Kincaid's long search came to an end. And he knew finally the meaning of all the small footprints on all the deserted beaches he had ever walked.

After the ecstatic lovemaking, Robert tells Francesca, "This is why I am here on this planet . . . to love you . . . through all those years, I have been falling toward you." He begs her to join him—in a manner reminiscent of Madame Bovary's fantasies of everlasting bliss with Rodolphe in some exotic location: "Come travel with me. . . . We will make love in desert sands and drink brandy on balconies in Mombasa, watching dhows from Arabia run up their sails in the first wind of the morning. I will show you lion country . . . on the bay of Bengal . . . and little inns . . . high in the Pyrenees."

For Francesca, too, their unexpected encounter and ecstatic lovemaking is an awakening and reminder of the undreamed-of possibilities of the body and spirit: "It was far beyond the physical. . . . Loving him was . . . spiritual." Her reflections, like those of Robert, once more bring to mind D. H. Lawrence:

> What was the barrier to freedom that had been erected out here? Not just on their farm, but in the rural culture. Maybe urban culture, for that matter. Why the walls and fences preventing open, natural relationships between men and women? Why the lack of intimacy, the absence of eroticism?[43]

The essential tragedy of Robert and Francesca's relationship is that they never meet again and—except for one exchange of letters and a posthumous one from Robert—never communicate again. He wills her his photographic equipment, and she keeps it as a sacred relic. At his request, his ashes are scattered at the covered bridge he photographed during his brief sojourn with her.

Death looms large in the story: first Francesca's husband dies, then Robert, finally Francesca. The reader is left with memories of an unfulfilled yet deeply moving account of the mystery of romantic love.

The persistence of romantic love in our times finds further expression in *The Bleeding Heart*, a novel by the late Marilyn French, the popular feminist author.[44] The story begins with the chance meeting on a train of Dolores, a divorced feminist academic, and Victor, a successful married businessman, both of whom are spending a year in England, he without his wife. The meeting leads to an impassioned love affair punctuated by the profound philosophical disagreements of the lovers. The relationship partakes of every attribute of the old-fashioned, stereotyped romantic love affair, combining obstacles of every kind with passion, intensity, and irrationality.

The barriers between the two are manifold. They have only one year in England, free of other obligations and social constraints; there is also physical space between them while in England: she lives in Oxford, he in London; the demands of his work reduce the time available for their meetings; most important, they have a clash of basic values, principles, and worldviews.

These obstacles feed the flames of passion: "After even the slightest separation, they came together tremulously, yearning after each other. . . . Be sensible, she told herself. It wouldn't be like this if we were together all the time, if we didn't have foreknowledge of the ending." She is right.

When they first meet on the train, without exchanging a single word "their eyes met, they locked . . . and would not let go. . . . She looked at him and he looked at her. . . . Blanking out what she had seen, eyes full of such longing that she could not abide by it, face full of such intensity that she could not resist it." After the wordless meeting on the train, he follows her to her apartment and they fall into each other's arms ("suddenly their bodies were together . . . until they felt like a single unit melted together"). The silence preceding the physical encounter intensifies it. As the female narrator reflects, "All the silence between them on the train, all the intensity, hadn't it been designed to make this feel cataclysmic, a tremendous romantic ecstasy? And it had worked, their sex was extraordinary."

As in many romantic encounters, lack of familiarity is, at least initially, an important component of the mysterious attraction. She thinks it is his "unknownness that made this encounter so marvelous." In turn, he says, "There was something in you—I don't know what it was—that drew me." The less than fully rational dimensions of romantic passion are further illuminated in these passages:

> They came together suddenly, violently. The violence was all inside but both of them felt it. They embraced, they kissed, it was even more desperate than the day before, as if then they had been separated for only a lifetime, but tonight it was a coming together after a millennium. They felt looped together by some power outside them, larger than they, manipulating them. . . .
>
> It was a loving war, a way of flesh to get beyond flesh, to get to something not palpable.

The conflict between the heroine's radical feminist beliefs and her lover's conventional attitudes adds a special element of drama and tension to the relationship, another obstacle that enhances the passion: "It was a shock to be involved with a man, any man at all, but especially a man who was her opposite in almost everything. It was like consorting with the enemy. . . . That's how insidious love was. It made you betray your principles."

The ease of nonverbal communication is another indicator of the mysterious power of their relationship:

> They did not touch, they did not speak. But their bodies cried out, sent out and received messages on the same line. Chemical, electrical, or romantic . . . whatever it was, it was so strong that when Dolores moved to allow a couple . . . to pass between her and Victor, she could physically feel herself breaking a field of force.[45]

It testifies to the persistence and strength of romantic ideals that even a feminist author, consumed by resentment and awareness of the endemic and chronic mistreatment of women by men, feels compelled to reproduce these ideals and to depict the romantic impulses as an irresistible force.

The next chapter will make clear that the romantic attitudes reflected in the novels discussed above have influenced contemporary American ideas and emotional aspirations. They are discernible both in popular culture and in the individual communications aimed at finding romantic partners. At the same time, as we shall see, this present-day "popular romanticism" has features rooted in American culture and social conditions, which distinguish it from the older European variety.

# CHAPTER THREE

# Popular Romanticism
in America

For generations of Americans during the first half of the twentieth century, romantic love remained perhaps our most fervent secular ideal. . . . Marriage would complement one . . . make one whole again. . . . The dream of a perfect lifelong mate expressed a longing for rescue from . . . living in an overwhelming and impersonal technological society. . . . For most of the twentieth century, popular culture . . . has conspired to portray this expansive feeling as paradise regained. Falling in love in a secular age . . . took on a spiritual dimension.

Michael Vincent Miller[1]

While romantic love may be dysfunctional . . . the fact that this luxuriant repository of pulp fiction finds a ready audience suggests that people can't get enough of it. In an endless stream of songs, novels, and movies . . . the same ideas about love and its woes are repeated over and over.

Brigitte Berger[2]

## American Modifications

A different kind of romanticism, modified to American tastes and circumstances—we might call it popular romanticism—today colors much of the quest for a partner in American society. Unlike its European forebears, this romanticism is not brooding, nor is it permeated by foreboding and melancholy; the tragic dimension is altogether absent. For many old-style romantics, both literary heroes and real human beings, emotional pain and suffering were an intrinsic part of the romantic infatuation: "preoccupation with pain was meant to serve a higher purpose. . . . Suffering was a gateway to a richer life, a door that led to a fuller understanding of the self and the world, a passage that opened out into the intensity of human experience."[3]

These beliefs in the benefits of pain and suffering also reflected the religious aspects of old-style European romanticism. But this is not the American way. As has often been observed, Americans are not disposed to a tragic view of life; they prefer to be cheerful and optimistic, inclined to the belief that there is a solution for every problem and that one may shape one's life by well-chosen means and the exertion of will. The idea of the self-made man (and woman) carries over from the economic realm to that of emotions and relationships.

A best-selling paperback by Nathaniel Branden, *The Psychology of Romantic Life*, offers an upbeat view of the accessibility and blessings of romantic love in our times, "not a fantasy or an aberration but one of the great possibilities of our existence, one of the great adventures and one of the great challenges. I am writing from the conviction that ecstasy is one of the normal factors of our emotional life, or can be."

Branden attempts to square the circle by suggesting that "one of the clearest requirements for a successful romantic relationship is that it be based on a foundation of realism. . . . This is the ability and willingness to see our partner as he or she is, with shortcomings as well as virtues, rather than attempting to carry on a romance with a fantasy."[4] He correctly points out that because America is an immigrant society, it has been easier to leave behind Old World traditions, which means, among other things, a greater freedom to marry on the basis of individual choice than in any other society.

The popular anthropologist Helen Fisher also offers an optimistic view of the place of romance in modern (and even premodern) society, arguing that romantic attractions have a biological basis and perform evolutionary functions, that "romantic love is universal human experience." Nor does age impose limitations: "Men and women in their seventies, eighties, even nineties also feel love's magic." She has come "to believe that romantic love is a universal human feeling, produced by specific chemicals and networks in the brain." On the other hand, "The very purpose of romantic love is to stimulate mating with a 'special' other"—which does not satisfactorily account for the fervor of senior citizens.

The results of Fisher's own study, based on a lengthy questionnaire completed by 437 Americans and 402 Japanese, led her to conclude that "age, gender, sexual orientation, religious affiliation, ethnic group: none of these human variables made much difference in the responses." Not unlike some of the romantic authors of the past, she finds that "contemporary men and women also feel the helplessness that accompanies this experience [of falling in love romantically]. 60% of the men and 70% of the women in my survey agreed with the statement 'Falling in love was not really a choice; it just struck me.'"[5]

The idea "that romantic love is essentially limited to or is the product of Western culture" has been criticized by two anthropologists who consider it a "Eurocentric" view. William Jankowiak and Edward Fischer argue that an "evolutionary perspective suggests that romantic love arises from forces within the hominid brain that are independent of the socially constructed mind." But even their account indicates that romantic love in non-Western, premodern societies was infrequent. Moreover ethnographic reports have encountered serious methodological problems, arising, among other things, "from the absence of any clear and consistent usage of the terms love, lovemaking, and lovers."[6]

While there are substantial similarities between the ultimate goals and ideals of old-style European and present-day American romanticism, the methods used in their pursuit are quite different. The very notion—prevalent in American culture—of *methods* that may be applied to a romantic quest is the most striking difference. Also characteristic of the American conception of romantic love is that it is readily and eagerly extended to marriage.

A student of present-day romanticism, Eva Illouz, has noted that "between 1900 and 1940, advertising and movies . . . developed and advanced a vision of love as a utopia wherein marriage should be eternally exciting and romantic."[7] It is a "vision" that testifies to a sturdy American optimism and high expectations.

The tenaciousness of romantic ideals and fantasies in America is also reflected in the undiminished popularity of romance fiction among women, notwithstanding the advances of feminism since the late 1960s.[8] It is indeed the case, as Miller puts it, that "our waning ideal of romantic love . . . offered a simplified . . . version of love to society that is fixated at the phase of adolescence. . . . American culture tends to be arrested at adolescence when it comes to social relations, especially intimate ones." The ethos of the 1960s, Miller adds, reinvigorated this utopian optimism:

> With that incorrigible, innocent . . . American optimism, a whole generation thought for a time that it could tame everything—wars, bureaucracies . . . racial differences—through love. . . . If monogamous marriage seemed confining . . . we would simply revise it and create open marriages, group marriages, spouse-swapping, and communal live-in sex without marriage.[9]

At the root of the American approach to romantic ideals and relationships is the conviction that all good things in life, and in sustaining personal relationships, are compatible: passion with reason, adventure with security, stability with excitement, beauty with brains, calculation with spontaneity, intense emotions with a routinized coexistence, and so forth. Hence most characteristic of the American approach to seeking intimate personal relationships is the attempted blending of the romantic with practical motives and considerations. While the basic values and aspirations may be traced to old-style European romanticism, peculiarly American cultural elements have been added, in particular the expectation that appropriate methods and determined efforts yield results, and that every individual is entitled to large funds of durable happiness and contentment.

The practical orientation is apparent in the tendency to gravitate toward people of similar backgrounds and sociocultural characteristics. To be sure, a substantial minority is indifferent to such considerations[10] and more preoccupied with elusive personal characteristics and compatibilities that are seen as independent of and superior to the mundane criteria of income, occupation, and education that define social class.

Helen Fisher suggests that two orientations converge when the romantically inclined seek to reconcile the appeals of the unfamiliar:

> Most people around the world do feel that enormous chemistry for unfamiliar individuals of the *same* ethnic, social, religious, educational, and economic background, who have a similar amount of physical attractiveness, a comparable intelligence, and similar attitudes, expectations, values, interests, and social and communicational skills. . . . Opposites attract—within the limits of one's ethnic, social, and intellectual sphere.[11]

Arguably there is a tension between the quintessential romantic disposition centered on the purity and intensity of feelings and the presumed essential compatibilities on the one hand, and practical considerations and criteria on the other. In the romantic frame of mind, decisive personal encounters and relationships are mysteriously preordained or determined by attractions and circumstances not fully understood or controlled by the protagonists. These attractions are often encapsulated in the word "chemistry." Those of a deeply romantic disposition doubt that intensely gratifying emotional connections can be established by some kind of cost-benefit analysis, calculation, and foresight.[12] Romantics disdain calculation. They believe in spontaneity and the free flow of feelings, and for similar reasons they disdain commerce as inescapably linked to material interest.

Dating is the archetypical American institution that incorporates these somewhat contradictory motives and considerations while providing the framework or structure for pursuing short- or long-term partners. It originated in the desire for privacy and freedom from supervision by members of one's family. It combines entertainment—"going out" to movies, theaters, nightclubs, and restaurants—with rational, market-oriented behavior designed to sample and evaluate the pool of potential partners. Notwithstanding the rational components, dating is usually expected to lead to a long-term romantic involvement.

Modern and especially American romanticism also departs from its European antecedents in its conception of physical beauty. Older attitudes toward romantic love and ideas of beauty were less standardized. By contrast, because of the rise of popular culture, the fashion industry, and advertising, images of beauty have become highly standardized, mass produced, and widely disseminated. Rougemont observes:

> Nowadays . . . a man who falls passionately in love with a woman he *alone* finds beautiful is supposed to be prey to nerves. . . . Admittedly, every generation forms a standardized notion of beauty as a matter of course. . . . But nowadays our sheep-like aesthetic tastes exert a greater influence than ever before, and they are being fostered by every possible technical . . . means. A feminine type thus recedes more and more from personal imponderables and is selected in Hollywood.
>
> The influence of standardized beauty is a double one. On the one hand, it preordains who shall be an appropriate object of passion. . . . On the other hand, it disqualifies a marriage in which the bride is not like the obsessive star of the moment. . . . A man who imagines he is yearning for "his" type, or a woman for "hers," is having his or her private wishes determined by fashionable and commercial influences.[13]

One of the consequences of these developments is that "intense exposure to images of attractive models produce decrements in men's commitment to their regular partner."[14] In other words, images of beautiful women appearing in advertisements or featured on televised entertainment offer standards of comparison that available realities cannot match, and may promote a sense of relative deprivation.

While, as noted above, there are areas of divergence between the traditional and contemporary popular American romanticism, American-style "expressive individualism" connects the two types. Andrew Cherlin has written about expressive individualism that it is "about personal growth, getting in touch with your feelings, and expressing your needs."[15] The emphasis on feeling is the first obvious connection between this type of individualism and the romantic worldview. More remarkable is that these notions of personal growth or self-development are rarely defined or specified. What exactly constitutes personal growth? Losing weight, changing one's hairstyle, ways of dressing, or occupation? Getting divorced or married? Learning another language, getting another degree? Moving to another location? Joining some type of support group? Presumably all these may be defined as personal growth. In the final analysis it seems that, in our anti-elitist culture, whatever the individual designates as personal growth is personal growth. Presumably a new relationship also promotes personal growth. The fuzziness of the concept adds to its romantic appeal.

The idea of personal growth is associated with the belief in the unique needs and capabilities of the individual. Today Americans are no less convinced about the uniqueness of their selves than were the nineteenth-century romantics. The endless preoccupation with "personal growth," self-development, and self-fulfillment—a product of the peculiar confluence of American egalitarianism, optimism, and individualism—has much in common with the past's romantic preoccupations with the self and its many needs. This preoccupation intensifies the importance and pursuit of understanding. The optimistic belief and expectation that there are, in every single individual, enormous intellectual and emotional potentials to be recognized and realized, and to be used to improve one's emotional life or occupational advancement, is the major American contribution to this modified romanticism.

## Popular Culture, Capitalism, and Romantic Love

Preoccupation with romantic attraction pervades American popular culture, as indicated by the profusion of Harlequin novels, television soap operas, women's magazines (and especially their advice columns), marriage manuals, and self-help books. Advertising massively reinforces and reflects this preoccupation. It disseminates, relentlessly and routinely, romantic images, clichés, and stereotypes, and raises expectations of all kinds, including that of romantic fulfillment. The basic, all-embracing message of advertising is that voracious consumption is the foundation of the good life, including loving personal relationships. Such relationships are shown to be fortified and enriched by various forms of consumption. Innumerable products promise rapid, miraculous physical and even mental transformation, and a dramatic increase in irresistible attractiveness.[16] Advertisements for many products and services explicitly assure their target audience of romantic benefits and wish fulfillment. Travel ads show lovers relaxing in beautiful settings; hotels, resorts, and cruises promise to enhance or help initiate romantic relationships. Television commercials for combating "erectile dysfunction" feature men and women gazing at one another enraptured; deodorants, perfumes, shampoos, hair coloring, toothpastes, and soaps promise rapid improvement of seductiveness. Cars, credit cards, and diet supplements routinely seek to associate their alleged benefits with personal relationships overflowing with warmth, joy, excitement, and contentment. Television commercials seek to convey the idea that users of these products are (or will be) deeply attached to one another and that their enhanced sexual attractiveness will be part of a unique relationship.

Advertising contributes to fantasies of romance by quite explicitly offering shortcuts to physical beauty and attractiveness, which are supposed to lead to or solidify relationships. Even shared consumption of certain foods and drinks is associated with intimacy, instant gratification, flirtation, good cheer, excitement, warmth, and joyful interaction between men and women, sometimes between different generations. Diamonds when given to women become symbols, even guarantees, of durable romantic relationships. Nature, the age-old romantic prop, is regularly enlisted:

> The ideal-typical romantic moment occurs in a remote place, on an exotic island . . . a dense forest, a serene lake . . . in a space symbolically cut off from the industrial and urban world. . . . The image of nature in contemporary advertising claims that consumption is a means to regain lost treasures, authentic self, genuine relationships. . . . The couples in such ads are absorbed in an intense gaze of nature as well as in each other.[17]

Using nature as an accessory to romance recalls the romantic images of nineteenth-century European romanticism. In such advertisements, authenticity and isolation are associated; human beings are often absent from these pictures except perhaps for an idealized couple feasting on the beauty and solitude around them. Not only are beaches invariably deserted in such commercials, even the decks of crowded cruise ships are bereft of passengers other than the man and woman shown gazing at the horizon and each other.

One may ask, how can romantic attachments, or an interest in them, flourish in a competitive, capitalistic, materialistic, and consumption-oriented society such as ours? Did Marx misjudge the corrosive influence of the "cash nexus"? Did he exaggerate the part played by material interest, the disposition to evaluate everything, including intimate personal relationships, by economic criteria? It is tempting to question the possibility that disinterested romantic attachments and dispositions could flourish in this kind of society; instead it might be argued that there are only *appearances* and gestures of a romantic orientation, which are based on self- and mutual deception and reflect a massive false consciousness. More convincingly, it may be proposed that romantic pursuits and attachments proliferate in modern American society as a reaction against the corrosive ethos of capitalism. Thus people seek to escape and transcend this grubby reality in romantic, intimate personal relationships that they hope will be free from the taint of the cash nexus, or "commodification."[18]

In other words, the values of a consumer society influence personal attachments and relationships without fundamentally or completely corrupting them, as illustrated by the connection between dating and consumption. "Dating," writes Eva Illouz, "appeared alongside the rise in real income of the early twentieth century. . . . These developments moved the romantic encounter from the familiar confines of the home to new locales that were both public and anonymous. . . . These circumstances made consumption an inherent element of any romantic encounter." She further suggests, "Although the market does not control the entire spectrum of romantic relationships, most romantic practices depend on consumption, directly or indirectly. But can we conclude from this that the quality of the romantic bond has been debased?" In her view the marketplace has "colonized" but not "debased" romantic relationships.[19]

Thus even in a capitalistic consumer society, romantic impulses and expectations remain widespread, but they lack the intensity captured in classical literary works. Advertising can only cheapen the ideal of romantic love by routinely suggesting that it can be realized by using the right product. The same applies to the flood of cheery self-help books and implausible romantic stories that are at the core of popular culture. Popular psychology too has made its unintended contribution to undermining and demystifying romantic love: "The model of love as an intense and spontaneous feeling has lost its power," Eva Illouz observes, "partly because it is now subsumed under a model of liberated sexuality, partly because a slow and progressive knowledge of the other is thought to be the only reliable way to build romantic attachments."[20]

Further light is shed on the connections between popular and old-style romantic love by Norman Mailer's novel *The Deer Park*, which is focused on the love life of Hollywood notables and aspiring celebrities, and set in the resort they frequent.[21] The male heroes of the novel share attributes of the heroes of popular film culture such as Humphrey Bogart, James Dean, Marlon Brando, and Clint Eastwood, among others. These movie characters, like some of those in *The Deer Park*, have in common a taciturnity, quiet strength, uncompromising determination, and a mysterious integrity. All are outsiders, exceptionally self-sufficient, solitary men of some deep but not necessarily revealed purpose.

They are risk takers and often court danger. Most important, they radiate authenticity. Unlike romantic characters of the past, they are doers rather than talkers. They are capable of great passion and strong feelings but can also get along just fine without women—part of their self-sufficiency.

Mailer's male heroes are further distinguished by their sexual prowess and concern with their performance in bed. Sex for them is a major form of authentic self-expression and self-realization, proof of self-worth, and a basis for making important connections with other people. Charles Francis Eitel, the main character in *The Deer Park*, represents an important strain of American romanticism. He is a filmmaker, creative artist, deep thinker, tragic hero, womanizer, and tortured soul. He is torn between his ambition to make great, artistically demanding films and his desire to be a Hollywood success with all its material indicators and mass-media-generated fame. He wants everything, including a reputation for being great in bed:

> Like most cynics, he was profoundly sentimental about sex. It was his dream of
> bounty, and it nourished him enough to wake up with the hope that this affair
> could return his energy, flesh his courage, and make him the man he had once
> believed himself to be. With Elena beside him he thought for the first time in
> many years that the best thing in the world for him was to make a good movie.

Elsewhere Mailer intimates that Eitel is not a true cynic but rather a frustrated idealist who found it difficult to fend off the enticements of Hollywood and the corrosive pressures of American-style success. He personifies the modern American romantic who is consumed by doubt about his way and the purpose of his life, and knows that his romantic aspirations are ultimately doomed. Nonetheless he pursues them with ambivalent hope:

> Now his life seemed stripped of interest. The inevitable progress of a love af-
> fair, Eitel thought. One began with the notion that life had found its flavor,
> and ended with a familiar distaste of no adventure and no novelty. It was one
> of the paradoxes he cherished. The unspoken purpose of freedom was to find
> love, yet when love was found, one could only desire freedom again. One went
> on, one passed on from affair to affair . . . and each provided its own way of
> promise of what could be finally found.

Eitel shares with romantics of all generations a highly unoriginal idea of human nature:

> The core of Eitel's theory was that people had a buried nature—"the noble sav-
> age" he called it—which was changed and whipped and trained by everything

in life until it was almost dead. Yet if people were lucky and they were brave, sometimes they could find a mate with the same buried nature, and that could make them happy and strong.

As perceived by the young narrator, the other major character of the book, "Eitel drank a lot, but I never saw him drunk . . . he took drugs . . . his reputation with women I would have been ready to share. . . . All the same he was forced to be a lonely man." Eitel's loneliness, like that of all romantic characters, is supposed to be an obvious mark of distinction.

There are actually three romantic, or romanticized, characters in *The Deer Park*. Besides Eitel, there is the narrator, a former fighter pilot (Korean War vintage) and boxing champion who decides for reasons not clear to live in the desert resort frequented by the Hollywood celebrities. He is totally self-absorbed, taking himself very seriously (as all romantics do): "I always thought there was an extra destiny coming my direction. . . . I never felt as if I came from any particular place, or that I was like other people." He was convinced "that to know oneself was all that was necessary." He is an incipient renaissance man: toward the end of the book he dabbles in bullfighting (in Mexico), aspires to write a novel about bullfighters, and sets up a bullfighting school in New York City; he also spends up to twelve hours a day in the public library devouring "all the good novels I could find" as well as literary criticism, history, philosophy, anthropology, and psychoanalysis. He studied French, Italian, and "even a little German because languages were natural for me, and two months I spent reading *Das Capital*." While ambivalently rubbing shoulders with the celebrities in their desert hideaway, he manages to pull off a torrid love affair with a Hollywood celebrity: "We were great lovers. . . . This was the best. I was superb. I told her the things I never told anybody else." During one of their passionate encounters she tells him, "I feel like a woman for the first time."

The third romanticized figure is a pimp. Mailer manages to romanticize him (and his calling) on the grounds that he is totally free of self-deception, a loner and risk taker, possessed of a ruthless sense of reality ("the whole world is bullshit") and the unromantic belief that "life was a battle against sentiment"; he is a champion of honesty, an unusual embodiment of authenticity:

> At twenty-four he was very special. He had an arrogance . . . staring at you, measuring your value. . . . He was a pimp. . . . When he came out of the Army, he refused to work, he refused to do anything he did not care to do . . . he was an amateur, he dabbled. To work at a business was to be the slave of a business. . . . Therefore he kept his freedom and used it to drink, to push dope on himself and to race his foreign car through the desert, a gun in the glove compartment instead of driving license . . . he drove like nobody I ever knew.

Most importantly, he is not a "phoney" and to be one is worse than being a "bastard," as another minor character speaking for the author insists.[22]

These heroes shared the aspiration to be (or appear to be) tough and hard-boiled; they were hard drinkers, occasional gamblers, and, above all, loners. They also were impulsive, self-absorbed, easily bored, and cherished a self-destructive streak. Each in his own way was intended to personify authenticity and a protest against the corruptions of American society, which pollute pure emotions.

A recent collection of interviews[23] sheds further light on the love life of Americans and provides glimpses of some unexpected similarities between the attitudes portrayed in The Deer Park half a century ago and those of present-day Americans. My interest in this book was sparked by a long and sympathetic article devoted to its editor in the New York Times.[24] The Los Angeles Times praised the collection as "a profound, touching work . . . a kind of self-help manual," allegedly "forcing readers to examine their own longings, failings, and assumptions about love."[25]

The volume contains a preface and forty-four interviews grouped according to the length of the relationship described in each—"one month to five years," "40 years to 60 years," and so on. The editor claims to have been motivated by the desire "to research other people's romantic experiences" (my emphasis). But he makes no discernible effort to achieve the goals attributed to him by the Los Angeles Times, instead assembling a jumble of unrelated, sometimes juicy stories about people falling in and out of love and often encountering various misfortunes. Some of these tales are quite mundane, while others are enlivened by an attention-catching twist; many are narrated in a spectacularly inarticulate manner, sometimes laced with profanities.

The apparent premise of the collection is that love has countless forms and manifestations, and each is as good as the other. Whatever people call love is love.

The stories were not selected according to any discernable theme or criteria. They include tales of unusual misfortunes and heartbreaks, unexpected terminal illnesses, drug addictions, and heavy drinking alternating with the occasional uplift provided by devout Christians of long and blissful marriages.

Each interview begins with the same question: "Please, tell me about the person whom you have loved the most." The editor explains that he wishes "to avoid theorizing and hypothesizing . . . and [wanted] to simply document a representative sampling of Americans . . . in all their variety, carrying on about romantic love." The criteria of selection is both highly subjective and vague: "We selected our stories on the basis of whether or not the interview augmented our understanding of romantic love," and edited them "with an eye toward highlighting each person's unique preoccupations and insights."

The editor apparently believes in the random availability of such insights. "I don't like experts and authorities," he tells the *Times*, "and I don't like writing about stuff in the normal way they consider news," explaining that "non-celebrities" and "non-experts" do a better job of "helping us understand the human condition."[26]

This collection reinforces the impression that there is a huge amount of confusion, insecurity, and free-floating discontent in American society regarding love and the creation of durable, intimate relationships. The only things most of these seemingly randomly chosen narrators have in common are their confusion, impulsiveness, and unstable personalities. Most of them seem to be impelled in their emotional pursuits by this instability and a reluctance (or inability) to defer gratifications and by a shallow individualism. They also share the conviction that whatever feels good is sufficient foundation for close personal relationships.

One interview begins with this revelation: "My definition of love is just being with someone who makes you feel good about being who you are." Another concludes, "I want to live the best life possible. If a woman contributes to my happiness, then I want to be with her. If a woman does not contribute to my happiness, I don't want her." The author of this confession claims to have dated three hundred women since his wife died. A twenty-seven-year-old man says, "Honestly, I think that when you fall in love, you pretty much know right away. You just know. And then, as far as keepin' it going, it's just waking up each morning on the same page. There's not really much more to it than that." Another respondent has this to contribute: "Theoretically everything was perfect. And then it wasn't. And that's really hard because I never had anybody that I thought I'd fit that well with. . . . Like, we were this really, really great idea. And then it didn't really work out."[27]

The thus-far favorable reception of the book suggests that the reviewers did not question the taken-for-granted moral relativism that permeates the interviews and the editor's outlook, including his apparent conviction that whatever people consider "love" is "the real thing."

This collection is another reminder of what I call the dark sides of individualism and its proximity to self-centeredness, isolation, and loneliness.

## New Challenges to Romanticism

While individualism and popular culture support the idea of romantic love, it has encountered new challenges in recent times.

Romantic love is under attack by radical feminists who consider it a form of false consciousness on the part of women, or "an agent of cultural orthodoxy."

They nonetheless admit—seemingly puzzled—that is has "endured all the philosophical and political attempts to discredit it." These feminists resolutely reject the "essential premise of popular romance . . . that a woman is not complete without a man." Feminist writers such as Fay Weldon, Angela Carter, Margaret Atwood, and Margaret Drabble seek to demonstrate the "deceptiveness of the way in which [popular romance] portrays women's relations with men." They intend to show that "the ideology of romance damages women, by giving them false expectations that the key to lasting happiness is the 'right' husband." They argue further that "romantic thinking blinds women to reality."[28] One may ask, why only women? The answer from these quarters would likely be that only women are so blinded because men cynically use romantic ideals to manipulate and dominate women. While Rodolphe's bombarding of Madame Bovary with romantic platitudes in his campaign of seduction is a good illustration of such uses of romantic ideals, it is hard to avoid the impression that the heartfelt romantic idealization of women by men is far more common than any corresponding idealization of men by women.

Megan Marshall writes on the same subject: "Love itself was branded as an advertising gimmick intended to lure women into the sexual slavery of marriage," referring to Caroline Bird's charge in *Born Female* that "[r]omantic love [is] a put-up job utilized to trap woman into giving up their identities."[29]

Christina Nehring, a champion of romantic love, is well aware of its feminist critiques: "It was in the 1970s that the anti-romantic chorus really swelled. . . . Articulate, energetic, and often best-selling feminist writers declared sex a glorified form of rape, and romance a patriarchal ploy to enslave women. . . . To look at love as the sublime union of souls . . . was to succumb to the fictions of the oppressor."

Nehring has taken a pessimistic view of the present condition of and prospects for romantic love:

> Romance in our day is a poor and shrunken thing. To some, it remains an explicit embarrassment, a discredited myth, the deceptive sugar that once coated the pill of woman's servility. To others, romance has become a recreational sport . . . another innocuous pastime. It has become "safe sex," harmless fun, a good-natured grasping for physical pleasure with a convenient companion. . . . Romantic love . . . is cause for embarrassment. . . . Undermined by cynicism, marginalized by recreational sex, rendered suspect by our culture's obsession with safety, and displaced, in part, by the worship of family values, it has also suffered . . . gravely from the side-effects of feminism.

There is a striking convergence in Nehring's understanding of romantic love and its nineteenth-century renderings. She writes, "At its strongest and wildest and most authentic, love is a demon. It is a religion, a high-risk adventure. . . . Love is ecstasy and injury, transcendence and danger, altruism and excess . . . a divine madness." Elsewhere she refers to romantic love as a "spiritualized sort of euphoria . . . a combination of sexual and metaphysical transport" of "consuming intensity," which "transcends ordinary expectations and experience." She too embraces the classical notions of obstacles that intensify passionate love: "At its core love is about breaking boundaries . . . between people and . . . and boundaries of propriety. Arrogant and intense, it disdains . . . the narrow playpen of bourgeois convention." Werther's protestations come to mind.

Nehring ignores the idealization and attendant distortion of the perception of the beloved produced by romantic infatuation: "What we see when we are in love is not a chimera . . . or an optical or emotional illusion. It is as close as we get to perfect sight, as close as we ever come to grasping the essence of another human being"—a highly questionable proposition. She believes that the major threats to romantic love in present-day America are to be found in the confluence of feminism and egalitarianism:

> It is the rare lover who genuinely thrives on the egalitarian, suspenseless brand of love touted today by our media and institutions of higher leaning. The heart craves adventure. . . . It is precisely equality that destroys our libidos, equality that bores men and women alike. . . . A man wants what a woman wants: someone compellingly different. . . . It is with the enigmatic Other . . . that we dream to join, not with a brother, not with a familiar, and not . . . with an equal.

Nehring is well aware of the tension between modernity and romantic love:

> Almost everything in modern society militates against our falling in love hard and long. It militates against love as risk, love as sacrifice, love as heroism. As presented to us in dating books, matchmaking sites, and advice columns, love is—or ought to be—an organized adult activity with . . . a clear, clean destination: marriage.

She rightly points out that marriage used to be considered "the very anti-thesis of romance. Adultery was romantic, adultery was spiritual, adultery was idealistic; marriage was just an arrangement of physical and financial convenience."[30] But this is not the American way. The innovation of American culture has been to insist on the essential compatibility of romance and marriage—another example of the American yearning for all good things to be compatible.

In a letter to the *New York Times Book Review*, a professor of psychiatry at the Harvard Medical School took issue with Nehring's message and the favorable front-page review her book received. "Nehring," he wrote, "supports impulsive, unthinking, and self-destructive behavior in the service of what she calls love. . . . What is described could serve as an illustration for a manual of emotionally disturbed living."[31] Nehring's book was also criticized by Martha Nussbaum for propagating "the adolescent view . . . that love is improved by suffering" and for exaggerating the role of modern feminism in the decline of romantic love.[32]

A more fact-based, if similarly pessimistic, view of romantic love in our time is put forward by Barbara Whitehead:

> A classical language of romance . . . has been supplanted by a scientized "relationships talk." Finding lasting love is never easy, but it seems to be especially hard for women today. Evidence of romantic frustration is everywhere: in popular television shows . . . in the gargantuan appetite for self-help dating and relationships books; in the endless talkfests about men's frailties and failings; in the hit movies and best-selling novels. . . . For woman today . . . the dating world is full of chaos and confusion. No one knows what the rules are. . . . No consensus exists on . . . romantic conduct, such as who should take the initiative in dating, when to have sex, when to live together . . . who proposes marriage, what constitutes commitment . . . what it takes to make love last.[33]

But Whitehead also observes, "Men and women alike say that they want to marry a 'soul-mate,' someone who fulfills their needs and desires at a sexual, emotional, and spiritual level." She notes another source of tension— between the development of romantic relationships and the ethos of work in American society, given the connection between leisure and love:

> Love offers a respite from the world of work. It creates a place where workplace values and expectations cannot intrude. . . . The very values traditionally associated with love stand in opposition to work. Love is indolent and inefficient. It is careless with time. Love has no billable hours . . . romantic love flourishes in the midst of leisure. This is why the personal ad placers, who are trying to save time and extend their prospects, still conjure a romantic vision of "walks on the beach," lazy evenings in front of the fire with a bottle of Merlot.[34]

People who are preoccupied with their career often don't have enough time for social life. Matchmaking businesses promote their services by offering to save time for busy professionals.

These varied comments highlight the complex and contradictory attitudes toward romantic love in America today. Romantic interests and impulses clearly persist, and no longer only among younger age groups: "The emerging relationship system . . . endows everyone with romantic privileges once reserved for the never-married young," Whitehead observes.[35]

Structural obstacles nonetheless interfere with the realization of these widespread and, arguably, often confused and contradictory aspirations.

As the following chapters will demonstrate, ideals of romantic love survive, even if in somewhat attenuated forms, as countless Americans seek to carve out a precarious space between the wish to acquire the unique soul mate and a realistic search for someone who will meet their carefully calibrated, more down-to-earth needs.

# CHAPTER FOUR

# Expert Advice on
# Dating and Mating

If you can't find the guy you want, or don't know how to fix the guy you got, you and I are about to change that in a major way. . . . I am about to let you in on some secrets and strategies. . . . You are about to master the art of relating.

Dr. Phil[1]

No more lonely Saturday nights, no more waiting for the phone to ring. . . . To be adored and secure at last! That's the incredible payoff you get when you do *The Rules*.

Ellen Fein and Sherrie Schneider[2]

This study seeks to shed light on not only the nature of the aspirations and expectations of individual Americans who seek romantic relationships but also the broader social and cultural forces that influence their hopes and dreams. Individual beliefs and attitudes are rarely unique or totally self-generated. Important beliefs and preferences are widely shared in every society and thus have common sources. But it is not easy to identify these sources and the processes that influence individual values and beliefs, especially in modern societies in which there are a great many such influences.

In traditional societies it was relatively easy to locate the sources of widely held beliefs: it was the family, the community, and the church (or individual representatives of religion) that inculcated and transmitted them and promoted what were considered appropriate attitudes. As traditional societies changed and modernized, these beliefs came to be reinforced (and sometimes challenged) by educational and legal institutions. In contemporary societies, and especially the American, the influence of family, community, and church has greatly diminished and been partially replaced by other forces. The family and religion still exert influence on the aspirations and behavior of many Americans, but these influences must now compete with others. As the following chapters will show, religion plays a much smaller part in the lives of some groups than in others.

We all are born into a society that supports certain values and beliefs, and few of us make a substantial and original contribution to them. As Barbara Whitehead observes:

> The successful search for a life mate is a social as well as an individual pursuit. Mating, or . . . romantic courtship, has customarily relied on social supports as well as individual efforts. . . . No known society leaves mate selection and marriage up to lone individuals. . . . Our choices in love, as in other areas of our lives, are structured by social influences . . . by social class, law, custom and technology.[3]

The books discussed below reflect these social influences. Laura Kipnis, a feminist author, notes that "relationship advice is a booming business these days: between print, airwaves, and the therapy industry, if there were any way to quantify the GNP in romantic counsel . . . it would certainly amount to a staggering number." She thinks that present-day American society seeks to indoctrinate its members with the importance of love, conventionally defined: "Consider the blaringly omnipresent propaganda beaming into our psyches on an hourly basis; the millions of lovestruck couples looming over us from movie screens, televisions, billboard, magazines, incessantly strong-arming us onboard the love train. Every available two-dimensional surface touts love."[4]

Kipnis also writes that "contemporary coupledom does have its hidden risks, or so our popular culture keeps warning us. . . . For every film that ends with a happy pair in love-affirming embrace . . . another shows us the anxiety, perversity, boredom, sadism, and frustration that riddle coupled life."[5] If so, the alleged brainwashing by popular culture is far from seamless since it also alerts its audience to the dangers and difficulties that abound under the conditions it supposedly idealizes.

Among the products or manifestations of modernity, American popular or mass culture (including advertising and self-help books) is the most obvious and direct influence on the attitudes we would like to better understand. It should be conceded at the outset that while mass culture influences widely held attitudes, its purveyors did not invent the values or attitudes they propagate. Rather, they reflect or elaborate beliefs already held. Even so, if popular culture reflects attitudes and beliefs it did not invent, it does strengthen, deepen, and legitimize prevalent attitudes, aspirations, and beliefs, whatever their source.

Writings that offer advice about dating and durable personal relationships ("relationship books") are the most tangible sources of cultural influences, especially those among them that are widely read. It is not difficult to place this literature into the broader currents of American cultural and social history in which egalitarianism seamlessly combines with individualism. These books serve up a reincarnated myth of the self-made man, but the self-improvement they champion is not aimed at getting rich but getting the love we supposedly all deserve.

Today's widely recognized confusion and uncertainty over the best ways to establish and maintain close personal relationships create a strong demand for advice and instruction. When traditional sources of guidance are weakened and discredited, as they have been for some time, the wisdom of "experts"—with credentials or self-styled—will be sought. As Barbara Whitehead points out, now "there are no models to follow or guides to direct [young women]. . . . The process of finding a life partner is often chaotic, unintelligible. . . . There are no common standards or codes of behavior."[6] Laura Kipnis adds: "Eager to be cured of love's temporality, a desperate population has molded itself into . . . advice receptacles. . . . Check out the relationship self-help aisle in your local bookstore chain."[7]

Whitehead includes popular fiction aimed at young women (also known as "chick lit") among the sources that reflect the mind-set and disappointments of young women who seek more substantial relationships with men. In most of these novels, "the heroine is isolated from a settled social world. . . . She has to figure out how to reach her romantic destination entirely on her own."[8]

Whereas "in the past societies had recognized sets of rules and expectations that helped women think about what they wanted when it came to love, sex, commitment, and marriage," a study by Norval Glenn and Elizabeth Marquardt of the dating and mating practices of college women found that

> there are few widely recognized social norms on college campuses that help guide and support young women in thinking about sex, love, commitment, and marriage. . . . As a result the culture of courtship . . . and expectations that once helped young people to find pathways to marriage, has largely become a hook-up culture with almost no shared norms or expectations. . . . Each young woman today tends to see her choices as wholly private and individual.[9]

Under these conditions it is not surprising that there is a large market for the wisdom dispensed by "relationship experts," dating manuals, and the televised advice of their authors.

In the following sections I will examine mostly best-selling "relationship books" and dating manuals (the two categories overlap) that dispense advice about finding a romantic partner and and enduring relationship. I have employed two criteria in selecting them. First, I wanted to maximize the number of popular or best-selling books. Their popularity suggests a greater public interest in their messages, and they are presumably more influential and informative of prevailing social and cultural values and trends. Second, I tried to diversify the sample of these books by including those addressing different audiences: women only, black women, Christians, and others. Several of these books combine a discussion of finding a partner with suggestions for improving existing marital relations. I also include books that deal only with improving marriage since many of the same issues—notably the qualities or traits essential for finding partners and maintaining durable relationships—are dealt with in both types of writings.

These books have been written by both men and women, but probably more by women and most of them *for* women. Most of the authors are therapists, psychologists, and psychiatrists, with or without PhDs, as well as freelance writers and journalists who believe themselves qualified to dispense such advice. We do not know how many of these authors lead exemplary married lives, or what proportion of them enjoy serial monogamy, or, more generally, how many exemplify the advice they offer.

It is noteworthy that even in our times marked by the success of feminist movements and beliefs, it remains a prevailing assumption in much of this literature that women are more interested in creating and maintaining romantic relationships than men are, and more eager recipients of advice that supposedly will help them achieve this goal.

The influence of these authors is enhanced by their lecture tours, seminars, and frequent appearances on television. While we can never know precisely how much influence ideas exert on popular belief and behavior, it is plausible that widely read and widely watched authors wield considerable power. People vote with their money and express trust in their message when they buy their books, enlist in their seminars, and watch them on television.

These books share one dominant feature: a focus on methodology, on techniques and carefully specified steps or stages in the process of finding a partner and developing a good relationship. They say much less about what people should look for or expect from such a relationship, or about the human qualities that deserve to be valued and sought.

Dr. Phil McGraw (also known as "Dr. Phil") is a preeminent authority on matters of the heart. Author of twelve self-help books (including three on diet and weight loss), his work often appears on the *New York Times* bestseller list, and he is "host of the nationally syndicated, daily one-hour series, *Dr. Phil.*" McGraw obtained a PhD in clinical psychology from the University of North Texas but stopped practicing in 1990 after he set up a trial consulting business. His claim to fame is closely associated with his friendship with Oprah Winfrey and his frequent appearances on her television show before he began his own. In the acknowledgments he profusely thanks her for her "friendship and endless belief and support of my work. You make this world a better place. . . . You have made a difference not only in this country, but also in the cradle of humanity by leading by example and living with completeness and honesty."

Dr. Phil's credentials include a great marriage of thirty years that he extols in the acknowledgments in his book *Love Smart*: "Robin, you are the culmination of what anyone reading this book would pray for. Our relationship has been the crowning achievement in my life." He makes no reference to an earlier failed marriage that lasted for three years. A seemingly detailed self-presentation (in which he offers himself as an example for the reader) includes questions addressed to himself and a listing of "committed relationships before" his current marriage. It also includes the question, "How did other significant relationships end?" but there is no reference to his previous marriage.

Like several others of the same genre, this book is written for women. Its surprising premise—in twenty-first-century America—is that, unlike men, women long to marry and badly need instruction about the ways they can accomplish this goal.

Dr. Phil does not shy away from bold claims and promises delivered in a folksy style, which brings to mind the proverbial used-car salesman—all the more so since he favors the metaphors of salesmanship. To wit:

> The problem is *not* you. . . . I believe, to the absolute core of my soul, that you are about to discover a huge secret . . . YOU.
>
> To get you where you want to go, we're going to absolutely rewrite the script of your life, and you're going to be the star.

In a section titled "Your Defined Product," Dr. Phil advises mastering "the first rule of the game, which also happens to be the first rule of sales: If you're not sold on your product, you won't be able to sell anyone else on it either." The same message is repeated later in different words: "Thinking like a winner, feeling like a winner, and behaving like a winner are essential to victory."

At the end of the book he writes, "Here is the chapter where you cash in your chips. The one you have been waiting for on how to reel him in. . . . Now it seems time to . . . close the deal." He offers "power tools for closing the deal" as well as "the formula for lasting love." This formula excludes a belief in the durability of romantic love: "floating on that romantic high feels great but . . . eventually you will wake up . . . and plant your feet on the ground."

The bulk of Dr. Phil's exhortations are remarkably unoriginal and may be reduced to repeated self-confidence-building mantras:

> You will not succeed in the highly competitive dating game unless you are *convinced* that you are absolutely fabulous. . . . I'm going to show you how to discover the fabulous parts of you. . . . If you will embrace the concepts that I'm about to lay out, adopt the behaviors that I'm going to prescribe, and employ the strategies that we're going to create together: problem solved!
>
> And what's more, we are going to have an absolute ball doing it. It's time to get what you want! . . . You have to decide that you are fabulous . . . that you are deserving. . . . If you truly want to get the fish into the boat, you're going to have to fall in love with yourself.

More specifically, he advises:

> You think you're fat and ugly—baloney! Who told you that? To the right guy, those extra pounds look like feminine curves. And while that face you see day in and day out may have worn out its welcome with you, in the eyes of the right man, it's unique, character-filled, quirky, or wise. . . .
>
> A great self-image will beat out collagen injections and silicone implants. . . . If you want to show the world that you have everything to give and nothing to lose, follow the example of powerful people.

Donald Trump is one exemplar then mentioned.

Dr. Phil's other major piece of advice (equally unoriginal) is playing hard to get:

> You are moving along and are actually dating this guy. Here is where you've got to be willing to play some poker. Some people may call this playing "hard

to get," but that's not really it. . . . You want him come to you, like a deer comes to the feeder.

You need to stay on your guard. . . . That means not seeming too eager. It means not always saying you're free when he calls up. . . . You need to remain that carrot on a stick—elusive and always just barely out of reach.

Methodical Dr. Phil tells the reader to make an inventory of her strong points: "What I need you to discover during . . . this personal inventory is who you really are: a great partner, a fantastic catch, and one of the world's best-kept secrets." He also recommends writing "an online dating profile . . . consider this step practice in self-promotion. After all, online dating is all about marketing yourself."

An abundance of practical advice includes making lists of all sorts of things to ponder and, most of all, specifics of self-presentation.

Eye contact is an especially powerful presentation tool. . . . You choose what type of presence you want to radiate in a room. . . . Don't just show up at a social situation. Show up with a plan. . . . Create your sound bite. Explain who you are in twenty words or less. Make yourself sound as exciting as possible. Hit all your strongest attributes and exclude anything that sounds negative. . . . Define four or five things you can talk about at any time to anyone. . . . When you are in conversation, avoid nervous habits like twirling your hair. . . . There are positions that are likely to get you in someone's crosshairs in no time: sitting at the center of interaction in a heavily trafficked area; sitting at the bar; facing the crowd, looking around for opportunities.

Dr. Phil's confident exhortations are firmly rooted in the boundless American belief in the capacity of the individual to remake or reinvent herself. The past is irrelevant, as are our genes, upbringing, and environment; the power of our free will is unlimited ("Now that you've got those naysaying saboteurs out of your system, it's time to figure out what is so wonderful about you"). All of us have something wonderful about us.

No one could accuse Dr. Phil of promoting old-style romantic ideas of perfect compatibility and unrealistic beliefs in the persistence of passionate love in marriage. He advises lowering your expectations, cautions against "going for the dream guy . . . set[ting] the bar so high that nobody measures up. . . . The 199% perfect candidate doesn't exist . . . the perfect fit is a myth." Still, he suggests looking for "a healthy, functional partner who is uniquely compatible with you."[10]

It is not easy to imagine and impossible to know how a book of this kind will help its readers establish rewarding and durable relationships.

*Mars and Venus on a Date* is subtitled "A Guide for Navigating the 5 Stages of Dating to Create a Loving and Lasting Relationship."[11] The author, John Gray, also wrote the best-selling *Men Are from Mars, Women Are from Venus.* His dating manual is a typical how-to book that instructs the reader in great detail about what to do—or not do—in the process of finding a "loving and lasting relationship." The book is relentlessly focused on techniques, good communication, the sober calculation of ends and means, and the profound differences between men and women. Each sex is coached about the kinds of compliments it should offer to the other. Several pages list specific places, occasions, or activities recommended for meeting "your soul mate." They include "hanging out on an airplane near the rest rooms and strik[ing] up a conversation while waiting in line." Further, "In a restaurant a woman should get up several times and walk to the restroom so that a man has a chance to see her and be interested." The reader is also advised that "by baby-sitting for a friend and strolling with a baby in the park a man will attract women like bees to honey."

Along with romantic notions of love, there is much talk about "chemistry." Gray writes, "When soul mates fall in love there is simply a recognition. It is as clear and simple as recognizing that the sun is shining today." He proposes that "we cannot create emotional, mental, or spiritual chemistry. It just is." Elsewhere he writes, "There is something special about every woman, but what makes a woman more special to a particular man is the special chemistry he feels for her." Gray is among the optimists who believe in romantic marriage with "a partner with whom our love and passion can grow." More conventionally, he also believes that women should "play hard to get"—or, as he puts it, "when a woman is too eager to please, a man doesn't experience the distance he needs to pursue her."[12] Little is said about desirable human qualities people should look for or cultivate in themselves.

Dr. Joyce Brothers, author of several best-selling books, is described on the jacket of *What Every Woman Ought to Know About Love and Marriage*[13] as a "celebrity and a unique authority figure in the lives of countless people." Her book also concentrates on method—how to establish and maintain a long-term, loving marital relationship, and how to avoid specific missteps. Like most advice manuals, it begins and ends on an upbeat note: "The good news is that . . . there are hundreds and thousands of Mr. Rights for each and every woman." Dr. Brothers is convinced that "the early ecstasy" and "rapture" of sex can be recaptured with prudent initiatives such as weekends away from home or a "second honeymoon"; "recharging sexual batteries . . . is easier than you think."[14]

Her approach combines hard-nosed practicality with somewhat old fashioned notions of the manhunt: "The office is not the only place where eligible men abound. Hospitals are full of male doctors and medical students, male patients and visitors. You might think of volunteering . . . at your local hospital a few hours a week." Dr. Brothers also recommends buying stock and going to meetings of stockholders to meet men. A great believer in being methodical, she urges the reader to "write down ten ways you can meet men." In one chapter, she acquaints readers with "the five ingredients of the Intimacy Formula" (opportunity, selectivity, receptivity and initiative, desirability, and intimacy) developed by a professor of psychiatry at the University of Pennsylvania.[15]

Readers are not only instructed in the techniques of the manhunt but are told what to watch for: "The qualities to look for in a man are sincerity, warmth, integrity, courage, gentleness, perseverance, sympathy, intelligence." Written in the early 1980s, *What Every Woman Ought to Know* shows few signs of radical feminism: it repeatedly advises women to cater to male egos, take the extra step to make their spouses happy (for example, have sex even if they don't feel like it), and treat marriage as more important than their career (if they have one). She opposes women having an affair more on practical than on moral grounds ("the competition is too keen for a woman to risk an affair") but is more tolerant of men engaging in one. She is well aware of the importance and fragility of marriage at a time when it is the target of historically unprecedented expectations while its economic functions have shrunk. On one hand, she writes, "We start out with unrealistic expectations that marriage will meet all our needs and make us happy." On the other hand, she maintains that "marriage offers a refuge from stress. It gives us strengths to cope with the world. . . . This has become crucially important in an impersonal world where so many of us feel anonymous."[16] She struggles with reconciling these two attitudes: unrealistic expectations and the hope that with wise planning and proper methods they can be met after all.

As common sense dictates, Dr. Brothers advises that successful marriages require substantial prior knowledge of the future spouses. It is preferable, she suggests, to choose a man with a similar socioeconomic and cultural background (including race and religion) and of similar age; it is also important not to choose someone who is "far more attractive." Less obviously, she proposes to find someone who is "your psychological opposite" and would therefore provide stimulation and complementarity. A "premarital checklist" is offered to help accomplish these goals.

The optimistic approach permeating much of this book finds expression in an emphasis on the redeeming value of communication that leads to problem solving: "Sex is not that complicated a deal. If you tell each other in a loving way what is good and what leaves you cold, you will be surprised how fast things will improve."[17] This is one of many similar books which both reflect and reinforce American cultural values and attitudes: optimism, practicality, a belief in being methodical, and high expectations tempered by sober calculation.

A popular book by Greg Behrendt and Liz Tuccillo, also made into a movie, is dedicated to the proposition that women make poor judgments about men and deserve better treatment than they get from them. They need advice and help, which the authors offer. The volume is titled *He's Just Not That Into You: The No-Excuses Truth to Understanding Guys*.[18] According to the jacket information, the book is based on an episode of *Sex and the City*, the popular television program. The authors also appeared on the *Oprah Winfrey Show*. While much of the book abounds in good-natured, humorously presented, commonsense advice, more unusually the authors insist that "if a man is not trying to undress you, he is not into you," and "if a man likes you, he's going to want to have sex with you." They advise their readers that they have a "right to have a fantastic sex life."[19]

This book raises the question: why is there such a large demand and receptivity for advice predicated on the poor judgment women make about men? The book suggests that women who complain of mistreatment by men display traditional, submissive attitudes and suffer from insufficient self-esteem. The apparent existence of a large pool of such women is counterintuitive in our era of liberated women

Most of these books are manuals on how to sell oneself, imbued with the spirit and terminology of the marketplace. The authors of *The Rules*, Ellen Fein and Sherrie Schneider, declare, "When you do *The Rules*, you don't have to worry about being abandoned, neglected or ignored!"[20] They promise that "abuse doesn't happen in a *Rules* relationship because when you play hard to get and he works like hell to get you, he thinks you're the most beautiful, wonderful woman in the world, even if you are not. He treats you like a precious jewel." Adopting *The Rules*, say the authors, will result in "living painfree."

This highly popular best-seller written for women has in common with most others a didactic and repetitive style and an unabashedly manipulative approach: "*The Rule* is that as long as you don't outright lie, you needn't be honest to a fault either"—as in writing a personal ad. *The Rules* also has in common with similar books an emphasis on techniques, the building of self-esteem, and a purported belief in the limitless possibilities available for all those willing to abide by the advice proffered. Its main distinction lies in its focus on the unembarrassed advocacy of the "playing hard to get" strategy and a largely conventional view of sex roles: "the premise of *The Rules* is that we . . . trust in the natural order of things—namely, that man pursues woman." Women "should be a mystery," not an open book—seemingly unattainable, somewhat distant, and emotionally reserved in their self-presentation: "Your job . . . is to treat the man you're really . . . crazy about like the man you're not interested in." He should always "feel that he is in love with the girl of his dreams."

These manipulative and tough-minded admonitions make *The Rules* an exceptionally unromantic text that endlessly warns against the dire results of spontaneity, openness, and sincerity ("letting it all hang out . . . is counterproductive to your goals"). It advocates relentless calculation, pretense, and "go[ing] against your feelings," at least in the early stages of the dating campaign. Sex should be withheld or carefully rationed; women should not "give it away" prematurely but use it as part of the grand strategy of marrying the most suitable partner.

Fein and Schneider "believe in treating dating like a job, with rules and regulations. Just like you have to work from nine to five, no matter how you *feel*, we believe you have to silently train men to make plans with you (elusive, busy, happy you!)." The authors also insist that women stop dating a man who does not buy "a romantic gift for your birthday or Valentine's day." They warn against discussing their book with a therapist, who is likely to consider it "dishonest and manipulative." A good guess.

The endless confidence building exhortations of *The Rules* merge into unabashed manipulativeness and the conflation of "is" and "ought":

Act confident even if you don't *feel* it.

Being a creature unlike any other is . . . an attitude, a sense of confidence and radiance that permeates your being. . . . It doesn't matter if you are not a beauty queen, that you never finished college, or that you don't keep up with current events. . . . Of course that is not how you really *feel*. This is how you *pretend* you feel until it feels real. *You act as if!*

On a date, you never show that getting married is foremost on your mind. . . . When you go to singles dances or parties, you pump yourself up. You pretend you're a movie star. You hold your head high and walk in as if you just flew in from Paris on the Concorde. . . . You act as if everything is great, even if you are on the verge of flunking college or getting fired. . . . You tell yourself "Any man would be lucky to have me" until it sinks in and you start to believe it.

What the authors fail to tell the hapless reader is how she will be able to conjure up these flattering and unrealistic self-conceptions and the determination to change her self-image abruptly. They can only advise the reader to repeat to herself how terrific she is and urge her to "read this book over and over until you have practically memorized it, then practice the principles as much as possible." Another practical piece of advice is to subscribe to *Seventeen* and *Glamour* magazines "to see what is hot and not" since men "like girls who wear what's on MTV and in *Seventeen*."[21]

The huge commercial success of *The Rules* inspired *The Rules: More Rules to Live and Love By*, published two years later in 1997. Interestingly, in the sequel the authors insert a disclaimer at the outset: "We are not licensed to practice psychology, psychiatry, or social work, and *The Rules* is not intended to replace psychological counseling, but is simply a dating philosophy based on our own experiences and those of thousands of women who have contacted us."[22] The new book was written (they explain to the reader) to address more specific issues not discussed in its predecessor, in chapters such as "Rules for Turning a Friend into a Boyfriend"; "Rules for Getting Back an Ex"; "Long-Distance Relationships"; "You Can Ask Your Therapist to Help You Do *The Rules*"; "Rules for the Office Romance"; "Don't Be a Groupie, Rules for Celebrities"; "Use a *Rules* Support Group"; "Rules for Same Sex Relationships," and many others (there are thirty-three chapters in all). In the introduction the authors respond to critics and reaffirm their core convictions and philosophy: "*The Rules* are based upon the basic truth of human nature! . . . The man must be attracted to and then pursue the woman. It simply doesn't work any other way. . . . *The Rules* is not just a dating book . . . but a way of building a full life and dating with self-esteem."

They also continue dispensing commonsense advice: "Make sure you are wearing fashionable suits and shoes [at the office]—you want to look as good as you can! Don't wear pantyhose with runs in them—keep extra pairs in your desk drawer. . . . Don't kiss or hold hands at the office. . . . Think positive. Keep your mind occupied with interesting ideas, activities, people, and reading material and you will be interesting."

Manipulation remains essential. To nudge a prospective husband to propose, "go away for a weekend with a girlfriend. Cancel a Saturday night date,
get very busy at work, mention that you are renewing your apartment lease
and be mysterious about your activities."[23]

Fein and Schneider have also published a follow-up volume, *The Rules
for Online Dating*, which largely duplicates the advice offered in their earlier
books. Not surprisingly, "the good news is that *The Rules* apply to online
dating."[24] They reaffirm the importance of thinking of oneself as a "Creature
Unlike Any Other" (CUAO). To achieve this blessed state of mind they
advise:

> You play hard to get on the internet as in other real-life situations described
> earlier. Certain words never to use in email: soul mate, dream man, commit-
> ment, anything about sex, ex-boyfriend, ex-husband, marriage, connection,
> intimacy or anything about game-playing (e.g., "I don't play games").[25]

*The Five Love Languages*[26] is one of eight books by Gary Chapman that has
achieved best-seller status. At my writing it has been on the *New York Times*
paperback best-seller list for 137 weeks.[27] It is not addressed to readers seeking a partner but to those who want to improve an existing marital relationship. The author is director of Marriage and Family Life Consultants, Inc.
He travels around the world presenting seminars, and his radio program airs
on over a hundred stations—as the jacket informs the reader. As the book
title indicates, Chapman focuses on communications, to wit, "We must be
willing to learn our spouse's primary love language if we are to be effective
communicators of love." The "five love languages" are "words of affirmation,
quality time, receiving gifts, acts of service, and physical touch." Each gets a
separate chapter.

The author takes a hardheaded view of romantic love ("it tends to disen-
gage our reasoning abilities") and cites studies showing that it rarely endures
for more than two years. He quotes M. Scott Peck, who has written that
"falling in love . . . is a genetically determined instinctual component of
mating behavior . . . the temporary collapse of ego boundaries. . . . Falling
in love is the stereotypic response . . . to a configuration of internal sexual
drives and external sexual stimuli, which serves to increase the probability
of sexual pairing."

The goal of Chapman's book is to keep love alive in marriage after the romantic fog dissipates and the couple returns to the real world. He offers a great deal of specific advice about the methods to be employed, as for example:

1. To remind yourself that "Words of Affirmation" is your spouse's primary love language, print the following on a 3x5 card and put it on a mirror or other place where you can see it daily:

   Words are important!
   Words are important!
   Words are important!

2. For one week keep a written record of all the words of affirmation you give your spouse daily. At the end of the week, sit down with your spouse and review the record.[28]

Numerous other exercises and lists will supposedly help achieve the objectives pursued by author and reader.

Alan Loy McGinnis, who died in 2005, was a popular Christian therapist and the founder and director of the Valley Counseling Center in Glendale, California. Several million copies of his books remain in print; he often appeared on radio and television. His religious beliefs notwithstanding, most notable in McGinnis's message is a refreshing common sense and an absence of jargon and semantic gimmicks. In *The Romance Factor* he writes simply and clearly and does not convey the image of the backslapping salesman or expert guru. He begins with a series of important questions:

Can old-fashioned romantic love work in this age of one-night stands and quick divorce?
What *is* that initial rush of elation that causes two people to stay up all night talking? . . .
Why does romance die? Is it possible to hate someone you once loved? Or could it be that you never actually loved that person in the first place?[29]

McGinnis shares with authors of comparable books the belief that winning "at the game of love" depends chiefly on the "skill at creating love," that "*becoming* the right person" is far more important than "*finding* the right person." In his examination of current conditions conducive to romantic infatuation, he highlights the connections between modernity, social isolation, and the search for a love object. The lonely individual, unhappy with himself or herself, is a "prime candidate for falling in love, and anyone handy can be the object of such projections. . . . The stranger can take on an unlimited number of our idealizations." Further, "We have been programmed by our culture, by the depiction of love on the screen and by popular song to think of love as the major solution to all our problems." At the same time, McGinnis observes, mass culture and its entertainments provide a panorama of negative role models, that is to say, social pathologies that are increasingly presented as normal. He mentions the popular television program *General Hospital*, in which the seventeen major characters "were involved in four divorces, two premarital pregnancies, two drug addictions, and four illicit affairs."

The main thrust of this book is unromantic: the author questions notions of "irresistible attraction" and being "at the mercy of passion." He believes that people make choices about the person with whom they will fall in love. He offers an interesting observation about a major source of intimate problems based on his twenty-five thousand hours as a therapist listening to his clients: "The longer I listen, the more I'm convinced that most of us have very little idea what makes us happy. . . . We have never taken a close look at our emotional makeup and its peculiar needs."

He might have added that, given the prevalence of individualism, most people believe they have numerous needs that must be urgently gratified, even if their own understanding of these needs is limited. The growing cultural relativism of modern society provides little help in determining what needs are legitimate and what are questionable.

McGinnis grasps the key paradox of modernity and individualism with regard to close personal relationships:

> One reason we fail so frequently [to achieve loving relationships] is that we enter the world, the dangerous world of male-female relationships, unaware and unprepared, urged on by a society that encourages everyone to pair off but offers almost no instruction in the art of bonding.[30]

It is not easy to imagine what such instructions would entail, who would provide them, and how they would help resist the pervasive influences of modern society that undermine solid, long-term relationships.

*The Complete Idiot's Guide to Dating*[31] is a serious and ambitious undertaking, despite its title. It "is intended for everyone looking for love—whatever your age, background, dating history, or sexual preferences or intentions." Even seniors are advised how to make "the most of the golden years." The author, Dr. Judy Kuriansky, admits to having tried to make "this tome an encyclopedia of sorts." Chapters include "Unraveling the Mystery of Attraction," "Diversity Dating," "Where to Meet People," "Putting the Best *You* Forward," "From Shy to Social Butterfly," "The Art of Flirting," "Handling Rejection," and many others.

In a preface she writes, "With every page of this book, feel my pledge to you for the hope, strength, and empowerment to free your spirit, enrich your soul, make your dreams come true, and give and receive the love you want and deserve." From the jacket we learn that "Dr. Judy," as she is supposedly referred to by her millions of fans, is a clinical psychologist, sex therapist, dating expert, and media personality. "A pioneer of radio advice talk . . . she answers questions from millions of callers." She has appeared on many popular television talk shows and also leads classes at various seminar centers on "How to Marry a Millionaire." This book also offers advice on how to do that.

Dr. Judy's essential message is that "the key to success is to be happy with *yourself*." One of her favorite phrases is "Whatever you believe and conceive you can achieve." Like other authors of the same persuasion, she cannot explain satisfactorily how sheer willpower or self-suggestion can create positive self-conceptions and attitudes. She is among the many writers of self-help books who seem to believe that no one has a good reason for an unfavorable self-conception.

The comprehensive, didactic aspirations of Dr. Judy's book are reflected in its organization, repetitiveness, and length (twenty-six chapters), and even in its graphics and format. It comes with both a table of contents and "contents at a glance." The messages of each chapter are summed up both at its beginning and end, suggesting (as do some other features of the book) that addressing the book to "idiots" may not be a total joke. The book is filled with eye-catching typefaces, titles, subtitles, sidebars, short paragraphs, pictures, exercises/quizzes, and "information boxes," which contain dating dos and don'ts. A long quiz and list of "resources" at the end of the book includes autographed color photos of the author, audiotapes, videotapes, and T-shirts autographed and personalized upon request—all of which the reader can order.

The author advises to "keep it [the book] by your bedside to read before you go to bed . . . [to] refer to relevant chapters before a date. Read sections and do the quizzes *with* a date." She uses what she considers catchy terms like "love script," "energetics," "eligibility score," "the mirror law of attraction," and "love antennae" (which turn out to be quite useless and in constant need of "retuning").

The overarching emphasis on method is exemplified by almost an entire chapter devoted to conversation openers, subdivided into "charming romantic openers, self-disclosure openers, conversation openers." Elsewhere we get acquainted with the "six rules and benefits of flirting" and "nonverbal ways to show you are interested." "Ten commandments" govern the initiation of sexual relations in addition to "nine phases of dealing with rejection" and "18 tips for letting go."

This mania to number everything is common to self-help books and is probably intended to make the instructions and exhortations easier to grasp and memorize, and to add a semblance of coherence, seriousness, and organization.

To her credit, Dr. Kuriansky belongs to the nonmanipulative school of relationship advisers, and opposes playing hard to get. Her "two basic rules of dating: 1. Your ultimate goal is . . . about being happy with yourself, getting to know yourself and someone else. . . . 2. Dating is not about playing games. It's about being yourself. If someone is going to love you, they will love you as you are." These and similar encouragements to nurture self-esteem are endless: "Sex appeal comes from self-appeal. . . . Would you rather date someone who is insecure and down, or someone who is vibrant, energetic, and fun to be with? . . . Do you consider yourself a catch? I hope so—because then others will want to be with you too!" While she conceives of dating as art or theater, she cannot resist the commercial metaphor: "Dating is about selling and is like a deal."

The chapter on "Putting the Best *You* Forward" offers familiar themes: "Become a master of attraction. The steps to building self-esteem. Exercises to discover the real you. How to develop body confidence. Talk yourself into self-love. Get over the need for approval." The reader is instructed to be her/his "own public relations agent! Think about what a public relations agent does to promote a product." We are told that "what you visualize is what most likely will happen, so visualize dating success."

Commonsense propositions abound. For instance, "We often wish in others what we wish for in ourselves. It is possible . . . to fall in love with a different 'type' of love partner. Ultimately the best partner is someone who is secure and who really cares about you. . . . Ideal sex is with someone you love, fulfilling both physical and emotional needs. . . . Understanding and good communications are essential for good sex."

Dr. Judy concludes by urging the reader to read more of her books.[32] It is difficult to put this book down without wondering whether or to what degree the author truly believes that it will make a difference in the lives of people who read it. For better or worse, it is likely that she does.

*The Complete Idiot's Guide to Perfect Marriage*[33] by Hilary Rich and Helaina Kravitz is of the same series and has the same format as Dr. Judy's book discussed above. Its authors assure the reader at the very beginning that "we will teach you everything you need to know to make *your* marriage strong, stable, and more passionate than you ever dreamed possible." The foreword refers to the book as a "step-by-step guide to marriage." The introduction advises the reader "how to use this book" and promises "a relationship makeover." Part I is titled "You Can Have the Marriage You Want."

Chapter titles suggest the nature of the book: "Profile of the Perfect Marriage," "Making the Ordinary Extraordinary," "Keeping the Passion Alive," "Soul Mates." Numerous chapters are devoted to practical matters such as money management, child-rearing, the handling of in-laws, drinking problems, and infidelity. "Hot date ideas" include the reminder that "some of the best things in life are free," such as "watching the sunrise, taking a walk, eating lunch under a tree . . . smiling at each other, telling jokes . . . [and] watching the sunset."

Once more, commonsense propositions and generalities proliferate:

> It is always important to listen to your spouse. . . . Compromising and agreeing to disagree will relieve a lot of stress. . . . A marriage is always growing and changing. . . . The more effort you put into your marriage, the happier you both will be! . . . Your marriage can and should be the most important relationship in your life; good communication is a key part of all good marriages. . . . Investing in your marriage will bring you a great return. The time and energy you put into your relationship will be well worth it. . . . Infidelity is usually a symptom of a troubled marriage.

A more unorthodox proposition that defies conventional notions of romance and demotes spontaneity is that "you can create passion by planning fun things ahead of time." Accordingly, women are instructed to "prepare a candlelit dinner and play beautiful music" to "set a romantic mood for your husband." The candlelit dinner appears to be firmly established among the paraphernalia of romantic settings and props, as is the walk on the beach and the sound of raindrops on the roof. Television commercials probably contribute to the popularity of these images.

Helpful quizzes abound in Rich and Kravitz, including a "think positive quiz," "a bother barometer," "an authentic happiness quiz," "expectations quiz," "intimacy quiz," "priority quiz," and others.[34]

The conclusion reaffirms that "there are five necessary qualities to every great marriage: good communication, real partnership, effort, adaptability, and total commitment."

*The Real Rules* by Barbara De Angelis[35] (also on the *New York Times* bestseller list) is distinguished by its no-holds-barred critique of *The Rules*, discussed earlier. *The Real Rules* was supposedly inspired by the strongly felt need to refute the *The Rules*, which is characterized as

> one piece of bad, recycled, antiquated advice after another—the kind of advice my grandmother gave my mother. . . . Each chapter got progressively worse. . . . These weren't rules for happiness—they were rules for messing up your love life and behaving like the worst stereotype of a superficial, submissive woman! . . . They are the very ideas that cause millions of women . . . to get into bad relationships.

In place of such rules, De Angelis offers her rather unoriginal "four laws of love":

1. The purpose of your life isn't to get married . . . [it] is to grow into the most loving, fulfilled, *real* woman you can be.
2. Your love life should not focus on getting a man but . . . on finding the *right* man.
3. Once you've found the right man the goal should . . . be . . . creating a healthy, loving, mutually respectful . . . relationship.
4. When you create . . . [such a] relationship . . . a loving commitment . . . will naturally occur.

The "real" woman (or real self) is never defined—it is part of the assumed individualistic premise that everyone has a rich, distinctive essence which is often concealed or suppressed by pretense or erroneous ideas. Once allowed free expression, it will triumph.

De Angelis at least briefly addresses the question of what character traits to look for in men, and it is hard to imagine that anyone would dispute her choices: "commitment to growing and improving; emotional openness; integrity, honesty and trustworthiness; maturity and responsibility; high self-esteem;

positive attitude toward life."[36] As is often the case, some of these attributes are rather vague and general.

The Real Rules is an improvement over The Rules, but it remains debatable how much help it may provide for those in need of it.

The Sistahs' Rules: Secrets for Meeting, Getting and Keeping a Good Black Man[37] is written by Denene Millner for black women. On the jacket it warns that it is "Not to be Confused with The Rules." Moreover "any real black woman can tell you that when it comes to African-American men, the oft-celebrated Rules is about as good as a pile of Monopoly money in Macy's."

Millner's humorous guidance is not significantly different from what is offered in the other books that do not have a racially defined audience. But there is a greater emphasis here on the importance of finding "a good man," that is, someone with qualities that "really matter"—personality, character, trustworthiness—rather than social status and things material ("money doesn't mean anything in the emotional scheme of things"). These oft-repeated exhortations suggest, not surprisingly, that many black women harbor mobility aspirations that may exceed those of their white counterparts. Nonetheless, Millner advises, lowering expectations is the key to finding the right man: "We've all too often held our potential mates up against the Knight of the Shining Armor standards . . . a fantasy wish list that's sentencing us . . . to the singles-only line." She also warns against the kind of man "who tells you he would have graduated from high school but he left in protest because the teachers were racist," or against the type who, "whenever a cop car drives by . . . slouches in his seat and pulls his hat down over his face."

The author avoids applying white standards of beauty: readers are assured that kinky hair and round bottoms are nothing to be ashamed of. In fact, "Black men will do anything . . . to please a woman with a big butt. And we as black women need to take advantage of that." No concern here with multiple racial stereotyping.

Under The Sistahs' Rules, the man to look for is "the considerate/hardworking/reasonably educated/mature/sexy/mentally stable/respectful/clean/drug and prison record free/fun/honest/trustworthy brother." The "potential Brother Mr. Right"—a version of the Renaissance man—"loves God and recognizes that there is a higher being in control of our destinies"—and "he likes oral sex—and loves performing it."

Unlike other books of this type, this one devotes an entire chapter to the importance of "a good home-cooked meal" as the "way to a man's heart" as much as showing an interest in sports. Other practical advices includes the stipulation—very much in the spirit of *The Rules*—not to linger with a new lover after sex but to get dressed and go: "Trust me, it will blow his mind." A chapter advises on how to get along with the mother-in-law. Most unusually, the acknowledgments begin with "All praise due to the Creator, who continues to cloak me in His unconditional love."[38]

*It Takes Two.Com: A Psychological and Spiritual Guide to Finding Love on the Internet Personals*,[39] by Kenneth and Beverly Appel, offers a generally upbeat view of Internet dating, which the authors consider superior in many ways to traditional methods. It differs from other books of this type by supposedly using information provided by one thousand Internet users. Unfortunately it provides no systematic, tabulated data about the information obtained. Instead, the book prints extracts from letters and from interviews with the participants in the study. The authors offer much advice on the use of the Internet but reveal very little information about the Internet users who were studied.

The pitfalls of Internet romance include the acceleration of romantic fantasies:

> The love relationship cycle, in the romantic form it usually takes, displays patterns very rapidly [on the Internet]. The ups and downs of emotions that might normally take much longer in "clock time" happen much more rapidly in "cybertime." When romance is condensed in this way, it feels more intense, even more exhilarating or disappointing. . . . Regardless of what the other tells us about their appearance, personality, intelligence, or interests, the image initially formed will not be the actual person. We underestimate, overestimate, or create an entirely different person depending on our needs.

The authors also caution against overemphasizing physical appearance and a refusal to talk on the phone. However, they seem not terribly concerned about deceptive self-presentation: "According to our data, once email passes from the superficial stage to some degree of self-revelation and intimate exchange, most people are sincere. . . . The most frequent problem encountered . . . is that he or she doesn't continue to match our fantasies." We learn nothing about the proportion of these communications that pass from the superficial to the more serious stage, or about the criteria the authors used to define and separate these two types of exchanges.

One finding is of greater interest, based on the undisclosed questionnaires, email correspondence, and phone interviews with participants in the study: the five key characteristics of those who succeed in "forming serious commitments to each other—perhaps even marriage." They are persistence, a positive attitude, mindfulness (by which they mean "being authentic, sincere, and genuine"), motivation, and visualization ("harnessing the energy of your mind to create your reality"). Persistence, a positive attitude, and motivation are overlapping qualities. All are obviously needed since, according to the authors' research, "the average length of time between beginning to use the internet personals and finding a partner is about 18 months."

The authors also asked their respondents, "What are the most important qualities you look for in the person you want to meet?" Not surprisingly, "sincerity and honesty" was the "resoundingly unanimous" response, but no quantitative data is provided about any of these responses.[40]

One of the authors of *Date Like a Man*,[41] Myreah Moore, is credited with helping "thousands of women find their soul mates through her personal training sessions and public seminars," according to the book jacket. The other, Jodie Gould, is "an author and writer specializing in relationships and popular culture." As the title of the book makes clear, women are advised to follow male strategies in dating in order to succeed, and to stop thinking of marriage as the ultimate goal. The very first paragraph exudes an upbeat tone as readers are congratulated for being single: "This can be the best time of your life. Being single allows you to discover who you are . . . and what you truly need from a man." What follows is the usual exhortation to avoid negative thoughts, which produce negative results, and the "promise that if you follow my advice and do the exercises in this book, you will feel better about yourself and the men you date. Once you learn to treasure yourself, people will move mountains to be close to you." The author believes "that every woman should date a minimum of one hundred men before she chooses a mate" and that "dating is a sport. . . . I hate it when women come to my classes and say, 'I don't want to play games,' Well, honey, then you don't want to date." She further advises, "Women should wait at least four months before they have sex with a man they are seriously dating. . . . A one-night stand is okay if you . . . don't care if you ever see the guy again."

Moore and Gould offer numerous specific instructions about the use of body language in order to attract men. They include the following: "stand with one hand on your hip . . . cross and uncross your legs when you are wearing a dress . . . wet your lips with your tongue . . . toss or flip your hair . . . play with a cylindrical object such as a pencil, pen, or stem of a wineglass. This reveals your subconscious desires. . . . Dangle one shoe while seated in a relaxed position."[42]

The book includes a survey of two hundred New York City men between the ages of twenty-three and forty-six who were questioned about their dating likes and dislikes (we are not informed how they were selected). A finding of some interest is this: "the characteristics that you want most in a woman in order of importance: 1. Intelligence/education. 2. Personality. 3. Looks. 4. Body. 5. Manners. 6. Dance ability. 7. Family oriented. 8. Sexual history. 9. Friends. 10. Similar taste in music." As is always the case, we do not know to what extent these preferences were influenced by what the respondents considered the respectable answers—as, for example, in rating education and personality higher than looks.

Given the enormous number of these books and their numbingly repetitive character, I will comment only briefly on a few additional offerings that address different audiences.

The best-selling *Ten Commandments of Dating: Time-Tested Laws for Building Successful Relationships*[43] is inspired by Christian beliefs. One of the authors, Ben Young, is a minister who directs a single ministry of five thousand at Second Baptist Church in Houston, Texas; the other author, Samuel Adams, is a licensed clinical psychologist. They claim that their book rests on "solid truths" and "moral foundations," not on surveys or opinion polls, and they reject moral relativism. They also believe that "the Bible has a lot more to say about successful relationships . . . than most people realize."[44] Except for their opposition to premarital sex and cohabitation, their commonsense advice is not substantially different from that offered in books of a secular orientation.

Another book inspired by strongly held Christian beliefs is *No More Sheets: The Truth About Sex,*[45] by Juanita Bynum, who is identified on the jacket as the "dynamic founder and president of the Juanita Bynum Ministries, in Waycross, Georgia, Prophetess [sic] Bynum travels the world over delivering an annointed message." The book "has sold millions of copies! She can be seen on her weekly television program on the Black Entertainment Television network." Bynum overcame a bad marriage and a nervous breakdown healed by a vision in which the Lord told her, "Keep your eyes on Me and as long as you do you will never fail." Most pages refer to God or

Christ or the Lord or a quote from the Bible. A more unusual feature of this book is a chapter devoted to masturbation (defined as "the bait that Satan uses to become a master over you").

Practical suggestions complement the spiritual exhortations: "If . . . there is any talk of marriage, always insist that he meet your pastor." During the first seven dates, visiting art museums is a good idea, or "professional sporting events, roller blading, and horseback riding." If invited by a man to his home, "always take a friend." The book includes a "Certificate of Accountability" that dating readers should sign. It includes the stipulation that "we promise to pray with each other before dates" and call each other after dates to ask, among other questions, "Did you do anything that's not pleasing to God?"[46]

William July's *Confessions of an Ex-Bachelor* is the product of a reformed playboy, now happily married and opposed to "playing games," who in his acknowledgments thanks God, "who powers my words." He too addresses women who want to get married and "have grown tired of . . . swinging bachelor types."[47]

*The Boyfriend Test* is written by Wendy Walsh, a former news anchor and "media personality" whose personal life "has been riddled with boyfriend candidates." In the acknowledgments she thanks her boyfriend "for 'hanging in there' while I figured out who I was." She also thanks her therapist. The book overflows with practical advice and includes an eight-page "Boyfriend Test Candidate Profile," "Pickup Lines That May Get a Good Grade," and "The Meet and Greet Score Sheet Report Card." Unlike many similar treatises, here the author affirms the obvious but important truth that "the search for a partner is, in some sense, a search for the parents we left behind."[48]

Neil Clark Warren, a clinical psychologist in California and author of best-selling books, claims to have written *How to Know If Someone Is Worth Pursuing in Two Dates or Less* for two major reasons: to help people "identify dead-end relationships quickly so you don't have to invest more time, energy, and caring than necessary," and "to learn to think clearly about yourself and the person you want to marry." It includes chapters on "How to Read Someone Like a Book," "The 25 Most Popular Must-Haves," "The 25 Most Prevalent Can't Stands," and "The Principles of Negotiating a Great Deal."[49]

*25 Words or Less: How to Write Like a Pro to Find That Special Someone Through Personal Ads* is written by Thornton Calvo and Laurence Minsky, "professional copywriters at one of the nation's largest advertising and marketing firms" (as the jacket informs the reader). It begins with the exhortation: "You're in charge of your destiny." The reader is advised to "look at yourself as a product" as well as "commit to the process [of advertising] and then persevere."[50]

Dawn Eden's *The Thrill of the Chaste: Finding Fulfillment While Keeping Your Clothes On* is a book by a Jewish-born rock journalist who at age thirty-one became a born-again Christian. As such she enthusiastically argues not only against pre- and extra-marital sex but also loveless sex. She blames American mass culture for corrupting young people and for popularizing the idea that sex by itself will lead to intimacy and love. She correctly points out that "the concept of deferring pleasure makes no sense in a consumer society."[51] Most of the "relationship books" do not encourage sex without emotional involvement, or at least the prospect of it.

Catherine Anne Lewis, the author of *Reborn Virgin Women: If You Wanna Be Happy Keep Your Pants Zipped*, lives in North Carolina with her husband and children and is a financial representative helping families become debt free. She too advocates chastity and includes a "Reborn Virgin Oath" and a ten-point guideline for the reborn virgin which argues that "bed hopping" doesn't follow from feminism.[52] Much of the book details the drawbacks of promiscuous, premarital sex.

Yet another book on the benefits of virginity is *Been There, Haven't Done That: A Virgin's Memoir* by Tara McCarthy, a music journalist, described on the jacket as "a Harvard educated, world-traveled, attractive young woman of twenty-five." This is not a how-to book but rather an autobiographical statement explaining why the author chose virginity. Her advocacy of chastity is based on her belief in the "combination of spiritual and physical connection." Her comment on the romantic imagination intersects with major ideas on modernity, high expectations, and the contemporary difficulty in establishing and maintaining durable relationships:

> *Romantic wanderlust—that irresistible impulse* to see what else is out there, that resolute belief that someone better is just beyond our horizon—has probably destroyed more viable relationships than Darren Star has acting careers.[53] No matter where we are in life, we can imagine a better place. Better weather, a bigger apartment, a better job, a bigger bank balance. And no matter who we are with we can conceive of someone who might somehow be better for us. . . . No mere mortal can compete with the ideal partners the human imagination is capable of creating.[54]

Finally, it is instructive to examine a book of similar purpose published more than half a century ago, Evelyn Duvall's *The Art of Dating*.[55] It was based on the author's effort to respond to the concerns of young people expressed in more than seventeen thousand questionnaires she collected. On one hand, this book shares with others discussed earlier a relentlessly practical, sober, and unromantic orientation. Much of the advice offered is commonsensical and predictable. But this book is distinguished from the others by its intended audience: high school and college students, and by its perception of dating as a well-defined, durable, and popular institution. Further, it displays a tone of moral certainty and an apparent conviction that sociocultural norms and standards have a robust, legitimate function, and individuals are rightly expected to conform to them. Duvall makes frequent references to what is and is not "socially acceptable" and to the importance of preserving a good reputation, especially for girls ("Fellows and girls who want to earn and keep a good reputation get home at reasonable hours"). The preoccupation with "reputation" is noteworthy and without parallel in present-day relationship literature. Reputation, of course, is an old-fashioned idea predicated on the belief that there is broad agreement about what constitutes acceptable conduct—a notion in conflict with the moral relativism and glorification of "transgressive behavior" of our times. Thus "responsible" and "responsibility" are among the most often used words in this book—rarely, if at all, encountered in today's "relationship books." (For example, "responsible fellows and girls feel that their homework comes first.")

The author strongly supports the idea of confining "one's social life to acceptable circles and one's friendships to those who are vouched for upon introduction." Relationships that spring up "without proper sponsorship," she suggests, can be hazardous.

Unlike most other books we have considered, this volume is permeated by a deterministic outlook: people are seen as operating within well-defined and benign cultural norms and conventions, paying attention to the opinions and judgments of their parents and peers; rebellious nonconformity is dismissed. At the same time the author also suggests that virtually everything is up to the individual, to his or her will and persistence to succeed.

In a section titled "How to be Popular," we learn that "young people like members of the other sex who are 1) careful of their personal appearance; 2) courteous and thoughtful; and 3) fun to be with." "Fun" is a concept often used but never defined, its meaning taken for granted, as are the propositions that *adults in charge of a party* (my emphasis) are a good source of information about the reputation of the participants, and that "some public places are just not suitable for young people . . . people you meet in public places are rarely suitable dating prospects." In particular, "public dance halls, places where alcohol is served, and parties at homes where you do not know the hostess can be hazardous." Further, "Going to a drive-in movie can be a real hazard for a girl."

Young readers are cautioned about "what is acceptable in this delicate area of a relationship"—that is, matters sexual. Premarital chastity is recommended (as opposed to "going all the way"), and, according to the author, "Research studies indicate that the majority of young persons feel strongly that premarital chastity is important."

The author's assumptions provide an excellent illustration of the sociocultural changes that have transpired over the past half-century and have made many of Duvall's ideas and injunctions quaint or obsolete. They include the proposition that "a man and a woman are expected to observe the sexual restraints of their society," and numerous references to the indispensability of parental approval of whom to date. For example, "If your parents disapprove, you will have to decline the invitation regardless of other favorable factors." Noted in passing is that "It is generally accepted that a girl won't be as intelligent as the boy she dates"; that "Marriage demands more of the woman than it does of the man"; and that "enduring, happy marriages are made by persons who . . . are conventional, trustworthy people . . . usually active in religious life." The book recommends serious preparation for marriage "in much the same way that any other job does."[56] Not exactly a romantic prescription.

Discordant voices may also be found among authors who address the striving for love in present-day American society. Unlike the great majority of the optimists who believe that proper methods and attitudes will yield the desired result, Laura Kipnis offers a dire diagnosis of the nature and prospects of "coupledom." With this term she refers to domesticated, monogamous, long-term relationships, either cohabitation or marriage, founded on the belief that two human beings can meet each other's basic needs forever. Kipnis is convinced that such relationships are doomed since they rest on unrealistic expectations and conflict with human nature and its need for freedom, variety, excitement, and experimentation. She chafes against society and its conventions that stifle the unfettered pursuit of meaning, satisfaction, and pleasure. She is a champion of rebellion and transgression, a true romantic in her own way, drawn to bohemians and the countercultural critics of society. She shares their belief that "all mainstream institutions are sitting ducks for artful saboteurs, [and] that all social forms invite creative violation and sneak attacks."

Kipnis—more a Marxist than feminist—aspires to integrate the critiques of American marital practices and ideals with a critique of American society and capitalism. In *Against Love* she proposes that Americans who believe in marriage and its romantic possibilities suffer from the false consciousness inculcated by the capitalist social order. The work ethic in particular (encouraged by capitalism) has invaded and subverted "all spheres of human existence," including close personal relationships, extinguishing spontaneity, passion, and playfulness.

> When monogamy becomes labor, when desire is organized contractually, with accounts kept and fidelity extracted like labor . . . with marriage a domestic factory policed by means of rigid shop-floor discipline designed to keep the wives and husbands and domestic partners . . . choke-chained to the status quo machinery—is this really what we mean by a good relationship? . . .
> Love is "the latest form of alienated labor."

As Kipnis readily acknowledges, her conceptions of present-day American society have been inspired by Herbert Marcuse. In this vision, manipulation and repression join forces to promote acquiescence by "seamlessly" transplanting social controls "into the guise of individual needs"—that is, the citizens internalize the goals of their manipulators. The repressive forces meet little resistance "as they ooze their way into the neighborhoods of daily life." The false ideals of everlasting marital bliss play an important part in the process: "Monogamy is required for general stability," and the citizens are molded into "busy worker bees and docile nestlers all."

Kipnis believes that these falsely idealized notions of love compensate—at least temporarily—for a wide range of frustrations and substitute for higher aspirations blocked by the social order. People are constrained to be preoccupied with their personal lives and (illusory) gratifications when large-scale social change is obstructed by dominant malevolent forces. Love in modern American society

> [is] harnessed to social utility . . . spouting the deadening language of the factory, enfolded in household regimes and quashed desires—an efficient way of organizing the acquiescence of shrunken expectations. . . . Love . . . in a commodity culture . . . conforms to the role of a cheap commodity, spit out at the end of the assembly line in cookie-cutter forms, marketed to bored and alienated producer-consumers as an all-purpose salve to emptiness. . . . Households . . . like the democratic nation . . . must be founded on the illusion of a loving partnership.

Her view of "coupledom" is dark: an entire chapter titled "Domestic Gulag"[57] is devoted to its specific horrors and deprivations:

Coupled life is either a barren landscape or a tense battleground or a nightmar-ish repetition, characterized by tedium, fighting, silence or unreasonable insa-tiable demands . . . cramming the entirety of a libido into those tight domestic confines. . . . Toxic levels of everyday dissatisfaction, boredom, unhappiness . . . are the functional norms in millions of lives and marriages. . . . From bathroom to bedroom, car to kitchen, no aspect of coupled life is not subject to scrutiny, negotiation, and rule formation. . . . Why not at least entertain the possibility that there could be forms of daily life based on something other than isolated households and sexually exclusive couples? Why not confront . . . the real-ity of disappointment and the deadening routinization that pervades married households? Maybe confronting the flaws in married life would be a route to reforming a flawed society?

Given this conception of "coupledom," it is scarcely surprising that its captives seek to escape "the rising tide of emotional deadness at home" through adulterous adventures. Here adultery is transformed into social criti-cism as it "refashions ordinary citizens into default social critics and heirs to Romantic protest." Such "love affairs *can* feel utterly transforming. . . . You get to surrender to emotions you forgot you could have: to desire and to be-ing desired." But elsewhere she writes, more realistically, that "if coupledom is society's sanctioned store-all for intimacy, property, children, and libido, then adultery is the municipal dumpster for coupled life's toxic waste of strife and unhappiness."

More plausibly, Kipnis argues that only recently did marriage become

the expected venue for Eros or romantic love [and one's spouse] the presump-tive object of romantic love. . . . Our age dedicates itself to allying the turbu-lence of romance and rationality of the long-term couple, hoping . . . despite all the evidence to the contrary, that love and sex are obtainable from one person over the course of decades and that desire will manage to sustain itself.

She correctly observes that "this modern belief that love lasts shapes us into particularly fretful psychological beings, perpetually in search of prescrip-tions, interventions, aids. Passion must *not* be allowed to die!"

Notwithstanding the prevailing romantic beliefs, she points out,

the majority of us select partners remarkably similar to ourselves—economi-cally, and in social standing, education, and race. . . . We choose "appropriate" mates, and we precisely calculate their assets, with each party . . . knowing exactly their own exchange value and that of prospective partners. . . . Scratch

the romantic veneer and we are hard-nosed realists. . . . Despite all the supposed freedom the social rules governing mate selection are as finicky and
precise as they were in Jane Austen's day. The difference is that it is now a
taboo to acknowledge them.[58]

This gloomy dissection of modern marital hopes and aspirations persua-
sively identifies numerous flaws and contradictions of contemporary American romanticism (as have been noted in previous chapters), but it fails to
explain its attractions and persistence. This persistence is probably a matter
of the alternatives. Adultery or endless affairs, no matter how passionate
and invigorating in the short run, cannot be sustained; staying single has
many self-evident drawbacks. Stability, security, and predictability—even if
inevitably weighed down by routinization and the loss of excitement—are
preferable for most people in the long run, especially when they are no longer
in their twenties.

In a more humorous vein, Maureen Dowd, in her best-selling book *Are
Men Necessary?*, also addresses the difficulties of present-day relationships
between men and women. She emphasizes the confusion created by the col-
lision of women's changed status with the persistence of traditional attitudes
and expectations among *both* men and women—that is, "the mass confusion
caused by the uneasy blend of retro attitudes about dating with modern
sexual freedom." Her firm belief is that women's greatly improved opportunities for a career have not altered traditional attitudes.

> Evolution is lagging behind equality . . . females are still programmed to look
> for older men with resources while males are still programmed to look for
> younger women with adoring gazes. . . . Men moving up still tend to marry
> down. The two sexes' going in opposite directions has led to an epidemic of
> professional women missing out on husbands and kids.

Dowd believes that by the 1980s many attitudes and beliefs associated
with women's liberation declined, and more traditional notions about social
roles and biologically determined differences between the sexes reemerged.
As she puts it, "Before it curdled into a collection of stereotypes, feminism
had fleetingly held out a promise that there would be some precincts of wom-
anly life that were not all about men."

One interesting finding that she cites in support of her argument is name
change upon marriage: "a study . . . found that 44% of women in the Harvard

class of 1980 had kept their birth names while in the class of '90 it was only 32%. In 1990 23% of college-educated women kept their own name after marriage, while a decade later the number had fallen to 17%." Dowd also notes the trajectory of *Cosmopolitan* magazine, a venerable source of advice for women and still "the best-selling monthly magazine on the newsstand," as it was decades ago. The magazine, in her view, has come to replicate "the original *Cosmo* girl's man-crazy, sex-obsessed image," instructing its readers on how to enchant and attract men.

Dowd sadly notes that the concern with physical attractiveness, scorned by feminists, has fully returned: "Professional strides have not made women less concerned about their looks, or curbed their compulsion to try to improve . . . on Mother Nature. . . . American women are evolving backward—becoming more focused on their looks than ever. Feminism has been defeated by narcissism." The striking increase of cosmetic surgery is among the indicators of these trends, with a "118% increase is cosmetic surgery since '97." As reported by the American Society of Plastic Surgeons, 9.2 million cosmetic surgeries and procedures were performed in 2004, a 24 percent increase since 2000.[59]

Dowd does not offer advice; she merely paints a picture filled with ambiguity and contradiction. It allows the reader to conclude that men are still sexist and that women cannot do much to change these ingrained attitudes.

One comes away from these books with a bemused disbelief, wondering if they could possibly have an impact on their readers, let alone provide effective help in establishing durable romantic relationships. With very few exceptions, most of these books are startlingly similar to one another, both in style and substance. They concentrate on methods or techniques, they are upbeat and cheery, radiate and recycle commonsense propositions, are highly repetitive and didactic. They oscillate between specific advice (where to meet men, or how many dates to have before sex) and benign generalities (giving priority to substance over appearance and goals other than finding a husband).

Most of the books are addressed to women and thereby reassert by implication—what came to be considered sexist stereotypes since the 1960s—that women are more interested than men in establishing long-term relationships leading to marriage. Also implied is that women need more advice on how to accomplish this goal, and that such an orientation is both natural and acceptable.

The other striking commonality among these books is the refusal to concede that human attitudes and behavior are to some degree socially and culturally conditioned or determined. Only *The Art of Dating*, published half a century ago, takes a more deterministic position. With that exception, all these books affirm and reaffirm that the individual can accomplish virtually anything she wishes, including a high degree of self-esteem and finding the most compatible, loving partner by using her free will as instructed. Thus these books fit into the long tradition of the American belief in self-help and self-reinvention that found expression in nineteenth-century self-help books dealing not with emotional fulfillment but with ascending the ladder of social hierarchy to wealth and power.

The major explanation of these messages is likely to be found in the persistence of individualism and the related therapeutic orientation—that is, the belief that most of our problems and difficulties have psychological origins and psychological remedies.[60] This orientation helps explain the firmly held unrealistic belief that improving self-esteem is the key to success both for socioeconomic advancement and emotional gratification, and that such improvement is within everyone's reach. This modern therapeutic approach has merged with the self-help tradition. The intact preservation of this tradition in these books is all the more remarkable since they were written in the last third of the twentieth century and the early twenty-first, periods marked by the spread and institutionalization of belief in the overwhelming social and cultural determination of individual lives and in the powerlessness of the individual confronted by social forces. Identity politics, affirmative action, political correctness, and associated policies have all been based on the conviction that individual will, wish, and determination count for little in shaping one's life. Evidently the writers of these books have not gotten the message, or they may believe that these axiomatic beliefs do not apply to intimate personal lives and relationships in which social position and background can still be overcome by individual will and determination, and by a properly positive outlook.

# CHAPTER FIVE

# Self-Presentation and Wish Lists in Printed Personals

For these individuals the personal column is a theater of fantasy where they can reach out for love and freedom.

Raymond Shapiro[1]

As belief in the essential selves erodes, awareness expands of the ways in which personal identity can be created and re-created in relationships. . . . As social relationships became opportunities for enactment, the boundary between the real and the presented self—between substance and style—is erased.

Kenneth J. Gergen[2]

## New Methods: Advantages and Drawbacks

This chapter seeks to connect broader sociocultural influences—and especially those associated with modernity discussed earlier—with the individual aspirations and expectations expressed in printed communications aimed at establishing intimate personal relationships.

Central to the romantic sensibility is the belief that somewhere out in the world is a uniquely compatible person to be discovered, someone who will gratify one's considerable emotional needs and will make one's life fulfilled and "meaningful." In our times and society, this elusive individual may be pursued in various ways, including the not very romantic devices of printed personals and electronic online messages. I begin with the printed variety found in the *New York Review of Books*.

Although the format of these communications conflicts with the spontaneity that true romantics cherish, the content of these personals is steeped in an age-old romanticism and is nurtured by the surviving congenial cultural values of the 1960s. These personals are also products of the high divorce rates of the past decades in America and the social isolation produced by modern, mobile urban life. The number of people living by themselves has greatly increased during the last decades of the twentieth century, the percentage of married people has fallen, and marriages last for shorter periods. Census figures indicate that between 1960 and 2009 the number of single-person households increased from seven million to thirty-one million.[3] Stephanie Coontz has noted:

> In the 1950s married couples represented 80 percent of all households in the United States. By the beginning of the twenty-first century they were less than 51 percent, and married couples with children were just 25 percent of all households. For the first time ever, there were more single-person households than those with a married couple and children.

Rebecca Davis too has confirmed that in the past few years "the percentage of married households dipped below 50 percent for the first time."[4]

The pursuit of romantic (or less than romantic) partners by printed and electronic advertisements is a rich repository of information about prevailing sociocultural values, ego ideals, and conceptions of desirable human qualities required and expected in close personal relationships. These communications also tell us about larger sociocultural currents and the nature of American society in the late twentieth and early twenty-first centuries.

These new means of date or mate selection have some obvious advantages and disadvantages. The key advantage is access to a vast number of potentially compatible individuals. Also these methods demand a focused, clear-cut presentation of oneself, his or her needs and requirements, and a corresponding specification of what we value in other human beings and what our priorities are in intimate or romantic relationships. Possibly these procedures could reduce the trial-and-error aspects of seeking and meeting romantic prospects and thus improve the chances of finding a compatible mate.

At the same time these new avenues of communication stimulate misrepresentation. The temptation to paint too flattering a portrait of oneself multiplies when advertisements are placed either in printed sources or online. It's tempting and easy to present a highly positive picture in order to draw attention—after all, people are "selling" themselves. As one study finds, "Self-presentational styles can be altered online. . . . Unhampered by normal constraints, users can self-present a more idealized self-image than they might otherwise. . . . Through self-presentational acts people may attempt to make their public selves consistent with their ideal selves."[5] Another study suggests that

> the notion "you are who you pretend to be" has mythic resonance. The Pygmalion story endures because it speaks to a powerful fantasy: that we are not limited by our histories, that we can recreate ourselves. . . . Life on the screen makes it very easy to present oneself other than who one is in real life.[6]

American culture encourages us to "reinvent" ourselves and helps legitimate such hopeful misrepresentations. But apparently these trends are not confined to American society. A British author observes, "Each of us feels that we can be what we like, and construct our own biographies."[7] The new ways of looking for a partner encourage high and often unrealistic expectations: "The people make up impossible shopping lists for what they want in a partner," says a psychologist who studies dating.[8]

Raymond Shapiro, business manager of the *New York Review of Books*, which pioneered the use of personals among liberal and well-educated readers, believes that those placing the notices are the

> creatures of that cultural upheaval of the late twentieth century that has swept all inhibitions to the dustbin. . . . The main fascination of the personal ads is the fresh view they give us of the human condition.[9]

In this new way of finding partners, "the pace of relationships is hurried, and the processes of unfolding that once required months or years may be accomplished in days or weeks." Many people may have the illusion that the exchange of detailed written communications will make it easier to get to know the other person more rapidly and thoroughly, but this may not be the case. Moreover, as a psychologist points out, "In earlier times one's range of available mates was geographically circumscribed." This is obviously no longer the case, and consequently far more potential partners are accessible. But these new possibilities and the abundance of prospects create new dilemmas and difficulties as "each new face may underscore the inevitable shortcomings of one's current companion, haunting one with doubts and issuing subtle invitations to yet another Valhalla of committed intimacy."[10]

A further problem is the tension between the apparent rationality of the new methods—involving the written specification of intimate emotional needs and attributes—and the romantic veneration of unpredictability and spontaneity. Making matters more complicated, the attempted rational specification of personal needs is often permeated by nonrational, romantic notions and aspirations. A final paradox, revealed by a close reading of these notices, is that the supposedly highly personal ego ideals, aspirations, values, likes, and dislikes are often remarkably standardized and formulaic.[11] Thus highly personal and socially structured preferences remain difficult to separate even in our individualistic society.

Studies of dating and marriage before the Internet age indicate that personal choice, or "the decline in conventions," played a key role in contemporary mate selection. Martin Whyte writes:

> We have gone from a situation in which there was a "right way" and a "wrong way" to conduct premarital relations, or to pattern one's marital relations, to a situation in which alternative ways of behaving lack such clear moral meaning. . . . There is declining consensus about what is acceptable and what is unacceptable.[12]

The wide variety of needs and preferences examined below further illustrate this "declining consensus." Conventions have been replaced, for the most part, by the injunction to pursue "whatever feels good." But this prescription seems to be an insufficient basis for a committed, enduring, and mutually satisfactory personal relationship.

Personals (printed or online) are a new departure in the pursuit of serious and important relationships; their rise reflects doubt about the efficacy of conventional methods, or an inability to rely on them. The communication of intimate personal needs via descriptive advertisements promises to be a more rational and effective approach to mate selection than the earlier means. The innovative "rationality" of the personals lies in the belief that specifying attributes and interests can be a shortcut to finding a compatible partner. The hope is that such communications can bypass the haphazard, superficial, and often frustrating contacts originating in introductions or the advice of friends, or initiated on the basis of superficial personal impressions, appearances, and chance. If you specify what kind of person (you think) you are, and what kind of person you are looking for—making clear, for instance, that your recreational interests center on Bach cantatas and vacations in Mediterranean fishing villages rather than country music and bowling— there may be a better chance to meet kindred spirits.

In the last few decades, conventional ways of finding a partner for romantic purposes have been abandoned by large numbers of people, including many who are apparently successful, attractive, and well-educated—if their self-presentations are to be believed. This development further illuminates the problems of modernity, especially the decline of community, the growth of social isolation, and the tension between the demands of professional work and emotionally gratifying intimate personal relationships.

## Personals in the *New York Review of Books* and Alumni Magazines

I began this study of the contemporary pursuit of durable romantic relationships by examining the personals in the *New York Review of Books*,[13] which have been published for more than forty years. I was unable to determine why and how these personals became a regular feature of the *Review*.

In these advertisements, individuals specify their own attractions and the attributes they seek in a romantic partner. The relationships being sought range from marriage to unmarried long-term relationships, affairs, dating, and afternoon trysts, mostly heterosexual, sometimes same-sex. (The latter is not included in this study.)

To the best of my knowledge, no comparable publication in this country (such as the *Atlantic*, *Commentary*, *Harper's*, *National Review*, *New Republic*, *New York Times Book Review*, *Weekly Standard*, etc.) prints such personals. *The Nation* publishes a small number of such notices in a column titled "Liberal Liaisons," written for the most part by serious environmentalists and middle-aged or older people of "progressive" political beliefs. Like the magazine as a whole, these advertisements are reliable indicators of the lasting cultural and political influence of the 1960s. The author of one of these notices in *The Nation* was engaged in "planning a five-year 'improve the world' project seeking romance with a like-minded female interested in participating."[14]

The *New York Review* is a leading intellectual biweekly journal which publishes mostly lengthy book reviews or review essays, political opinion pieces, and occasional reviews of movies or museum exhibits. It reflects and caters to intellectual and cultural trends popular among liberal academics and those in the educated middle classes influenced by them. These ideals and attitudes are for the most part derived from or part of the cultural legacy of the 1960s, a moderated echo of the counterculture of that period. Contributors tend to be prominent academics, well-known writers, and journalists, most of them American but supplemented by a regular British contingent. In its early years the *Review* closely reflected the radical trends and sentiments of the 1960s and early 1970s; over time this orientation has moderated.[15] The magazine remains liberal or left of center, but no longer shrill, and occasionally publishes articles critical of political correctness and radical left-wing views, movements, or political systems.

The *Review*'s total circulation is close to 140,000; the average age of its readers is fifty-six; 73 percent are males and 27 percent females (these ratios are reversed among those who contribute to the personals). Ninety-seven percent of readers are college graduates; 70 percent have graduate degrees or have attended professional schools. Sixty-eight percent are classified as professionals or are in managerial occupations. The median income of readers is $71,000; the average is $123,000.[16] Clearly this is both a highly educated and financially comfortable elite group of Americans.

It is noteworthy that many of those who use abbreviations in the personals, such as DWF (divorced white female), include the W. Apparently, even in this largely liberal group, specifying one's race is an essential piece of information. We cannot be sure exactly what is intended: to discourage nonwhites or merely to inform readers of the racial identity of the writer. But if race were irrelevant and only personal qualities and interests mattered, there would be no Ws.

The personals published in the *Review* provide an abundance of information for the sociologist or social historian interested in cultural values, sexual morality, ego ideals, aspirations, and widely shared perceptions of desirable human qualities. The very existence of these communications demonstrates the contemporary difficulties of finding a romantic partner. The resort to advertising is an implicit admission of the narrowness or unsatisfactory character of one's social life; it may also indicate a busy professional life that permits little time for face-to-face socializing.

The *New York Review* is an unusually rich source of personals, having published tens of thousands since 1970. These ads are highly specific and detailed in describing the types of individuals sought and the personal characteristics of those engaged in the search. Readers of a publication like the *Review* are preselected to some degree—that is, we know something about them by virtue of their being readers of the same publication. They have in common certain tastes, interests, outlooks, and political preferences, which provide some bases for generalizations. It is easier to generalize about readers of the *Review* than, for instance, those who post similar messages on Internet dating services.

It is of further interest that the *Review* is a highbrow publication, an elite journal read by well-educated people, many of whom are intellectuals or aspiring intellectuals; most of them are professionals of some kind, and a large proportion of them are academics. We do not know what percentage of the authors of these personals read the rest of the *Review*, or how much of it. But even if they do not read it, they have an idea of what kind of a publication it is and what types of readers it attracts.

Representativeness is not among the reasons for including the *Review* in this study. Its readers' social and educational backgrounds, tastes, cultural values, aspirations, and ego ideals are likely to differ substantially from those of the great majority of Americans who do not read it. Readers of the *Review* are also unrepresentative politically; most Americans are not liberal or left of center, unlike most readers of the *Review* who doubtless share its liberal editorial inspiration, as many of the personals make clear.

The readers of the *Review* are also unrepresentative demographically: far more women than men advertise; *at least* two-thirds are women.[17] The apparent geographical distribution of this group of readers is also atypical: the *Review* is published in New York City and is most readily available there; the personals themselves indicate that most readers live in the New York metropolitan area, though many do not reveal their exact location. (I was unable to learn the geographic distribution of subscribers or the proportion of subscribers versus those buying it at newsstands.) Probably more than half the readers of the *Review* live in the New York metropolitan area and the rest in various other metropolitan or academic settings, mostly in or around San Francisco, Los Angeles, Boston, and Chicago.

Finally, this is also an atypical group because it consists largely of the middle-aged, divorced, or widowed—at any rate, that's the impression conveyed by the personals. Many writers do not reveal their age or marital status while others provide approximations such as "fortyish" or "fiftyish" or "mature." By contrast, the age range of the people being sought is almost invariably specified and allows us to estimate the age of those advertising.

The apparent age distribution probably accounts for infrequent references to children or parenthood. Some writers make clear that they are "unencumbered," noting that their children are grown up; others may have children in the custody of a former spouse or are uninterested in having any, given their zest for living and their wide range of social, cultural, and recreational activities. With very few exceptions, also missing are indications of interest in pets. By contrast, the largest Internet dating site, match.com (discussed later), has a question that lists ten kinds of pets that advertisers may already have, like, or dislike. Arguably, there is a continuum between not having children and not having pets, though sometimes pets substitute for children—apparently not for those intensively engaged in self-realization and the attendant pursuit of a wide range of leisure-time activities, as authors of the personals in the *Review* seem to be.

It would be hard to find out how successful these communications are, how many face-to-face meetings they lead to, how many letters or phone calls are exchanged before people actually meet, and what proportion of the communications lead to meetings, lasting relationships, or marriage.[18] This is all the more regrettable since such information would help us learn about the relationship between self-assessment (conveyed in the ads) and the subsequent assessments of others, based on meetings.

Whatever their success, people have been publishing these personals for decades. Some individuals may find a degree of satisfaction in these communications themselves, without the meetings and relationships they are supposed to lead to. How "success" in such matters is to be defined or measured is another thorny issue; presumably a durable relationship (even short of marriage) in which both participants claim satisfaction or fulfillment could be considered a success. How to define "durable" invites further discussion.

I did not attempt a quantitative analysis of these personals for several reasons. To begin with, the advertisements are open-ended, that is, unconstrained by any uniform, external criteria. People tell as much or as little about themselves as they wish. All we know about the authors of the personals is what they choose to reveal, and that is largely limited to appealing personal traits they possess and seek in others. The only readily and regularly forthcoming information is *approximate* age and gender, essential for the purpose at hand. But age may be misrepresented. Perhaps for that reason, a photograph is sometimes requested, but it's possible that the photos used are not current. (I received anecdotal evidence supporting this possibility from a handful of veterans of personals and computer dating.) Given these circumstances, it would have been difficult to code reliably and uniformly much of the information provided.

There is also no way of knowing how accurate the self-characterizations are (this of course applies to all such notices and not only to those in the *Review*). Given the goal of maximizing the favorable attention of strangers, positive attributes probably are greatly overstated. Indeed, as will be shown below, at times these self-presentations verge on parody or fantasy. But even if this is so, *it is of great interest to learn what people consider desirable or attractive human qualities, whether or not they actually possess them.* A key value of the personals is that they invite little doubt in regard to the specification of *attributes sought in others.*

In light of these difficulties I settled on a qualitative analysis based on a generous sampling of the personals, many examples of which are provided below. I did range over the *Review* from its earliest days to the present, examining at least one issue for each year. I read far more than one issue per year published since the 1990s, when I have been a subscriber. Altogether I probably read several hundred personals that appeared between 1970 and 2009 (the number of personals published per issue ranged from approximately ten to sixty or more).

For the most part these personals were written by people looking for new departures, a large portion of them divorced or widowed—but again, information about marital status is not always provided. These age groups face greater difficulties in their search for partners, which helps explain their reliance on these personals and the strenuous efforts to offer a pleasing self-presentation.

The vast majority of advertisers appear to be over fifty, probably between their late forties and sixties. The relatively advanced age of these writers is the likely stimulus for projecting a youthful image of being active, adventurous, resourceful, enterprising, curious, spirited, and having a wide range of interests. To wit:

Classically pretty, smart CEO—athletic, trim, and very likeable, with ever-present touch of fun and self-deprecating humor. Gracious yet appealingly irreverent. . . . Easygoing travel companion, true explorer's spirit. . . . Passions include lazy afternoons on my dock in Maine, cooking fresh delicious meals, photography, sailing, literature. Kendall Square [in Cambridge, Massachusetts] movies, Italian hill towns, improving rusty French . . . and my Boston version of the Mediterranean pace of life. No big resorts, just little hotels, remote villages, city buzz, authenticity.

Savvy, sassy, sweet, and really good-looking, with lively intellect and mischievous sense of irony. . . . Slender, willowy, with shoulder-length hair—resemble younger, funnier Susan Sarandon in looks, politics. Fun, empathic, adventurous. Can talk travel, movies, baseball as seamlessly as economics, literature, politics. . . . Adore Clint Eastwood, Stegner, film noir, Picasso, Vermont tomatoes, swimming badly, exquisite discoveries.

Artist and outdoor adventurer. Graceful, natural; athlete. 49. Leggy slim figure. Chestnut hair. Mischievous and genuine with whimsical humor. Keep body and spirit in shape. Loves the challenge of elements: white-water canoeing, downhill skiing, winter camping, sailing, hiking, breathtaking views. . . . Warmhearted and playful with passion for ceramics, photography, architecture, Maine, Japan, spur-of-the-moment fun. . . . Authentic, game, fair-minded. Contributes to the community, sits on boards. Spunky, improvisational cook.

Pleasure-loving writer and intellectual; dark hair, nice slender shape. Academic with no time for academic hooey; immoderately literary, unexpectedly sexy . . . observer of rivers, trees, and tides. Flexible definition of high art:

The Sopranos on A&E. Martin Puryear at the MoMa. Grand Marnier souf-
flé in the Dordogne. Emotionally open and alert with an unguarded sense of
humor. Movies, meals, biking through the Cape Cod dunes; anhingas and
flamingos in the Florida 'glades. . . . Playful, stylish, and heartfelt; outgoing
and thoughtful.[19]

Blonde, slender, tall, willowy DWF very attractive (a younger Faye Dunaway)
with graceful lightness of heart, refined intelligence, smiling eyes. Ph.D./
academic. Optimistic, emphatic, elegant. Physically sensual, aesthetically attuned. Lovely profile, long legs. Considered great package: head, heart, spirit.
Puts people at ease. Loves exploring restaurants, architecture, performing arts,
hiking, yoga, Jacuzzis, narrative history. Europe any time. Thailand some day.
Seeks well-educated, attractive, kind man 5'11" plus, engaged with the world,
able to laugh occasionally at himself. [9/26/02]

Green-eyed blonde, toned, trim, and very pleasing to the eye. Adventurous,
appreciative, curious lifelong learner with humor that reveals a dry, sarcastic
side. Progressive worldview, passionate about social justice, stimulating conversation, reading, psychology, diversity. [12/5/02]

Dark, beautiful DJF with a passion for music and film. Anthropology Ph.D.,
international human rights experience combined with playful spirit, wry humor. NYC resident. Warm spontaneous smile, physical grace, calm presence,
trim figure. Keenly intelligent yet gentle, quietly affectionate, unafraid to
laugh. Also enjoys a good Bordeaux, canoeing, being near water, Marx brothers, playing pool, making amazing lemon cake, blues, live jazz, gospel, world
music. Seeks bright, thoughtful, secure, open man 49–65 with ability to laugh.
[11/7/02]

Inviting smile, beautiful bone structure, very pretty, slim Ph.D. with a real
spark (not hiding behind academic mask). Radiant, sensual, authentic, very
present, poised. Studied dance (Graham). Active in public speaking, fund-
raising, the arts, and lefty community work. Good networker, gentle risk-taker,
accentuates the positive. Loves making people laugh. Enjoys the Vineyard
anytime, Monteverdi-Mozart-Modern, blackjack, theatre, movies, champagne,
just looking at nature, learning something new. Seeks bright, active man 60s–
70s caring about the world, concerned about others. [12/5/02]

In contrast to such ample inventories of activities, interests, tastes, and
hobbies, objective characteristics—such as ethnicity, marital status, level
of education, occupation, and geographic location—are only sporadically
revealed. When specified, the occupation is often academic. Also represented are psychotherapists, physicians, businessmen, and people in publishing. Hardly anyone is, or admits to being, a lawyer. No industrial workers,

farmers, computer programmers, accountants, bankers, secretaries, nurses, or military personnel were found (though I may have missed some), but there were a handful of prison inmates reaching out.

Most of these personals do not dwell on prosaic and factual matters such as income or occupation—an interesting finding in itself. "Financially secure," "solvent," "independent," or "successful" are the rare concessions to matters involving socioeconomic status. Admission of being narrowly specialized in one's work or confessing to a limited range of interests is rigorously avoided. An apparent abhorrence of routinized activities complements bragging about artsy-artistic inclinations and touches of bohemian, sometimes whimsical non-conformity ("irreverent" and "mischievous" are recurring self-characterizations, usually by women). Veritable Renaissance characters abound, men and women with an amazing cultural reach, originality, and breadth of aspiration—free spirits possessed of a sparkling mind, a wide range of interests, and an impressive physique.

These advertisements led me to recall notices of similar purpose but very different character in newspapers published in Communist Hungary during the 1970s and 1980s.[20] Unlike the notices in the *New York Review*, they had a sober, material-existential focus and flavor. Scarcely anything was revealed about personal traits, favorite recreational activities, musical or other tastes, or artistic interests. Instead people provided factual information about their age, height, weight, occupation, educational qualifications, assets (such as apartment, car, telephone), and the neighborhood or town they lived in. They declared freedom from bad habits (mostly drinking) and said next to nothing about their personalities, feelings, tastes, and hobbies.

The messages in the *Review* are the exact opposite, reflecting the desires and needs of people with a high level of material security and comfort, even luxuries such as travel, and especially foreign travel to exotic and romantic destinations. For these Americans, the initiation of an important relationship has little to do with financial security but everything to do with the intangibles of (supposedly) unique personal needs, tastes, characteristics, and favorite entertainments.

Many of the authors of these personals in the *Review* also seek to establish their culture-consumer credentials by specifying highbrow tastes, and interests, often *in combination* with a predilection for simple or popular entertainments—thus hinting at a refreshing earthiness that is joined to sophistication ("refreshing" is another favorite adjective in these self-presentations). Good taste is a key attribute of the attractive personality portrayed in the personals. For example:

Are you the man I am looking for? Are you single, 57 plus, physically fit, secure, enjoy Matisse as well as Woody Allen, only missing the companionship of a warm, fun-loving, attractive, slender, blue-eyed blonde artist to share movies, museums, theater, ballet, travel, long walks, quiet dinners? [1/17/91]

Lover of life and laughter interested in meeting a man who values communication, spontaneity, and sharing. This publishing professional's interests range from the elation of discovering a first edition of Gide to the exhilaration of white-water rafting. If you're not afraid of romance, intimacy, and full moons this caring woman (40) may want to be by your side. [4/23/93]

Playful spirit. Natural beauty with great legs, warm intelligent dark eyes, long hair. Stunning, well-educated, sophisticated, fit. Feminine, sensual, unpretentious, successful DWF. Loves new adventures, interested in art, community, more. Avid reader, great Italian cook, works out, adores laughter, jazz, Mozart, Michelangelo, Italy, French/English countryside, raw beauty of the Maine coast and occasional fine Bordeaux. Seeks accomplished, interesting man 45–64 with compassion, humor. [1/20/00]

Serene, sweet, sensitive, sexy, sophisticated, spirited, petite, very pretty DJF (Manhattan) professional (medical research) seriously seeking divorced or widowed emotionally evolved, accomplished, financially secure, urbane, gentle male 49–60. Sense of humor essential and a (partial) passion for Puccini, pasta, Paris, Provence, and balmy evening promenades. [4/6/95]

Religious affiliation, belief, or preference is rarely mentioned, unlike political sympathies or outlook. Sometimes politically correct attitudes are spelled out, such as "liberated man," "politically concerned" (readers are expected to know what the appropriate concerns are), "environmentally conscious," "socially concerned jogging feminist," and so forth. Most writers assume a measure of political affinity that need not be spelled out for fellow readers of the *Review*.

In addition to a solid majority looking for long-term heterosexual relationships and a much smaller group of homosexuals and lesbians looking for partners, a third group of those already married (and apparently intending to stay married) wish to supplement an unsatisfactory (or satisfactory?) marital relationship with an affair. These unembarrassed invitations to participate in emotionally uninvolved sexual encounters are among the reflections of the moral relativism of our times. The requests invariably come from men (unless I somehow missed the females). To wit:

Handsome Chicago area married exec, fine background, good future, looks for down-to-earth engaging lady for discreet involvement finding summer's butterflies & winter dreams. [6/11/87]

Married, 33-year-old photographer-artist, affectionate, considerate, sometimes passionate, sincere, intelligent, well-educated, unsophisticated, athletic seeks compatible woman for enduring intimate relationship. [Shared] interests include movies, drawing, sculpture, music, outdoors, politics, philosophy, psychology and encounter groups, teaching children, walking, swimming, and open creative conversation. [1/25/73]

Does Alfred Brendel, Yo-Yo Ma, Juilliard Quartet, Oscar Peterson turn you on? Successful, attractive married professional mid-forties seeks a fun-loving professional woman interested in theater, art, chamber music, and stimulating conversation. [1/21/82]

Affectionate married man, 28, seeks slim, intelligent woman for mutual oral intimacies. [4/7/75]

Married, foreign-born professor and man of letters—with passion for annual pilgrimage to Caribbean—seeks woman (25–45) for discreet encounters. Special bias for Oriental woman. Must love reggae. [6/25/98]

Remarkably enough at a time when "lookism" is a bad word in feminist and politically correct circles, a large portion of the writers of these messages (mostly women) emphasize or boast of their appealing physical characteristics ("slender, slim, trim, fit, great legs, beautiful/sparkling eyes, hair," and so forth). The acclaimed physical attributes are almost invariably listed at the very beginning of the ads, to be followed by admirable traits of character and intellect. For instance:

Grace Kelly good looks. Stunning blonde. Doctorate. Humanist values. Slender 5'7" DWF. Young looking 44. Strongly values integrity. Adventurous, dynamic, accessible. Loves NY, theatre, music (Chopin to Gladys Knight to gospel), film, Egyptian art, impressionists, travel . . .

A younger, dark-haired more radiant Jane Fonda. Thin, smart, stunning, 40-something. Stands out in a crowd. Graceful, gracious, DJF. Long, beautiful, wavy hair, sensual smile. Interesting and interested, quick study. Art consultant, curator. Nature-lover but can do black tie at the drop of a hat. Interests: music, philanthropy, contemporary art, wine, hiking, film. Pilates. Runs daily. Loves laughter, surprise, giving small dinner parties. Open, unafraid, passionate, creative. Seeks NS, very bright man, medium-large build. 40s–50s, passionate about something in his life. [12/5/02]

A cross between Sigourney Weaver and JoBeth Williams: poised, sensual, warm-spirited with a shy grace that lights up a room. Slim body, exquisite face, fun humor, no artificiality. Interested in people and the world around. Easygoing good company, dazzling cook (makes divine bouillabaisse), something of an oenophile. Drawn to beauty in nature, art, theatre, music. Delights in generating/exchanging ideas, playing piano, hiking, travel to unexplored places. Seeks NS, vital, successful professional (49–64) with warmth and sense of discovery. [11/7/02]

An attribute often sought by women is "comfortable with himself." This requirement suggests that men are often believed to be uncomfortable with themselves, that is, suffering from identity problems associated with the extremes or excesses of individualism. The sources of such discomfort may include insufficient accomplishments, lack of material success, or falling short of their own ego ideals or of prevailing sociocultural expectations. Whatever its source, the concern is appropriate: people not comfortable with themselves are unlikely to be comfortable with others, especially in a long-term intimate relationship.

A large portion of these ads specify the preferred recreational or leisure-time activities of the writers. Many messages allude to consumption patterns that are also reflected in the stylish or artsy advertisements in publications such as the *New Yorker* or the *New York Times Magazine*—intimate dinner parties, luxurious "hideaways," contemplative walks on the beach, pastoral retreats "off the beaten path," second homes, and accommodations fit for connoisseurs of the good life. References abound to gourmet cooking and good wines nurturing body and spirit.

The most often recurring attributes allegedly possessed as well as sought are (in alphabetical order): accomplished, adventurous, affectionate, attractive, authentic, bright, creative, caring, curious, down-to-earth, earthy, easygoing, fit, funny, fun-loving, gentle, honest, intelligent, irreverent, lively, mischievous, open, passionate, playful, radiant, responsive, self-aware, secure, sensitive, sensual, serious, slender, slim, smart, sophisticated, spirited, stunning, stylish, successful, tender, trim, vibrant, vital, warm, well-educated, and witty. Many of these attributes overlap with traditional romantic values and virtues such as sensitivity, creativity, strong feelings, warmth, vitality, exuberance, tenderness, openness, sincerity, honesty, spontaneity, innocence, and arresting physical beauty. Sense of humor is another frequently mentioned desirable trait, as is relaxed.

In an age and culture in which a degree of skepticism and a refusal to take anything at face value are widespread and deeply embedded, it is surprising to find a phenomenon (such as these personals) predicated on honesty and truthfulness. In our culture few things are taken for granted, and there is a sharp awareness of the gulf between appearance and reality, especially among people who consider themselves sophisticated. Since the authors of the personals are trying to sell themselves under intense competitive pressure, their self-assessments should invite the kind of skepticism stimulated by flamboyant salesmanship or television commercials. But the personals demand that we believe what people say about themselves. How many "stunning" women such as those described below could be out there awaiting eager partners?

Stunning academic DWF, 55, slender dark hair and eyes, seeks S/DWM 55–63 for LTR. Me: striking, charming, intellectual, witty, serious, sophisticated, self-aware, open, cultivated. You: humane, good-looking, honest, well-educated, urbane, interested in art, classical music, films, candid conversations, travel. [9/26/02]

Exuberant, warm, witty, most attractive, intelligent, cultured, elegant woman, 40s, seeks open, sensitive, literate, affectionate, successful, urbane, unattached male counterpart 45–55. Prefer tallish, music-loving, nonsmoking, for whatever pleasures may result. [6/25/81]

Striking Southern California woman, strawberry blonde and newly single, thrives on imaginative sex, animated conversation, controversial politics, Brahms quartets, and the Moody Blues. Invites uninvolved intelligent male 40–60 similarly nourished to mutual feast. [4/14/77]

Woman of intellect and sex appeal, literate, sophisticated, thoughtful, helpful, gentle, vulnerable, very attractive 49 of European extraction. Seeks strong-minded, refined, reasonably handsome man capable of sustained friendship. [1/17/85]

Boston SWF artist/therapist 48, attractive, passionate lover of life and nature, vegetarian seeker of wisdom, Himalaya trekker seeks authentic, spiritually aware, self-actualizing man 40+, accomplished in his field, open to new experiences, willing to explore and enjoy life's many wonders. [7/19/90]

Hopelessly intellectual Berkshire farm-dweller, 5'6" brunette, 66. Passionate about the word written and spoken. Serendipitous discovery is my principal joy on the page, in travel, in people. I am interested in someone who is unattached and liberal who is fifty plus, well read, and considers himself funny, healthy, and happy. [7/12/99]

Adventurous, lovely, connected, fit, funny and smart Jewish woman (academic 52 NYC) seeking male counterpart to share loving and joyful aspirations. Searching for a man with good mind, deep heart, full laugh, and a social conscience. [4/26/01]

World-class professor, divorcee, elegant, attractive, vivacious, earthy, caring Manhattan resident. Seeks accomplished, well-educated, dynamic man 45–55 to share life's pleasures, travel, warmth, and love. [4/13/89]

I have a weakness for Bach's English Suites, the beach in the later afternoon on a summer day, singing in the shower, cutting dahlias for the dinner table, cooking the perfect roast chicken, Chopin nocturnes, making love in the moonlight. Me: beautiful, slender, writer, 65 NYC. In search of a vigorous man 63–75, witty, kind, with an intellectual mind, an adventurous heart and a lambent touch. No anhedonia please. And no wife in the next room. [1/14/10]

Men too are capable of implausible self-presentations:

Responsive, gentle, reflective, genuine, bright, stable, flexible, attractive, slim, 5'6" nonsmoking professional SWM seeks serious, intimate, potentially lasting relationship with slender SWF of similar qualities. I enjoy movies, theater, dogs, humor, verbal and nonverbal communications. [4/28/83]

Joys to be shared, sights to be explored, and adventures others can only dream about. You: attractive with inner beauty, responsive, considerate, affectionate, understanding, companionable, with substance, style, multiple interests, and integrity, SWF. n/s over 5'4" and irresistibly lovable. Me: SWM, n/s, tall, successful, no dependents, attractive, generous, intelligent, responsive, idealistic, principled, considerate, with a passion for adventure, nature, travel. [5/14/98]

Man 40s characterized by an encounter group as creative, complex, caring, authentic, intuitive, intense, impatient, durable, wise, searching, tentative, distinguished, not paranoid, not pretentious, not cynical, in transition, sharing, open, politically concerned, effective. Would like to meet woman with some of the following: stylish, slender, elegant, sensate, spontaneous, spirited. [1/25/79]

These messages are by no means atypical. We do not know if the authors had considered the danger of overselling themselves, or how they reconcile their idealized and colorful self-presentation with the more mundane and realistic impressions and assessments a personal encounter is bound to create. Similarly unknown is how readers respond as they evaluate the outlandish claims. Many will discount the more extraordinary assertions while others may give the benefit of doubt to even the most implausibly alluring self-presentations and reserve judgment until further communications or a personal encounter. It also remains unknown to what extent these flattering self-conceptions are genuinely held and internalized, as opposed to being deliberately burnished and distorted.

The powerful and pervasive cultural legacy of the 1960s is most likely to account for the patterns in these self-presentations. Authors of the personals in the *Review* appear to be descendants or veterans of the counterculture of earlier decades. In their communications, 1960s values and attitudes blend with an old-style romanticism made more widespread (and cheapened) by mass culture. This romantic individualism was part of the counterculture of the 1960s. The ideal personality of that period was one "in touch with his or her feelings," as well as playful, expressive, nonconformist, irreverent, adventurous, and open. The ethos of the period rejected regimentation and advocated love of nature and everything "natural." Expansive notions of self-realization (rarely defined) have remained integral to these ideals, supported by a belief in the uniqueness of oneself.

Current trends and attitudes toward objective truth and a stable identity may also help explain these questionable self-presentations. The social psychologist Kenneth Gergen writes:

> The increasing awareness of multiplicity in perspective undermines attempts to justify any transcendent criterion of the correct. . . . The very concept of an internal core—an intentional, rational agent—also begins to fray. . . .
>
> One's identity is continuously emergent, reformed, and redirected. . . . "Who am I?" is a teeming world of provisional possibilities.[21]

The personals in the *Review* yield an unexpected finding: when aggregated, the desirable attributes possessed and sought reveal a uniformity, a highly standardized set of cultural values, tastes, and ego ideals which undermines the stated or implicit claim of the unique individuality the advertisers supposedly possess. At a time when "diversity" is extolled, the specifications of ego ideals and ideal partners sampled above expose the narrow and stereotyped nature of widely held dreams and ideals, the limitations of true diversity. It is not easy to be a unique individual in contemporary American society. Attitudes and beliefs once considered unusual, innovative, daring, or nonconformist, or experimental ways of life, have become the new conventions of "nonconformity," transformed into a trend and taken up by large numbers of people who coalesce into a discernible subculture.

The personals in the *Harvard Magazine* and the *Yale Alumni Magazine* are strikingly similar to those in the *New York Review of Books*, as if they had been written by the same computer program or the same service that composes such messages. At least one such service does exist and helps account for the stunning uniformities in the style of these personals, including recurring adjectives, phrases, and characterizations:

> Many of the ads [in American publications] are now written by professionals such as Susan Fox of *Personals Work!* For 12 years she has been penning glowing descriptions of people, often with celebrity references ("head-turning good looks—evocative of Diana Riggs . . ."). She says she never lies; she is just selective about what she includes. This is advertising, after all. "They have to . . . put their best foot forward."[22]

In an advertisement placed in the *AMC Outdoors* (January/February 2008), Ms. Fox explained her undertaking:

> Personals work! You can find the person you want to meet. Our professional staff will write and place successful ads in publications best for you, devise Internet strategies, screen respondents, develop your online presence, provide invaluable skilled coaching, and help prevent burnout. We consult to men and women, all ages. We are not a dating service! All the help you need to make the personal work for you! Let us maximize your success and save your time. Call personals work! 617-859-0720. pw@latoile.com

Elsewhere Susan Fox estimates that "she's written more than 1000 personal ads for the *Harvard Magazine*—and many more in other magazines," charging $125 per hour.[23] Her handiwork is all too apparent in the personals posted in the *New York Review*, the *Harvard Magazine*, and the *Yale Alumni Magazine*.

One of her Yale clients claims to be "Smart and beautiful yet unequivocally cute. Playful intelligence, international sophistication . . . expressive sexy eyes, head-turning presence." Others possess "natural radiance . . . [combine] adventurous[ness] with calm, warm demeanor . . . laugh a lot, think deeply."

There are further claims of "whimsical humor" (a Fox favorite) possessed by a "graceful" "outdoor adventurer" who seeks a "mature" man "young at heart." A "bright and beautiful [woman] with a dash of mystery" offers "slender feminine allure, incisive humor and spontaneity" and is "always up for adventure" in addition to being "charitable" and "passionate." Not surprisingly, she "values authenticity."[24]

We also have a lady with "sparkling eyes" who is "refreshingly authentic" "with lots of heart and passion for the outdoors . . . curious with a wonderful smile, lively humor, and touch of mischief." "Mischief," "dash of mischief," "mischievous," and "natural radiance" are also among the Fox favorites, as well as "romantic at heart."[25] Sometimes the same personals appear in both the Yale and Harvard magazines.

> Artist and outdoor adventurer. *Graceful*, natural athlete. 49. Leggy, slim. . . .
> *Mischievous* and genuine with *whimsical* humor. . . . Love the challenge of the
> elements: whitewater canoeing, downhill skiing, sailing, hiking, breathtaking
> views. . . . Warm hearted and *playful* with *passion* for photography, ceramics,
> architecture, Maine, Japan, spur of the moment fun, the environment. Authentic, game, fair-minded. . . . Spunky improvisational cook. Contributes to
> the community, sits on boards. [Words italicized recur in the personals posted
> in the *Review* and the two alumni magazines.]

In *Harvard Magazine* we encounter, among others, these specimens:

> *Slender* published author, outgoing and *warm* with *passion*, a sense of *fun*, depth
> of thinking and a natural kind of beauty. . . . *Curious, authentic, adventuresome*
> yet unassuming enough to *laugh* at herself . . . drawn to the beauty of the natural world, game for just about anything. . . . Known for ability to see the bright
> side of life and for *humor* and *easygoing* unpretentiousness. Enjoys exploring
> Costa Rican rain forests and backroads of Maine, riding a camel in the Sahara,
> an evening at the BSO or local restaurants. Enjoys science museums, conversations that explore the mystery of life. . . . Prefers small, charming hotels to
> Hiltons. [November/December 2007]

A woman in her early fifties offers "*sparkling* green-blue eyes" and a "*sense of adventure and spontaneity* . . . can talk to a Nobel prize winner or janitor." She is competing with a similarly disposed woman, "strikingly attractive and *irreverently funny* . . . friendly, relaxed good company . . . in great shape, quietly charming, *easygoing* and eclectic conversationalist . . . with *lively* smile, a *wry* twinkle in the eye and *passion* for art, good coffee and wine" [November/December 2007].

There are further offerings of "*natural radiance* . . . calm demeanor and genuiness of character" as well as beauty "with dash of *mystery*, hilariously *dry wit* [and] contagious *laugh* . . . [as well as] *slender* feminine allure, incisive *humor* and *spontaneity*." Other recurring characterizations include "insightful irreverence," "ever-present dash of self-deprecating humor," "contagious humor," "adventurous yet down to earth," "easygoing allure," "dash of mischief," "light-hearted," "passionate connection to the natural world, magical ability to play," "graceful," "passionate interest in things active and intellectual," "natural radiance," "natural athlete," "easygoing great looks," "mischievous," "genuine, sexy and comfortable with herself," "loves challenge of the elements," and enjoys "spur of the moment fun."

Among all the women who advertise in the *New York Review of Books* and the alumni magazines, the reader will note a pronounced resemblance. The similarities encompass character traits, accomplishments, and pastimes, and make it hard to distinguish one person from another. These profiles reflect both stereotyped conceptions of female attractiveness and the stylistic quirks of the prolific writer of these personals.

It is hard to escape the impression that many ads in all three publications greatly and sometimes grotesquely overstate the personal qualities and attractions of the individual advertisers. They seem to be endowed with every conceivable trait that is highly valued in our culture. They are good-natured, good-humored, open-minded, cheerful, witty, lively, easy to get along with, warm, adventurous, playful, accomplished, physically attractive, highly educated, and have broad interests. The women in particular convey a personality that combines appealing and authentic simplicity with great sophistication. The inflated and implausible self-presentations are more common among women than men.

Why would such impressive human beings decide to invest time, energy, and money in a highly organized and costly search for suitable partners? Are these self-presentations largely wishful fantasies, exaggerations, or reflections of the copywriter's beliefs and style? The implausible self-presentations are clearly attention-getting efforts; overselling oneself is a response to keen competition for partners, reflecting the pressures of a competitive culture and a competitive marketplace of personal relationships, especially among older age groups and especially older women, who, as statistics indicate, are more often without partners.

Some broader conclusions may be drawn. Being alone in middle age or older is a difficult experience that prompts efforts to escape this predicament and gives rise to the personals in the *Review* and elsewhere. One must try to stay, or appear to be, "young at heart" until the bitter end. The youth cult permeating American society encourages these efforts.

The heightened expectations central to modernity also help explain these self-presentations and the yearnings they express. They originate in ways of life that provide an abundance of "options" and are free of pressing material concerns but are weighed down by an imbalance between material needs that are easily gratified and emotional ones that are largely unmet. Modernity intensifies expectations and the quest for intimate relationships which, it is hoped, will compensate for the loss of community and a stable worldview.

## The *London Review of Books*

The idea that national character is a useful concept[26] finds support in a comparison of the personals published in the *New York Review of Books* and the *London Review of Books*, its British equivalent. The similarities between these two publications are not limited to their title. Both lean left-liberal, in both most of the contributors are academics, and both address well-educated readers. There is one important demographic difference: possibly two-thirds if not three-quarters of those advertising in the *New York Review of Books* are women, whereas the proportions for the *London Review of Books* are 51 percent male and 49 percent female.[27]

The differences between personal advertisements in the two publications are striking and highly patterned. Unlike their American counterparts, British men and women placing these personals don't seem to take themselves very seriously; they do not meticulously list their accomplishments and attractions. Their style and approach is humorous, playful, quirky, self-deprecating, and dominated by displays of eccentricity. There is scarcely any serious reference to recreational activities or hobbies. To wit:

[H]ave two great talents. One is writing superb adverts like this, the other is cage-free chicken farming. If either of those appeal, please write.

If we fail to hit it off on our first date, you will at least appreciate the brutal efficiency with which I let you know. No hidden meanings.

As a frequent attendee at LRB Bookshop events, I spend most of my time wrestling with my internal monologue jokes and summoning up courage to articulate these before an audience. . . . By the time my anxieties have subsided, the shop has emptied and I am once more alone. My sexual experiences mirror this.

Sulky M, 68 seeks acquiescent wife or punctual urologist. Preferably one in the same. No perverts/slackers.

Bald, short, fat, and ugly male, 53, seeks shortsighted woman with tremendous sexual appetite.

Mature gentleman (62), aged well, noble grey looks, fit and active. Sound mind and unfazed by the fickle demands of modern society seeks . . . damn it I have to pee again.

Either I am desperately unattractive, or you all are lesbians. Bald, pasty man (61) with nervous tick and unclassifiable skin complaint . . . holds out hope for dominant (yet straight) fems at box.

Shy, ugly man, fond of extended periods of self-pity, middle-aged, flatulent, overweight, seeks the impossible.

Too much sex, not enough vitamin B12. Vegan love-god on the brink of mental and physical collapse (M, 26) seeks pallid, calcium-deficient F for nights of apathy, depression, and headaches.

I am not afraid to say what I feel. At this moment in time I feel anger, giddiness, and the urge to dress like a bear and forage for berries at motorway hedgerows. Man 38.

I intend to spend the summer stewing over failed relationships. You can join me if you like.

Your buying me dinner doesn't mean I'll have sex with you. I probably will have sex with you though. Honesty not an issue with opportunistic male, 38.

I use this column principally as a sounding board for my radical philosophical theories. This time, however, I would like some sexual intercourse.

Reply to this advert, then together we can face the harsh realities of my second mortgage. M 38.

Ladies: naturally apologetic man, 42, predisposed to accepting the blame. Whatever it was, it was my fault. Sorry. Sound like heaven?[28]

How to account for these differences between London and New York personals if not by national character? The British, or at any rate those among them who devise these notices, are clearly less individualistic, less narcissistic, less competitive, and less anxious to make a favorable impression—or their notion of what makes a favorable impression is very different from that of the American writers. Another possibility is that these ads serve an altogether different purpose, that they are just a game, an expression of playfulness and not of the desire to make contact with another human being in order to initiate a romantic relationship.

According to the editor of the *London Review of Books* collection, "For some LRB advertisers, meeting a partner is no longer even the main objective of placing a personal ad. Creating these silly little flourishes has become an art form. . . . They are a frolic, a bit of whimsy. . . . Pitching oneself in LRB is no longer about trying to locate one's most attractive aspects. . . . The ads in the LRB aren't necessarily about saying anything at all; they are little statements of absurdity."[29] Even if this is so, the British personals illustrate the profound differences between their authors and their American counterparts. The Americans would not waste time on such seemingly pointless games ("little statements of absurdity"), if that is what they are. It is indeed possible that for the British these personals are a form of playful, whimsical self-expression divorced from any serious desire to find a partner.

## The *Village Voice* and the *Valley Advocate*

The *Village Voice*, published in New York City, used to be another major publisher of personals. It ran scores, possibly hundreds of them in each issue from the 1950s until 2006. Those discussed below appeared between 1974 and 2004. For reasons similar to those explaining the absence of a quantitative analysis of the *New York Review of Books* personals, the following discussion is also qualitative but is based on a reading of hundreds of these notices.

The character of these personals is significantly different from those published in the *New York Review* and the alumni publications discussed above. The *Voice* personals reflect lower levels of education and more diverse sociocultural backgrounds. Spelling mistakes are not uncommon, and some of the ads are poorly written. These notices are shorter, more matter of fact, provide more ethnic identification and preference, and include far more references to matters sexual, probably because the writers are generally younger than those who advertise in the *Review* and the alumni magazines. A broader age range may also be seen in these ads.

In a large number, possibly half, of these notices, weight and height are specified (they rarely are in the publications discussed above). On the other hand, many *Voice* ads do not indicate occupation; "professional" is sometimes used as a desirable attribute possessed by the advertiser. Occupations mentioned include teacher, professor, college student, artist, belly dancer, songwriter, real estate broker, photographer, musician, businessman (or executive), advertising executive, social worker, former monk, opera singer, lawyer, and prison inmate (a large category). But most writers don't consider occupation important enough to mention (as in the *Review*). This may be a reflection of an underlying romanticism that judges attributes of personality as far more important to compatibility than how one makes a living and with what results. Overlooking occupation is also a reflection of the individualistic belief that occupation (and social roles) is not a major determinant of personality.

What makes the *Voice* ads interesting is the wide variation in what is sought and offered, and the fact that important emotional needs, ego ideals, and self-revelations are compressed into short messages (in most cases twenty to twenty-five words), presumably to save money.

A wide variety of social, ethnic, and demographic backgrounds is reflected in these notices, making it difficult to generalize and to discern patterned connections between social background, ego ideals, and expectations. Moreover, as in the *New York Review*, the amount of information provided about oneself varies greatly. Some of the 1960s terminology and attitudes are apparent but are not nearly as pervasive as in the *Review*'s notices. The sensibilities of the 1960s are more often reflected in "liberated" sexual attitudes and requirements displayed in the *Voice* than in more elusive longings or dreams of self-realization found in the *Review*. Still, residue of the 1960s may be found in the high value placed on "sensitive and caring" individuals and on the pursuit of "sincerity"—possibly the most oft-mentioned quality, either as something possessed or sought after. "Attractive" is probably even more frequently mentioned, notwithstanding its inherent vagueness. We don't know, in most cases, if attractiveness refers to appearance or character—most likely to the former, possibly to both. Desirable political attitudes, including environmental concerns, are rarely mentioned.

It is worthwhile to ponder why—unlike the authors of the personals in the *Review*—so many writers in the *Voice* offer or demand "sincerity," the attribute central to the romantic disposition. In all probability, "sincerity" as used here is a substitute for the more esoteric concept of "authenticity." The requirement of sincerity could be an expression of apprehensions inspired by the possibility of being deceived, manipulated, or taken advantage of. In a modern, impersonal, competitive, capitalistic society like ours, such apprehensions are not groundless. More generally there is a heightened awareness of the gulf between appearance and reality, resulting from the ubiquitousness and prominence of commercial advertising and the practices of the "public relations" industry. This concern is particularly justified when people seek to "sell themselves" by advertising their virtues and assets and when there is no way to know, at least initially, how truthful these communications are. It remains to be explained why those advertising in the *Review* do not express interest in sincerity and appear less concerned with deceptions and misrepresentations. They may feel that belonging to higher-status groups and possessing social and intellectual credentials confer protection against such deceptions.

Many of the messages in the *Voice* are vague and general as to the type of person or relationship being sought; others are highly specific about needs and requirements. The types of relationships sought vary greatly, ranging from the all-embracing and intense to the highly specialized and unemotional, from a hoped-for lifelong commitment to short-term, sometimes kinky and paid sexual encounters. Often the writers are content to express interest in "a relationship," "a warm relationship," "a relationship of significance," "a discreet relationship," "a mutually beneficial or rewarding relationship," or a "mutually satisfying relationship." None of these characterizations helps discern what they have in mind. Others seek a "romantic, passionate relationship," a "passionate and true relationship," "someone special," a "soul mate," or a "partner for loving relationship."

There are also frequent expressions of interest in "fun or romance," "friendship," "fun and friendship," "friendship and romance," "friendship and fun," "sincere friendship," "friendship and possibly more," "companionship," or, more vaguely, "sharing good things in life."

At the other end of the spectrum are those who seek merely a "discreet weekday liaison" or "fun only" or, even more moderately, a "clean, disease-free" partner. Modest but specific requirements are exemplified by wanting to meet an "attractive female between [various ages specified]" or a "busty blonde 26 years old and 5'9" who seeks men over 40 for discreet, mutually rewarding relationship" [1-1-94]. Another man is looking for a "full-figured" woman. An M.D. "with a good sense of humor" limits his interest to "an Oriental female with a simple life style" [1-10-84]. A "nice-looking" white executive seeks "attractive, educated, light-complexioned black woman for meaningful relationship" [1-7-86]. A "well-built" black male of thirty-three seeks a "down-to-earth" black or Hispanic female "who is looking for a relationship" [1-3-95]. A "motorcycle enthusiast" is anxious to meet a woman who is "interested in weekend or week-long cycle trips," and has no other requirement [7-11-74]. A "single white male 39, Ph.D. seeks attractive woman, race not important. Slim, long hair a plus" [7-9-80]. It is hard to know why this writer expects his Ph.D. to impress this largely undefined woman. Race is also "unimportant" for the "Hot Italian guy [who] seeks buxom woman. Race unimportant" [1-3-95]. "Hot" and "buxom" signal that sex is at the heart of this message.

More unusual requirements include those of a "Single white male in his late 20s seek[ing] single white female who resembles one of the following: Demi Moore, Louise Brooks, Joan Jeff." He notes his own liking for blues and rock music as well as basketball and baseball [1-5-93]. Vague and specific requirements are combined in the case of "White male seek[ing] pleasant lady of *subtle good nature* and Russian-Jewish descent or other loving types" (emphasis added).

It seems widely assumed that the desire for "fun" or "fun times" needs no further explication, as in the ad of a "tanned handsome man (25) seeking attractive female companion who likes to sunbathe, have fun times with lovely people & live" [7-11-74]. A "successful athletic attorney" seeks "independent, intelligent woman 25–36 to share good things in life," and assumes consensus as to what they are. "MD/medical school professor with sense of humor, wonder & personal honor seeks female with nice personality, nice smile, nice hair & nice body" [7-9-80]—here everything hinges on the interpretation of "nice." More ambitious is an "idealistic & affectionate professional man, close 40, secure, selective, witty & good company [who] needs an accomplished woman to complete long-range plans for a civilized existence" [7-14-75]. He does not reveal his conceptions of such an existence. A more unusual request is made by the "SWM 28, professional [who] seeks intelligent attractive muscular woman into body building or weight training" [1-5-93]. Other special interests include "candlelight dinners" (also a favorite of many who advertise on the Internet), "older woman" (requested by a surprising number of men), a "dancing partner," and someone for "intimate late-night conversations."

Also unusual is the "Blonde . . . 30 years old SWF nonsmoking, nondrinking [who would] like to meet single American or Mid-Eastern Christian male 25–30. Social activities, good clean fun, and sincere relationship" (a rare expression of religious preference) [7-9-80].

A few revelations of physical handicaps appear, as in the ad of "Male social worker. 34. Sensitive, into conversation, theater, physically handicapped but independent, mobile, seeks caring relationship" [5-10-76]. Other unusual requests include "Sincere, desirable, 6' tall generous guy seeks athletic, swimmer, gymnast runner type female to share fantasies in a relationship" [5-10-76]. "Trim successful white M 45, seeks not overweight lady under 45 who would like being escorted to the movie 'Servant and Mistress'" [7-3-78]. By contrast, "Fat lover, 45 years old, divorced, 6'2" 290 pounds seeks large lady between ages 30–60 for very romantic and hot times" [7-9-80].

The wide range of unusual interests includes an "Older female wanted 40–80. WM 40s, 6', handsome, business exec seeks F for sensual discreet relationship" [1-14-04]. "Female 37, interested in Iranian culture, anti-Shah, would like to meet gentleman for weekday companionship" [1-14-04]. "Tall, large-sized brunette beauty 30s seeks tall SWM (Mr. Wonderful) to share life. Must love animals & have a great sense of humor" [1-9-90]. "MWF (Deborah Winger type) desires witty, charming, intelligent & articulate SWM or MWM for intimate late-night phone conversations" [1-7-91]. "Famous musician/director/poet SWM very handsome seeks SWF 28–35 beautiful, intelligent model-actress-dancer" [1-6-98]. "Handsome, sexy, blue-collar Latin male wanted by very attractive, curvy, irreverent redhead [female] with green eyes for incredible adventures" [1-12-99].

More idealistic is an "attractive European woman" in her mid-forties, "ambitious, creative, affectionate, and caring," who wants "to grow on a more personal level . . . looking for a man with the same qualities who is in business or the medical profession" [1-10-84]. Somewhat similar may be the "SWM 27, 5'9" 150 [who] wants to live and give. Let's help each other to maximize our potential" [1-7-86].

"Intellectual athletic single male seeks intellectual type single female for friendship and possibly more" [1-7-86]. "Jewish princess wanted" by a "sexy, hot, Italian MWM 30"—nothing said about the writer of this ad. Also unusual is the "female teacher 34, warm, loving, and sensitive [who] seeks man not afraid to get involved and show feelings for close but not overly dependent relationship" [5-10-86].

The requirement of "discretion" is often attached to the *Voice* personals. There are two likely explanations. One is that many of those advertising are married and apparently wish to stay married while seeking an extramarital affair. The other possibility is that money changes hands in some of these relationships, and that too calls for discretion.

A large portion of these ads seek sex—for or without money: "Beautifully composed black woman 20s tall, slender, strong, passionate desires successful worldly, fit WM. Lawyer or law student welcome" [1-10-89]. "Mature black female seeks white male 50+ drug and disease free for a spontaneous no-strings-attached relationship" [1-1-03]. "Affable married man 34 seeks pleasant female for occasional mutual enjoyment" [6-4-77]. "White male, 40s, handsome business executive seeks female for sensual, discreet relationship" [1-9-80]. "Laid back, financially secure real estate developer 38, fit, is looking for a knockout white female with a Dolly Parton figure to share some of the better things with" [1-5-88]. "Married white male 45 real estate broker seeks female for day or evening romance, no pros, must be discreet" [1-13-87]. "Couple, white, late 20s, warm, attractive, affectionate professionals seek attractive woman, perhaps couple, for intimate weekends at our mountain retreat" [1-10-89]. "Married white couple 33, 31, look for same for enjoyable evening" [1-9-90]. "Wealthy $$$ handsome single white male seeks unique fem: e.g. busty muscular young etc." [1-1-94]. A more unusual writer inquires: "Are you a married lady who deserves more pleasure? Has your romantic frequency dropped from seldom to never? I'm your married male counterpart. If you seek a safe, sensual encounter, take charge of your needs, & call" [1-1-94]. "An adventurous, attractive, exhibitionistic male seeks exhibitonistic female who is unafraid of her passion, sensuality, fantasies, or special intense friendship" [1-1-94]. "A hot lover! Male seeks curvaceous/full-figured vixen for sensual times" [1-1-94]. "Tall black female, model-type figure seeking extremely successful male age 40 and up" [1-6-98]. "Single black female, voluptuous and sensual, seeking discreet relationship. Professional man only. Drug and disease free" [1-12-99]. "Beautiful, sensual, intelligent Chinese/Hawaian sweetheart looking for wealthy CEO Exec enterpreneur for discreet, personal, one-on-one fun" [7-2-02]. "Busty Latin Venezuelan Beauty 30 years old looking for a generous & affluent gentleman for casual discreet fun relationship" [1-1-03]. "Latin Korean single female 40, sensual, with an Asian touch of sexiness, seeks older gentleman over 50 for safe and discreet times" [1-6-98].

There is no ambiguity in the ad of a "pretty English black girl 37" who seeks "wealthy white gentleman for good times" [1-2-02]. Sex for financial benefits is proposed by the "very sexy single black female college student looking to go shopping to exotic clothing and jewelry stores" and for "discreet or regular relationship. Professional man only" [1-12-99]. More unusual in this category is the "attractive belly dancer, ex-medical student, Turkish airline hostess" who wishes to meet "professional man, doctor, lawyer, author for sincere friendship" [1-12-99]. Many of these *Voice* ads, specifying the wealth, affluence, or professional status of men, represent a classier form of prostitution.

Also noteworthy are the unembarrassed invitations to adultery, as in the *New York Review*. A "Good-looking man, 39, born and educated in Europe, married, seeks attractive white woman, with sense of humor, to spend afternoons in a pleasant companionship" [7-4-77]. "White Latin married man seeks married woman to explore emotional/sexual intimacy" [1-13-87]. "Married white male 41, 6'2" attractive, health-conscious, seeks married female for intimate, sensuous & discreet daytime fun" [1-7-91]. "White male 50s tall, handsome executive seeks single or married woman in 40s for ongoing relationship. Available evenings. Some weekends and business trips" [1-10-89]. "MM [married male] seeks MF [married female] 30–50 . . . for discreet diversion. Oral is my specialty. Dominant and kinky women welcome" [1-9-80].

Several patterns emerge from these ads. One is the hard-nosed, consumerist approach, shopping for attributes carefully specified, suggesting that the writer knows exactly what he or she wants and needs. The specifications need not be realistic and may represent some fantasy. Demands for specific sexual gratifications or services are a subcategory.

Another pattern is unabashed romanticism, reflected in such notices as "Wanted . . . needed, independent, compassionate, athletic, mystical, difficult female. . . . Do not send photos or phone numbers, send poetry" [1-5-93]. To this category belongs the ad of a "beautiful and sweet" woman "looking for a man that makes me complete. . . . I'll keep searching till I find you" [1-7-03]. "A truly beautiful slender, angelic, blond singer, 46, with smarts, curves, and sweet soul wishes for handsome loving soul mate 40 + for loves [sic], sweet dance" [7-2-02]. "Male (mid 20s) in advertising who enjoys oceans, trees, and poems would like to meet sensitive career woman" [5-10-76]. "White male seeking beautiful young white girl for total relationship & affection. Sweet, romantic affair with lots of love" [7-4-77]. A "female accountant and artist" describing herself as "romantic, lively, and affectionate" would like to meet "congenial & idealistic man for hopeful lasting relationship." "Attractive NYC police officer SWM, 31 would like to develop a committed lasting relationship based on mutual trust and affection. . . . Looking for that special person to share special times" [1-10-84]. More unrealistically, a "shy romantic male poet 29, not rich or handsome, into classical music, sci-fi seeks very beautiful, gentle, imaginative, caring woman" [5-10-76]—an example of unreasonable expectations unlikely to be met by women of the attributes listed. Such ads are a small portion of the total.

A third pattern resembles a projective test: expressions of interest in desirable but highly unspecific attributes like "attractive," "caring," or "nice," and hoping for the best. Perhaps people who are unspecific about their needs and requirements are not sure what they really want, apart from escaping loneliness.

Attributes most often encountered (both possessed and required) in the *Voice* personals include (in alphabetical order) athletic, beautiful, bright, busty, caring, classy, considerate, creative, fun-loving, generous, honest, intelligent, laid-back, mature, passionate, pretty, professional, secure, sense of humor, sexy, shapely, smart, successful, upbeat, warm, and youthful.

Another source of printed personals is a weekly publication distributed free of charge in western Massachusetts, where I live, called the *Valley Advocate*. The geographic area is often called the "Pioneer Valley," and it includes five colleges, the cities of Springfield and Holyoke, and a number of smaller cities where the colleges (and the University of Massachusetts) are located: Amherst, Northampton, and South Hadley. The area is politically and culturally left-liberal due to its large academic population as well as the presence of many former students who settle here; others are drawn to it because of its countercultural reputation and natural beauty. In spite of these circumstances, the personals in the *Advocate* have little in common with those in the *New York Review* since apparently most of those advertising are neither students nor faculty but "ordinary" people, several of whom take pride in owning and using Harley-Davidson motorcycles, and none of whom aspires to (or boasts of) vacations in Provence or Tuscany. A female "Harley owner" is looking for a "hardworking, blue-collar type, who is honest and kind and trustworthy."[30] A "hardworking [male] nonsmoker enjoys hiking, fishing, camping, music. . . . Seeking a nice easygoing SF [single female] to share the simple times of life." A construction worker seeks SF 30–45 "who knows how to love, laugh, and have a good time!" A truck driver would like to meet a "SF 50+ to hang out with and get to know. Friendship first, may be more." The needs catered to seem simpler in these notices, as, for example, those of a "male [who] likes rock and country music, cooking, going to the movies, swimming, and more. Looking for WF for dating and possible LTR [long-term relationship]." A self-described "real gentleman" "enjoys walks in the park, quiet nights at home, watching movies, the mall." He seeks that "special someone, 18–45."

These ads have more in common with those in the *Village Voice* than with their counterparts in the classy publications considered earlier. They are short (like those in the *Voice*) and concentrate on down-to-earth basics; the wants expressed are more straightforward, as are the hobbies or recreational preferences; absent are the implausible claims of physical attractiveness, sparkling intellect, and all-round, magnetic personalities. Unlike the personals in the *Voice*, those in the *Advocate* do not include sex-for-money offers (the *Advocate* has a separate section for escorts and massage where such offers may be found, but so does the *Voice*).

There are many indications that the *Advocate*'s readers are a younger, less-educated group, capable of (as the writers themselves put it) "enjoying the simpler things in life" or "the simple pleasures of life," including and especially "quiet evenings at home" as well as "boating, cooking, watching movies at home" or "dining out, beaches, shopping, movies." Shopping, eating out, movies, and beaches seem to be the most popular recreational activities mentioned; men almost invariably are interested in outdoor activities. Not every ad is upbeat; some of the writers reveal the pain of loneliness, as, for example, the "very lonely SWM 41, on disability for depression, but doing ok, into 60s rock music, desperately reaching out for single female for LTR."

Many self-presentations include reference to or affection for a football or baseball team such as the Red Sox or the New England Patriots, and seek a "sport companion" since it is "no fun watching sports alone," a woman writes. A lover of the Patriots "seeks honest, down-to-earth, independent, secure White Male, to be my special someone." Being a fan of a particular athletic team may be a sign of an encouraging normalcy or "ordinariness" as well as a bond shared by strangers belonging to a virtual community of fans (when no other community is available). The shared support for these teams seems to be a precondition or component of becoming a soul mate for some of those who advertise.

Many advertisers sensibly enough propose "friendship first and see what happens from there," or "friendship, possible romance." This is not to say that interest in romantic relationships is absent. Many are unabashedly looking for a "soul mate," or for "passion for life," or "a romantic, loving, mature, honest guy who loves the Red Sox and the Patriots."

The attraction of beaches is widespread among those advertising in the *Advocate*, as it is among online writers considered in the following chapters. The reference to beaches signals a romantic disposition and romantic possibilities, popularized by television commercials that endlessly depict happy couples strolling or frolicking on a beach used as a setting for a wide range of advertised products, none of which has any connection with being on a beach. Apparently the abundance of such advertisements leads to an association of the beach with happiness, companionship, good cheer, playfulness, spontaneity, natural beauty, and endless possibilities and opportunities.

Another prop of romance that often appears in both printed and online notices is the "candlelight dinner," or candlelight on other intimate occasions. Why this association of candles and romance? Perhaps because candles symbolize simpler and better pre-industrial times and because they provide little light, allowing pockets of darkness, flickering images, and room for the imagination.

It is noteworthy that some attributes or characteristics are never or rarely mentioned in the printed sources surveyed in this chapter. Desirable attributes of men, as specified either by the men or the women, rarely include "ambitious," "achiever," "responsible," "good provider," or "hardworking," suggesting that these traits are considered less important for a good relationship than being caring, honest, sincere, sensitive, playful, romantic, open to new experience, warm, and fun-loving, among others. If people are interested in social status and earning power, they certainly play down or decline to reveal such a disposition. Likewise, among desirable male attributes there is scarcely any reference to courage, decisiveness, generosity, and stability.

Attractive female characteristics rarely include nurturing, gentle, generous, or being a good mother, a good cook, or a devoted homemaker. There is also a surprising restraint regarding references to sensuality: few women describe themselves as amorous, sensuous, sexy, seductive, or allude in any way to being good in bed. Nor do men express a desire to find such women, except in the *Voice* ads. The closest men or women come to hinting at sexual attractiveness or needs is in using attributes such as "buxom" or "curvaceous" while expressions of interest in physical intimacy are limited to "cuddling."

These personals reflect a wide variety of needs and requirements which have only one indisputable common denominator: the desire to escape loneliness. The vast majority of the advertisements play down the importance of socioeconomic status (and by implication that of income) and concentrate instead on personal qualities. Higher social status and educational attainments (such as possessed by those advertising in the *New York Review* and the alumni publications) are communicated in codes and by referring to certain leisure-time activities and places chosen for travel. The self-conceptions and the individualistic values espoused are often contradicted by the standardized notions of what constitutes a good relationship and its recreational accessories.

Broader American cultural influences are apparent in many of these notices: high expectations, the blend of romantic and pragmatic considerations, and the values of the 1960s with their emphasis on self-realization.

❦

# CHAPTER SIX

# Looking for Love on
# the Internet: Massachusetts

Self-presentation on line . . . allow[s] lonely individuals to self-present a
more idealized version of [them]selves.

Janet Morahan Martin and Phyllis Schumacher[1]

Our fate in love and marriage seems to be driven by factors such as looks,
height, weight, and income that are hard or impossible to change.

Gunter J. Hitsch[2]

## The Growth of Online Dating

Many Americans would strongly disagree with the proposition that their love
life is determined by factors over which they have little or no control. After
all, they are engaged in ceaseless efforts to remake themselves with the help
of cosmetics, exercise, wardrobe, or psychotherapy. How successful such efforts
are is, of course, another matter. More Americans may agree that idealized self-
presentation in print or online (and even in the course of actual dating) can
seriously conflict with the reality of the existing personality being presented,
and that the discrepancy can make it difficult to establish an enduring intimate
relationship. As in so many other areas of life, the clash between ideals and realities is endemic and especially pronounced in a culture of high expectations.

For the first time in history, in recent years an extensive written record
has become available about the desires, preferences, and expectations of
millions of people who are seeking intimate personal relationships. These
aspirations find expression in both printed and electronic sources.

At the start of the twenty-first century, electronic dating seems to have become the prevalent method of searching for a romantic partner in American society. Tens of millions of people now rely on a multitude of dating sites and services catering to a variety of specialized interests and tastes. Reportedly "74% of single Americans searching for partners used the Internet to facilitate their romantic pursuits."[3] According to the *New York Times*, "16.6 million people visited matchmaking Web sites in September [2002] alone, a figure [that] has made internet dating seem almost stigma free"; the same figure was provided by the Pew Internet Project in 2006.[4] Another estimate put the number of Americans who visited online dating sites in 2003 at 40 million.[5] These numbers also reflect population growth, the high incidence of divorce, and the longer life span of the so-called baby boomers, many of them divorced or single. Census Bureau data reveal that more than 18 percent of the 76 million baby boomers are divorced, 10 percent have never married, and 2.8 percent are widowed. According to Helen Fisher, of 46 million single women and 38 million single men in the United States, 25 percent have joined a dating service, adding up to 21 million people.[6]

Stephanie Coontz, the historian of marriage, reports that "many women tell me they feel 'desperate' to find a man. Running into potential partners gets harder once you are out of school and no longer spend most of your waking hours in a concentrated pool of singles in your own age-group. Also, when women work in predominantly female work settings, as many still do, they have few opportunities to meet potential partners at work."[7]

It is not easy to generalize about people who use the Internet for these purposes, except for the finding—not altogether surprising—that "loneliness has been associated with increased Internet use. Lonely individuals may be drawn online because of increased potential for companionship, the changed social interaction patterns online, and as a way to modulate negative moods associated with loneliness."[8] Studies have also shown that "those who are more likely to be online are richer, have more education, are not disabled, are more likely to live in a suburb or a city, and are more likely to be white."[9]

Electronic personals differ substantially from their printed counterparts. They usually are longer and have a standard, structured format that seeks to elicit the same basic information, such as age, sex, occupation, ethnicity, and religious and political preferences. Internet dating sites represent a more systematic attempt to match compatible individuals than the haphazard, open-ended self-revelations in printed sources. Online questionnaires restrain, to some degree, the hype and misrepresentations found in many of the printed messages discussed earlier, but they also provide their own new temptations and opportunities for misrepresentation.[10] One study finds that "the lowered accountability levels of online interactions and the inability to pinpoint an online persona to [sic] a solid offline identity might foster . . . façades and lower people's inhibitions about lying."[11] Another study points out that "self-presentation online is altered not only by disinhibition, but also by the reduction of online role constraints, social expectations, and interpersonal barriers found in face-to-face communication. These . . . allow lonely individuals to self-present a more idealized version of self."[12]

Whether online expressions of romantic interest are superior to older, conventional methods of making contact is debatable. Are they more helpful in screening and selecting compatible partners than the old trial-and-error procedure that begins with meeting potential partners in school, college, or the workplace? Is online dating superior to connections that result from introductions by third parties? Are pickups in public places necessarily inferior to electronic methods? Subjective, online self-presentations may not be the best sources of information for initiating and establishing long-term relationships and may be inferior to visual impressions, face-to-face interaction, or *reliable* information about basic sociological or demographic markers such as age, ethnicity, level of education, religion, and political outlook.

Advocates of online dating focus on its perceived advantages: "You can remain anonymous as you deem necessary. . . . You can be as specific or nonspecific as you like. . . . You can do it all from the comfort of your home. . . . You can save time by avoiding face-to-face liaisons with people who are clearly not going to be compatible."[13] But Internet communications are severely limited in their capacity to shed light on the more intangible components of personality, including self-conception and personal history, that shape attitudes toward the opposite sex. They cannot provide much information about important matters such as the need for security versus adventure and variety, the balance or imbalance between emotional and sexual needs, mobility aspirations, and many others. As we shall see, in the most widely used dating service (match.com) there are few if any questions that address these matters. Personality traits and expectations are the most important influences on the unfolding of romantic relationships, but it is difficult to learn about personality from information volunteered online (or for that matter in print).

The major drawback of online dating is the absence of a social context, as is found in the conventional settings (school, work, organizations, etc.) which provide baselines or objective realities and thus help assess potential dates or partners.

Several trends have led to the expansion of online dating: the requisite technology and growing computer literacy; demographic changes resulting in an increase in the number of people seeking romantic partners; and a greater social acceptance of Internet dating.[14] A *Dating Site Advisor* list illustrates the expansion and growing specialization of such sites. The list includes the Dating Site Reviews Index with more than eighty dating sites; 8 Best Sites for Dating U.S. and Canadian Singles, catering to thirty-three million singles; Alternative Dating Sites for Every Kind of Quest ("pet owners, seniors, big people, military personnel, millionaires, people with STD, and other alternative dating services with a specialized focus"); Best Asian Dating Service; Black Dating Web Site; Christian Singles Dating Web Site; Gay Dating Service; Lesbian Dating Service; Foreign Dating Service; Interracial Dating Service; Jewish Dating Service; Top Latin Dating Services; and the Dating Resources Directory, among others.[15]

Given the great numbers of people using many different sites and electronic dating services, it is difficult to find aggregated, comprehensive, and representative data about their attitudes, values, and social background. Only a few attempts have been made to collect information about these groups or at any rate about some of their attitudes and attributes.

According to the Pew Report (based on a representative national sample), 64 percent of those involved in online dating consider it helpful because it provides access to a large pool of potential dates. The survey further revealed that 75 percent of single adults looking for a romantic partner are Internet users compared to 56 percent who are not looking. Forty-three percent of these online seekers made dates and 17 percent reported resulting long-term relationships or marriage. But, significantly, the study also found that "most internet users who are married or in committed relationships met each other off line: 38% at work or school, 34% through family or friends, 13% at a nightclub, bar, café, or other social gathering, 3% through internet, 2% at church."

Nor surprisingly, the Pew study indicates that younger people are more likely to use the Internet. Thus 18 percent of these online daters were 18–29, 11 percent 30–49, 6 percent 50–64, and 3 percent over 65. Sixty-six percent of Internet users "like to try new things" as opposed to 49 percent of the general population, another finding indicative of a less conservative disposition than can be found in the general population.[16] Only 29 percent of online daters describe themselves as "a religious person," compared to 46 percent of all Americans, supporting the impression (gained from my own research, discussed below) that online date seekers are a more liberal and secular segment of the population.

Another study examined in 2003 "a major online dating website" with twenty-three thousand users in Boston and San Diego. In this group men were overrepresented while minorities and those over sixty-five were under-represented. It found that "Both men and women prefer partners with higher incomes, but this preference is much more pronounced for women." The researchers concluded that "the online dating site attracts users that are typi-cally single, somewhat younger, more educated, and have a higher income than the general population." Thirty-nine percent joined the dating service to find a long-term relationship, 26 percent were "just looking/curious"; 14 percent of men but only 4 percent of women were interested in casual rela-tionships. Site users were concentrated in the 26–35 age range. Fifty-seven percent were single, 24 percent divorced, and 4 percent separated. Fifty-four percent had college degrees or higher qualifications. Ninety-three percent identified themselves as heterosexual. Respondents in this sample preferred a partner with a similar level of education; men had a strong distaste for a woman better educated than they were, while women wished to avoid less-educated men. Across the board there was a preference for a partner of the same ethnicity, but this preference was stronger among women. Looks, in-cluding height and weight, were of great importance: "Among women . . . the average stated weight is less than the average weight in the U.S. population. The discrepancy is about 6 lbs." These findings indicate that many respon-dents understated their weight in order to enhance their appeal. Those who posted a photo received more responses. Height mattered greatly in the con-ventional way: men wanted shorter women, women preferred tall men. The study reporting these findings noted, "Our estimates imply that compared to a man who is five inches taller than a woman and earns $50,000 per year, a man who is five inches shorter than a woman would need to earn slightly more than half a million dollars per year to make up for his shortcoming."

Income (reported by 64 percent of men and 51 percent of women) was another important variable strongly affecting the success of male seekers (measured by the number of emails they received). Women "place almost twice as much weight on income as men" while "the online success of women is at most marginally related to their income." Similar double standards ap-plied to educational qualifications: "higher levels of education increase the online success of men but not of women. . . . The outcomes of women do not improve with their educational attainment." On the contrary, women with greater educational credentials "incur a slight outcome penalty." Women had a strong preference for men with equivalent education, but "men with college or graduate degrees do not seem to base their choices on a women's education." Likewise, women's occupation had little influence on their suc-cess in these Internet transactions.

A notable difference was found in the stated preference for ethnicity: 38 percent of all women but only 18 percent of men preferred to meet someone of the same ethnic background. Forty-eight percent of white women and 22 percent of white men preferred whites, but only 25 percent of black women and 8 percent of black men expressed a corresponding preference for black mates—a finding that might be interpreted as a reflection of the legacy of racism and the implied higher value placed on being white, even among blacks. Overall, women discriminated more readily against members of other ethnic groups than men. For example, "African-American and Hispanic men receive only about half as many first contact emails from white women as white men." Other, conventional gender-related preferences included men who wished to avoid older women and women just as eager to avoid men younger than themselves.

In summing up, the authors observed, "Many readers will find some of our results sobering."[17] Studies cited earlier confirm these findings of stereotypical differences between the preferences of men and women, such as the male preoccupation with the physical attractiveness of women and the far greater interest of females in the male's occupation and financial assets and prospects.

These studies strongly suggest that the conventional gender determination of many attitudes and preferences persists, stubbornly resisting the goals and values of contemporary feminism.

## Regional Samples: Massachusetts

To learn more about the preferences and personal attributes of online daters, I examined samples of individuals in four different states—Massachusetts, Nebraska, Alabama, and California—representing four distinct regions of the country—New England, the Midwest, the South, and the West. I chose the match.com dating site, said to be the largest of these services with fifteen million subscribers.[18] It is of some interest that match.com recruited Helen Fisher, the anthropologist and a strong believer in the biological bases of romantic attachments, as "chief scientific adviser" for its spinoff website, chemistry.com.[19]

Match.com membership is largely middle class: "82% attended college and 21% have advanced degrees; 52% are employed in managerial/professional fields; 52% earn more than $40,000 per year . . . 79% have no children; 58% are single and have never married; 30% are divorced."[20]

I chose Massachusetts users to represent New England, Nebraska the Midwest, Alabama the South, and California the West. These choices were made on the assumption that each of these states and their surrounding regions reflect distinct cultural values which are likely to find expression not only in the religious and political attitudes of their residents but also in their nonpolitical preferences and expectations for personal relationships.[21] Needless to add, these samples are not representative of all women and men of the same age groups in these states, and not even of all those looking for partners online since match.com is not the only such service.

Given the problems involved in tabulating and analyzing the enormous quantity of data available on match.com, I decided to sample these communications by selecting smaller subsets, defined by gender, age, and location (state). I chose two age groups, 20–39 and 40–60. The samples also provide information about education, religious beliefs (or their absence), and political attitudes, but I made no systematic attempt to try to explain the preferences by these three variables. (See appendix 1.)

The data not only reveals attitudes about the personal qualities that Americans value and associate with successful relationships, it also provides insights into larger cultural currents and characteristics of American society.

Match.com considers certain questions useful for identifying the key characteristics of individuals in order to establish compatibility. These questions allow the browser to conduct a "custom search," that is, to specify traits he or she offers and seeks in others.

The questionnaire begins with two open-ended sections of special interest for our purposes. One is called "In My Own Words" and is divided into overlapping questions such as "For Fun," "Favorite Hot Spots," "Favorite Things," and sometimes "My Ethnicity" and "My Education" as well.[22] The second open-ended section is called "About My Life and What I Am Looking For." This question allowed us to learn about the human qualities and traits most highly valued and sought in a potential partner. In order to tabulate the answers to these open-ended questions, their numbers had to be reduced, that is, grouped according to their shared properties and designated by certain headings. The choices were reduced to fourteen, and the responses were tabulated according to the categories they fell into. (See appendix 2.)

While the information sought in the questionnaire is quite substantial and provides a basis for the attempted assessment of compatibility, numerous elusive attributes relevant to establishing and maintaining a romantic relationship are not probed. For example, there are no questions about the respondents' familial upbringing. Did they grow up in an intact or a one-parent family? If the parents divorced, how old were the children at the time? Was there ample contact with the noncustodial parent? Admittedly, such questions could make many people uncomfortable and reluctant to respond. Another related matter of obvious interest is the (perceived) *quality* of the respondent's relationship with his or her parents, of which we learn nothing. It would also be useful to seek information about the parents' occupation and education, assuming that socioeconomic background influences personality and compatibility.

Other information that would have been useful but difficult to elicit: Have the respondents any experience of psychotherapy, and if so for how long and for what reasons? Do they have, or think they have, *close* friends? Many references are made to friends in the responses, but it is difficult to know how people define friendship, or close friendship, given the disposition of Americans to use the concept rather broadly and generously. A question probing the capacity to compromise would also have been informative and highly relevant.

Finally, it would have been of great interest to learn something about what the respondents consider to be the weaknesses of their own character or personality in addition to the ample inventory of their strengths or attractions. The numerous options listed under *appearance* and placed ahead of other indicators of compatibility such as *background/values* suggest that physical appearance is considered a very important aspect of attraction.

The areas left untouched by the questionnaire illustrate the limitations of learning about potential partners without face-to-face contact and communication.

## Younger Women, Massachusetts

The first of our samples from match.com consisted of five hundred women ages 20–39 who provided photos of themselves and lived in Massachusetts. (I used responses only by people who provided photos.) This information was accessed in March 2009. Following are the tabulated responses of this group:

*Education*
> high school, 2.6 percent
> college, 47 percent
> graduate school (anything above a BA), 51 percent

*Religion*
> Christian, 50 percent
> spiritual, 31 percent
> agnostic/atheist, 12 percent
> Jewish, 8 percent

*Political attitudes*
> liberal, 89 percent
> conservative, 11 percent

*Want children*, 84 percent

*Prior marital relationship*, 9 percent

This is an atypical group in the general population of American women of the same age, and probably is also atypical of women of the same age in Massachusetts who don't use the Internet for dating. These women are better educated, more liberal, and probably also less religious (depending in part on the interpretation of "spiritual") than women of the same age in the same state and in the country as a whole.

Some of these atypical characteristics are likely to be a reflection of living in Massachusetts, a politically liberal state with a better-educated population, almost half of it in the greater Boston area. It is also likely (and other samples support this point) that the cost of using match.com ($30–$50 per month) leads to the underrepresentation of those with lower incomes and lower education, two attributes closely related. Those with lower incomes are far less likely to own or have access to a computer or to be computer literate.

Almost everyone in this group is white and has never been married. While the occupations were not tabulated (and not everyone responded to this question), three occupations are most frequently mentioned: schoolteaching, social work, and nursing. There are also graduate students, people in sales and marketing and other administrative positions, a handful of physicians (or students in medical school), and a few lawyers.

If the photos enclosed are realistic and up to date, these are, for the most part, attractive young women. They also seem lively, active, cheerful, open-minded, and good-natured. Many of them express idealistic or mildly countercultural impulses. They have a wide range of interests and entertainments, including many outdoor activities, travel, and a fondness for socializing (the expression "hanging out" with friends recurs). Enjoying good conversation is among the sources of pleasure along with frequenting bars, coffee bars, and pubs, and eating out in restaurants of various kinds. Many respondents dwell on the different kinds of food they like. Virtually all profess interest in some sports and report well-established exercise habits. The range of recreational and cultural interests is wide, often combining high and popular culture, occasionally reminiscent of the claims of the "Renaissance women" appearing in the personals of the *New York Review of Books*.

Breadth and versatility is a major theme in many of these self-presentations, but they are never as implausible or pretentious as those found in the *New York Review of Books* and the alumni magazines. Thus many in this group claim that they love both going out to eat and cooking something simple and interesting at home; more generally, they "love" both going out "on the town" or "curling up with a book" or watching a DVD at home. "I am just as excited going to a bar as I am spending a quiet night at home," one of them writes. Another claims to be "open to just about anything." A patent attorney writes that she is "laid back but can get hyped up about things I am passionate about. Active and love to try new things, but I'm also super happy sleeping in on the weekends."

Breadth of character or personality is often emphasized. A "therapist/ teacher" thinks of herself as "grounded yet idealistic; romantic yet wry," and is favorably impressed by people capable of balancing "irreverence" and "sensitivity." A twenty-eight-year-old "Construction Project Manager of PUMA" writes, "I am the type of girl who in the same day can watch a football game in a t-shirt and jeans . . . then the same night get all dressed up for a night on the town." (As it turns out, most women in all regional samples claim to have this capability.) Another dimension is conveyed by a thirty-one-year-old teacher of young children: "I can be serious and funny, thoughtful and goofy. Sarcastic and tender . . . have strong opinions but also very open-minded. . . . I like to have fun but I also respect when it is time to take life seriously."

The tabulation of highly valued traits in potential partners is based on a random sample of 80 drawn from the total of five hundred. These traits are derived from the coding of the open-ended self-presentations and similarly coded open-ended descriptions of personality traits these writers are looking for. (Words in parentheses refer to the cluster of interchangeable traits that were subsumed under one designation. For example, "fun-loving" included several other traits used by the respondents and listed below.)

*Highly valued traits*
    fun-loving (good cheer, sense of humor, valuing laughter, makes me
        laugh, cheerfulness, positive thinking), 88 percent
    open to new experience (willing to try new things, try anything
        once, many interests, adventurous), 68 percent
    intelligent, 65 percent
    long-term relationship (interested in), 51 percent
    short-term relationship, 49 percent
    honest (sincere, trustworthy, no games), 42 percent
    ambitious (purposeful, achievement oriented), 40 percent
    kind (warm, good-natured, sensitive), 37 percent
    easygoing (laid back, down to earth), 35 percent
    romantic (passionate, in touch with feelings, seeks soul mate), 32
        percent
    independent, 22 percent
    idealistic (civic-minded, compassionate, environmentally con-
        scious), 20 percent
    no identity problems (knows who he is, comfortable in skin, etc.),
        12 percent
    religious, 1 percent

The most striking feature of these communications is that the desirable partners are entirely defined by their personality traits, not their occupation, education, income, social position, ethnicity, or political or religious values. Preference for complementary traits is occasionally expressed, such as the same ethnicity (white), the same political disposition (liberal), and similar age (or somewhat older). There is an apparent tolerance for different religious beliefs and affiliations as most of the writers find acceptable both believers and nonbelievers, and people of different religious faiths. Apparently religious affiliation (or its absence) is not seen these days as a salient matter—neither a source of conflict nor compatibility—by this group of young American women.

These self-presentations are generally upbeat. The women describe themselves for the most part as lively, cheerful, fun-loving, sociable, open-minded, flexible, adaptable, and interested in new experiences ("always looking for exciting new things to try," as one puts it). Many express a strong interest in and dedication to their work, especially the teachers and social workers.

The respondents are almost evenly divided in their preference for long- versus short-term relationships, but often their intentions are ambiguous when interest in a short-term relationship is qualified by comments such as "let's meet and see how things might develop." Thus even those who express interest in less involving, short-term relationships leave the door open for the development of a more serious and enduring relationship. Probably many of these young women are cautious and do not wish to scare away potential long-term partners with a premature emphasis on commitment.

Many qualities of the desirable partner are predictable: honesty, sincerity, sense of humor, caring, sensitivity, being down to earth, ability to share, self-awareness, sometimes adventurous, "laid-back" or easygoing nature, open-mindedness, being a good listener. Some expect the eligible man to be "passionate about what he is doing," without expressing preference for his line of work. Desirable men are to be free of identity problems (not that this expression is used)—they will "know who they are," be "comfortable in their skin" or "comfortable with himself," "confident but not cocky," or "centered and mindful." "Looking for a down-to-earth guy who has his life in order," a therapist from Massachusetts writes. A teacher of writing "at a local college" is looking for someone "who is not afraid to put himself out there, as he truly is, someone who has a passion for being . . . who knows who he is" and also "likes to laugh." A student of social work wants "a relationship that is both challenging and supportive with someone who likes to work hard and play hard."

The preferred personality traits in the potential partner are quite similar to those the young women claim to possess or aspire to. Expectations of potential partners range from "soul mate" to "someone to have fun with" or "just find someone good to hang out with," but often the nature of the relationship is left cautiously unspecified.

Somewhat unexpectedly, "laugh," "laughter," "sense of humor," and "fun-loving" are at the top of the desirable qualities both in self-description and among the valued traits of a date or partner—listed by 88 percent in the sample. A twenty-nine-year-old lab worker is "looking for someone who sees the funny side anywhere and everywhere." A woman with a master's degree and a "fulfilling career in the medical field" writes that "the best feeling in the world is to make another person smile." Some of the women express interest in men who "don't take themselves seriously," that is, someone easygoing with a sense of humor, who is likely to be more flexible, adaptable, and easier to get along with.

Such preferences are not limited to those match.com users sampled here. A society woman whose marriage was given extended coverage in the *New York Times* told the reporter that she "thought from the beginning that Ben [her husband to be] was a very handsome man and later on I realized that there was nothing sexier than a person who makes me laugh."[23]

Sense of humor or the capacity for laughter is more a pragmatic than a romantic trait. Old-style romantic heroes and heroines were often inclined to gloom and a tragic view of the world rather than to laughter, smiles, and jokes. A graduate student in rehabilitation counseling writes: "I love to try new things . . . and like to go through life laughing and smiling." Her ideal partner "would be able to make me laugh every day."

"Openness to new experience," the second most highly valued quality in this group (68 percent), captures a stereotypical and widely observed trait of Americans that is also a characterological precondition of modernity. This openness amounts to a readiness to reinvent and transform oneself, and a belief in the endless choices and opportunities life offers. This attitude is probably also linked to what David Riesman decades ago labeled "other-directedness"—seeing oneself as lacking in a solid core of traits and interests, which may hinder the capacity to relate to others. Other-directedness has an approval-seeking aspect, the wish to be popular and well liked. It is easier to make friends and have an active social life if one is nonjudgmental and open to new experiences. A degree of moral and cultural relativism is a prerequisite of being other-directed, nonjudgmental, and open to new experience.

This attitude toward new experience is also associated with open-mindedness, with a favorable disposition to social, cultural, or political change, and with little concern as to the kind of change or the kind of new experience that is being sought. The strong preference for this trait among these young and well-educated women reflects major cultural trends in contemporary American society.

"Intelligence" is the third-most-preferred (65 percent) attribute. It expresses the desire to find someone educated, competent, and of comparable social status, especially since most of these women are college educated.

The demand for honesty and sincerity (42 percent) is among the most self-evidently desirable yet less highly rated than other traits preceding it. It is reasonable to be apprehensive about being cheated or deceived in a highly competitive, commercial society such as ours. In an individualistic society, such concerns are bound to be more widespread than in more stable, more collectivist, less competitive, and less success-oriented ones. Such fears need not be limited to business transactions; we can also be tricked or manipulated in personal relationships, hence the frequent warning "No head games" in these communications.

While hardly anyone uses the word "authenticity," many respondents probably have that quality in mind when referring to honesty and sincerity. The same applies to expressing a desire for meeting someone "who knows who he is" or who accepts the person he is. The requirement of sincerity stems from somewhat different sources: from the desire to know well the person one wishes to have a close relationship with, and from a belief in the importance of learning as much as one can both about oneself and one's partner.

"Easygoing, etc." is a quality chosen by 35 percent. It includes being calm, confident, unflappable, stable, solid, dependable, and sometimes also in control of resources of some kind—a preeminently positive male stereotype. The attribute also conjures up film and television stars whose images change little over time, from Humphrey Bogart to Clint Eastwood. These are tight-lipped males, strong, inscrutable, goal-oriented, and unshakably calm but capable of sudden outbursts of highly focused violence. A laid-back person is someone you can rely on, the target of conventional female interests.

I expected to encounter a larger volume of romantic attitudes and expectations in these communications; instead I found a typically American blend of romanticism and practicality. There is little doubt about the romantic disposition when self-presentations include attributes such as "passionate," or when "soul mate" is used to indicate interest in an all-encompassing, long-term relationship. More indirectly, a romantic disposition may also be discerned in extended musings in different sections of the questionnaire such as "About Me," "Favorite Things," "Favorite Hotspots," and even "My Job."

A thirty-two-year-old teacher's self-presentation belongs to this category:

> I make a point not to forget all the joys of a single day. . . . I am still learning and becoming more of who I am each day. . . . I love creating space and community. . . . I am compassionate, caring and thoughtful, sensitive and sincere. . . . I love all things beautiful . . . snowflakes, myth, forgotten treasures, laughter, stories, surprises, water . . . [She is looking for somebody] comfortable in his own skin . . . able to laugh at himself . . . not afraid of commitment or spontaneity. . . . Someone to explore all this beauty with.

The romantic outlook is also captured in the specifications of a thirty-four-year-old art history major who is "looking for a partner to share life with. . . . I think people should have some sort of bond of attraction from the first time they meet."

Another romantic self-depiction comes from a twenty-eight-year-old woman in Boston with a graduate degree who is "working on rekindling the kid in me" and seems to assume that this will be helpful in establishing a good adult relationship. Children have been romanticized at least since the early nineteenth century as uncorrupted embodiments of purity, innocence, and authenticity, as in *Werther* discussed earlier.

In the final analysis, the pragmatic and romantic elements are intertwined in these communications, as exemplified in the specifications of a twenty-five-year-old social studies teacher in a suburb of Boston:

> I am looking for someone I can learn from and . . . do things with—a running partner, fellow chef, and adventurer . . . who can challenge me . . . who loves to laugh, who is laid back and warm . . . enjoys running in the rain but also enjoys curling up . . . with a hot chocolate and reading.

"Running in the rain" is the romantic dimension of this message—a highly spontaneous act that sober and rational people don't ordinarily do. Advertisements often feature young lovers laughing or hugging in the rain; their intense emotional involvement and enjoyment of each other's company enables them to ignore getting wet.

The holder of an MA in an undisclosed field speaks for many of those with high expectations in describing her ideal partner:

> You are open to a long-term, stable, and emotionally healthy relationship. You have your own place. You are legally single and not going through a break-up. . . . You live life in balance and strive for physical, emotional, and spiritual harmony. You are affectionate, charming, chivalrous, and have a wonderful sense of humor.

You are reliable, gainfully employed, financially stable, intelligent, passionate about your career, but you know how to let loose and have fun. You care about your home environment and physical appearance. You feel at ease speaking to strangers and can command the attention of the room.

This same person also reveals a more unusual manifestation of the romantic disposition, listing among her favorite things "receiving massages by candlelight."

Unlike the older, stereotypical possessors of romantic beliefs, few present-day Americans believe they are predestined to meet someone who is uniquely compatible and suited to satisfy all their emotional needs. They correctly assume that there are many possible candidates for such relationships and that suitable mates are, within certain limits, interchangeable. This is not to say that pragmatic considerations overwhelm all the others. Thus, while match. com's structured questions include income, people rarely respond to this question or make any reference to the desirable income of a future partner. This suggests that people in search of compatibility—whether in print or online— give little weight to material considerations such as income and occupation.

Finally, it should be pointed out that it is not easy to display convincingly a romantic disposition in highly structured electronic communications, given the inherent practicality of the method. A passionate nature, which is an intrinsic part of the romantic mind-set, is difficult to convey in communications that seek to summarize desirable traits. The format of these communications predisposes one to convey the impression that he or she is compatible with a wide variety of personality types, flexible and open to a wide range of new experiences, with broad tastes and interests.

A similar observation was made by Monica Whitty about the central theme of self-help or "relationship books" discussed earlier: "The authors [of these books] make use of the romantic script of fulfillment, spontaneity, and passion whereas the process of acquiring a partner is depicted as a rational, calculated, and rehearsed series of acts in which spontaneity risks making oneself vulnerable to harm."[24]

Professions of spirituality, as distinct from conventional religious beliefs, have an affinity with the romantic mind-set. The designers of the match. com questionnaire include "spiritual but not religious" among the structured responses to religious preferences, and it is chosen by 31 percent of this group (and more often in other groups). Being spiritual means different things to different people, but there are commonalities rooted in the ethos of the 1960s. Such self-identification signals that you are neither a crass materialist nor beholden to old, stultifying religious strictures which may inhibit the drive for "self realization."[25]

Those who were imbued with the spirit of the 1960s were not religious in the conventional sense but nonetheless embarked on a quest for higher (spiritual?) values. They sought alternatives to the prevailing sociocultural norms and values, which they passionately rejected. They craved authenticity, deplored materialism and status seeking, worshiped nature and everything deemed "natural." This new, countercultural spirituality also rejected selfishness, competitiveness, violence, and notions of success associated with public recognition and high levels of consumption. For 1960s people, their descendants, and kindred spirits, "spiritual" came to refer to a diffuse idealism and social consciousness, to being religious in a new way, abandoning the old institutional structures and demands of organized religion and their core beliefs.

A graduate student at the University of Connecticut School of Social Work, who declares herself "spiritual but not religious," writes, "I like going to church occasionally and experiencing spirituality in community, especially when there is singing and dancing involved!" A "case manager for a drug diversion program" notes under "My Religion," "I believe in living an honest life and doing what's right . . . as opposed to doing what's easy! A quiet dock at a nice lake on a gorgeous day is my church!"—an example of what she would doubtless regard as a form of spirituality. Another "spiritual but not religious" teacher of language (not specified which) writes, "I believe in the joy of living, honoring many religious philosophies and at the end of the day taking time to say thanks. For me faith is not only something to reside in, but something to come into, out of, and back around through. Dizzy yet balanced." She exemplifies the confused yearnings that "spiritual but not religious" may encompass.

## Older Women, Massachusetts

Age is a major determinant of human attitudes and behavior, including those examined here. It is hardly surprising that only 14 percent of the older women sampled from match.com are interested in having children, given their age (40–60) and the fact that 80 percent of them have been previously married, and many have already had children. Eighty-four percent of the younger women wanted to have children.

On the other hand, age did not determine the educational levels of these two groups as the great majority of the older women are also college educated.

*Education*
     high school, 9 percent
     college, 41 percent
     graduate school, 50 percent

*Political attitudes*
 liberal, 85 percent
 conservative, 15 percent
*Religion*
 Christian, 33 percent (vs. 49 percent among younger women)
 Jewish, 12 percent (vs. 7.6 percent)
 spiritual, 40 percent (vs. 12 percent)
 agnostic/atheist, 4 percent (vs. 12 percent)
*Want children*, 14 percent
*Prior marital relationship*, 80 percent

*Highly valued traits*
 fun-loving, 91 percent
 open to new experience, 71 percent
 easygoing, 70 percent
 long-term relationship, 66 percent
 kind, 65 percent
 honest, 64 percent
 romantic disposition, 57 percent
 intelligent, 49 percent
 ambitious, 42 percent
 idealistic, 41 percent
 no identity problems, 35 percent
 short-term relationship, 34 percent
 independent, 25 percent
 religious, 3 percent

A few excerpts will illustrate the aspirations and expectations of this age group. A fifty-three-year-old part-time administrator from Plymouth writes, "My match would have a good sense of humor, love to laugh, be flexible, enjoy some travel and be a romantic type . . . even-tempered but passionate." To what extent the passionate and even-tempered dispositions can be reconciled is of course debatable. A fifty-year-old woman from a small town in eastern Massachusetts is "not into games" and is looking for someone with "a sense of humor" who is also "easygoing, romantic, and passionate about life and love." As is often the case, she too overlooks the latent conflict between "easygoing" and "passionate." The authentic romantic impulse is nicely summed up by a fifty-one-year-old woman from Cape Cod who is "looking for that one and only one that will take my breath away." She, along with virtually every other woman in this group, also values humor and laughter highly, as does another fifty-one-year-old from a small town in western Massachusetts who requires her match to have "an infectious smile and laughter" and the capacity "to question the world around you." Another fifty-one-year-old woman from a small central Massachusetts town describes herself as "down to earth" who wishes "to put a little excitement" in her life and is interested in a "playful man with a sense of humor."

To meet "someone special" is a recurring desire and arguably a major present-day expression of the romantic disposition. The special person is presumably unique in some ways and uniquely attuned to the needs and expectations of the advertiser. A fifty-six-year-old woman with a graduate degree from a suburb of Boston wants this special person "to make me smile when I think about him." The romantic disposition is also revealed in the desire of a sixty-year-old woman on Cape Cod who wants to find "someone to really know me"—a wish that implies the complexity of the task and of the personality to be understood. A forty-two-year-old social worker from a Boston suburb offers "incredible warmth, kindness, gourmet cooking skills, and an affectionate nature." In turn she expects "honesty, kindness, reliability [and] intelligence . . . through good times and bad and someone to go to Costco with." A forty-nine-year-old owner of a small company describes herself as "funny, gregarious. Fun-loving, sensitive, and giving person" looking for "someone who enjoys socializing, loves animals . . . and wants to enjoy life. Laugh with me!!" she urges. A fifty-two-year-old woman from West Springfield "loves to laugh and have fun." Described by her friends as "very compassionate and lovable . . . spontaneous and willing to try new adventures." She is looking for someone "energetic and has a great sense of humor . . . and who likes romance."

Table 6.1 compares the preferences of Massachusetts women, by age, as to traits they are seeking. These figures suggest that older women seek more stable, long-term, risk- and trouble-free relationships by expressing stronger preferences for an easygoing personality, honesty, warmth, lack of identity problems, romantic disposition, and long-term orientation. Older women also appear more idealistic, compassionate, and civic-minded, more interested in volunteering and getting involved in public affairs.

Harder to explain is the higher value placed on a romantic disposition and relationship by the older age group (57 percent versus 32 percent). It may be that younger women find a less committed, shorter, less emotionally demanding (hence less romantic) relationship more appealing precisely because they are younger and have less need for a long-term, committed relationship that is often romantic (though a durable relationship may also rest on pragmatic foundations). Younger women are also likely to be more experimentally oriented, more interested in "playing the field." On the other hand, it may be argued

Table 6.1. Comparison of Massachusetts Women

| Traits | Females (20–39) | Females (40–60) |
|---|---|---|
| Fun-loving | 88 | 91 |
| Open to new experience | 68 | 71 |
| Easygoing | 35 | 70 |
| Long-term | 51 | 66 |
| Intelligent | 65 | 49 |
| Honest | 42 | 64 |
| Kind | 37 | 65 |
| Romantic disposition | 32 | 57 |
| Ambitious | 40 | 42 |
| Short-term | 49 | 34 |
| Idealistic, civic-minded | 20 | 41 |
| Independent | 22 | 25 |
| No identity problems | 12 | 35 |
| Religious | 1 | 3 |

that being young and less experienced disposes people to greater naiveté, to higher and more unrealistic expectations. If so they would be likely to display stronger romantic inclinations—not the case with this group.

It would be more plausible for the older (as well as the divorced or separated) women to be more wary of a romantic involvement, having been disappointed in a failed marriage, but evidently this is not the case. Probably their interpretation of "romantic" does not conflict with what they consider stable and durable, and is associated with warmth and strong feelings, hence their greater affinity for a romantic disposition.

Another interesting difference is the far greater preference on the part of older women for the "laid-back" or "easygoing" attitude (70 percent versus 35 percent), which is more difficult to reconcile with a romantic disposition that values intensity and passion. But it is obviously easier to get along with a laid-back or easygoing person, as these attributes help avoid the difficulties and disappointments experienced in failed past relationships.

Finally, there is a notable difference between the ratings of "idealism"— twice as high among older women. This too is a somewhat counterintuitive finding insofar as we tend to associate idealism with youth and youthfulness. A possible interpretation may be that the coding captured forms of idealism, such as concern for the environment, volunteering, and civic-mindedness, that are linked to a deeper and broader sense of responsibility and to being less self-centered—attitudes more likely to be found among the middle aged or older than among the young. Perhaps older women are also motivated to participate in such activities for social reasons, because they present opportunities to meet like-minded men.

For both age groups the two most highly valued traits (a fun-loving attitude and openness to new experience) are almost identically rated.

## Younger Men, Massachusetts

*Education*
    high school, 3 percent
    college, 62 percent
    graduate school, 35 percent
*Religion*
    Christian, 51 percent
    spiritual, 25 percent
    agnostic/atheist, 20 percent
    Jewish, 3 percent
*Political attitudes*
    liberal, 75 percent
    conservative, 25 percent
*Want children*, 85 percent
*Prior relationship*, 8 percent

*Highly valued traits*
    fun-loving, 89 percent
    easygoing, 74 percent
    open to new experience, 64 percent
    long-term relationship, 61 percent
    ambitious, 48 percent
    intelligent, 43 percent
    romantic disposition, 46 percent
    short-term relationship, 39 percent
    honesty, 39 percent
    kind, 30 percent
    independent, 28 percent
    idealistic, 22 percent
    no identity problems, 11 percent
    religious, 4 percent

Many of these men expressed concern about being taken in or misled by women—like the thirty-eight-year-old "hardworking gentleman" who is "looking for that special woman that is done with head games." A more complicated requirement is presented by a thirty-two-year-old electrician from Hingham who wants "to meet someone who I can be myself with," presumably meaning that the relationship will allow him to be his real self (whatever that is), so that he will not have to pretend, or strain, to be something he is not—a familiar theme expressed in various ways by many users of match.com. A thirty-six-year-man from Brighton designates his "perfect match" as someone "who enjoys dinner and a movie as much as a basketball or football game . . . looking for someone who can be themselves behind both closed and open doors."

"A fun-loving guy" from Holyoke, working at the help desk of an information technology business, "just likes to hang out and have a good time." He "always enjoys a good laugh and making other people laugh." He would like his match to be "the same easygoing, funny, caring, and sweet." A "union electrician" thinks of himself as "a nice guy" who wants to settle down with someone whom he "could relate to." He described himself as "a huge Boston sports fan . . . anything regarding the Patriots, Red Sox, or Celtics is of interest to me." He also likes golf and working out and "cuddling on a couch, relaxing in front of a nice movie." He is looking for someone with "a sense of humor" and "good personality." A young worker in the "building trades" writes that according to his friends he is "honest, funny, stable, and responsible" as well as "a positive thinker" who likes "to explore new ideas . . . interested in new things [and] open to just about everything." A construction worker from New Bedford thinks of himself as "outgoing and hardworking" and "fun to be with." His favorite fun activities include roller-blading and "going to the outlets for shopping." A young man in landscape construction makes three references to his fondness for cuddling (preferably before a fire and watching a movie); roller-blading and hockey are other favored pastimes. He describes himself as "a romantic cuddly kinda guy . . . a little rough around the edges."

The owner of an electronics store likes "most outdoor sports and gets along with anybody except fake people." He describes himself as "honest, intelligent, strong, confident, caring, loyal, funny, and fun to be with." He owns a "fast boat, rides and races motorcycles [and] scuba dives with sharks." A romantically inclined "single dad" in Fitchburg is "looking for a woman of my dreams, the one 'true love' that most men dream of." He would like to meet "someone I can trust and give my whole heart to without worrying about it breaking." He wants "that love to be able to last a lifetime." By contrast, a young man from Fall River lets on only that he is "very easygoing to a point" and expects the same from his match. For fun he relies on mountain biking, jet skiing, and snowboarding.

An organic farmer from Shrewsbury ranks "intelligence, passion, and self-awareness" higher than "physical beauty" and especially values "a long engaging conversation with a sharp girl who knows who she is." He too is concerned about identity problems that may interfere with a stable, long-term relationship. He believes that "our main goal on this earth . . . is to develop as many deep relationships as we can." A thirty-seven-year-old carpenter from Medford "love[s] to laugh and . . . can mix well with just about anyone." He appreciates in women "a sense of humor, respect for man . . . and [being] in touch with their sensitive side and not afraid to show it."

One of the rare black respondents in these samples describes himself as "a laid-back guy, with a good job, honest, loyal, sense of humor. I like to have fun . . . looking for a nice female who knows what she wants out of life." His favorite things include basketball, sports in general, movies, music, playing pool, and bowling. A Hispanic correspondent characterizes himself as "outgoing, kind, romantic, lovable, and sincere who is looking for true love." Under "For Fun" he lists "movies, camping, bike riding, beach . . . stay at home and watch a movie, cuddle, relax and enjoy a romantic night with that special someone." Under "Favorite Things" he mentions "shopping at the mall," "listening to soft rock," and, again, cuddling.

A young man working in a house-painting business writes, "First off, I love to have fun." Skiing is in the forefront of his interests, but he also "loves watching movies, going out to eat." He sees himself as "extremely laid back and hardly serious," suggesting a less common conception of "laid back" and associating it with fun rather than a sense of security and stability. His only requirement is "a good personality and like having fun."

It is noteworthy that under "For Fun" and "Favorite Things," many of these match seekers list shopping, or shopping at the mall. Doubtless these preferences reflect what may be called "recreational shopping"—that is, shopping without a predetermined need or a clear purpose. Recreational shopping may involve looking for some goods to be acquired, or merely walking around, looking at displays, and allowing them to stimulate some desire or need. This attitude is an obvious expression of "consumerism" nurtured by a discretionary income, and especially the growing reluctance (or inability) to differentiate between necessities and luxuries. Advertising does its best to obliterate this distinction. Shopping as entertainment or recreational activity is also an attempt to escape boredom resulting from limited cultural resources. Few well-educated people regard shopping as an appropriate recreational activity, or would admit to its recreational value.

## Older Men, Masschusetts

*Education*
    high school, 11 percent
    college, 40 percent
    graduate school, 49 percent
*Religion*
    Christian, 46 percent
    spiritual, 41 percent
    agnostic/atheist, 9 percent
    Jewish, 4 percent
*Political attitudes*
    liberal, 72 percent
    conservative, 28 percent
*Want children*, 16 percent
*Prior marital relationship*, 61 percent


*Highly valued traits*
    fun-loving, 85 percent
    long-term relationship, 60 percent
    easygoing, 58 percent
    open to new experience, 48 percent
    romantic disposition, 45 percent
    kind, 52 percent
    intelligent, 51 percent
    honest, 42 percent
    short-term relationship, 40 percent
    ambitious, 35 percent
    idealistic, 24 percent
    no identity problems, 10 percent
    religious, 3 percent

Three notable differences emerge. Younger men have a more positive attitude toward a partner, are more open to new experiences, and are more easygoing. Warmth is more important for older men. Other differences are minor.

Table 6.2 highlights age-related differences among both women and men, in percentages seeking particular traits. On the whole, the differences between men and women of the older age group are modest, except for a

**Table 6.2. Comparison of Massachusetts Men and Women**

| Traits | Female (20–39) | Female (40–60) | Male (20–39) | Male (40–60) |
|---|---|---|---|---|
| Fun-loving | 88 | 91 | 89 | 85 |
| Open | 68 | 71 | 64 | 48 |
| Easygoing | 35 | 70 | 74 | 58 |
| Long-term | 51 | 66 | 61 | 60 |
| Intelligent | 65 | 49 | 43 | 51 |
| Honest | 42 | 64 | 39 | 41 |
| Kind | 37 | 65 | 30 | 52 |
| Romantic disposition | 32 | 57 | 46 | 45 |
| Ambitious | 40 | 42 | 49 | 35 |
| Short-term | 49 | 34 | 39 | 40 |
| Civic-minded | 20 | 41 | 22 | 24 |
| Independent | 22 | 25 | 28 | 32 |
| No identity problems | 12 | 35 | 11 | 10 |
| Religious | 1 | 3 | 4 | 3 |

handful of preferences. Thus women are considerably more public-spirited or civic-minded and value more highly a romantic disposition, honesty, an easygoing attitude, and openness to new experience. These differences suggest that older women are more invested in finding a compatible partner for a long-term relationship with the kinds of attributes and attitudes that are more likely to support such relationships.

The word "stable" is rarely used among the desirable traits, though "laid back" and "down to earth" may carry such connotations. The avoidance of "stable" may suggest its possible association with "boring" or "routinized."

An overall impression created by these profiles is that this is a fairly pragmatic group. If they harbor "extravagant expectations," their expression is muted. Probably the very choice of the Internet in pursuit of a partner suggests a disposition that strives to balance romantic and pragmatic considerations.

# CHAPTER SEVEN

# Looking for Love on the Internet: Nebraska and Alabama

I am clean cut, easy-going, humorous, intellectual, low maintenance, practical, quiet, romantic, serious, sophisticated, caring, honest. . . . I like positive happy people.

Male "technical manager," Nebraska

I love hanging out with my friends and laughing over margaritas or a bottle of wine. . . . I am typically up for whatever and have fun in most any situation.

Female teacher, Alabama

While it was not the aim of this study to prove that highly patterned differences may be found in the political, religious, and cultural dispositions of Americans in different regions of the country, the data confirms this, even among subscribers to match.com. For instance, while in Massachusetts most of those sampled identify themselves as liberal and a minority as conservative, in Nebraska it is almost exactly the opposite for men (women are evenly split in these attitudes). In Alabama the same political attitudes are reversed for both men and women.

Of course we know that these regions are politically and culturally different. The interesting question is how these differences manifest themselves in desirable personal relationships and the qualities desired in a mate. Given the broader regional differences, it is noteworthy that the attitudes toward dating or mate selection do not appear to be radically different among the four regions.

To begin with, in Nebraska and Alabama—as in Massachusetts—respondents define themselves largely by their personal traits, recreational interests, and activities and display a pronounced leisure-entertainment orientation. The emphasis is on "what I do" rather than on "who I am," though of course the two overlap.

## Younger Women, Nebraska

*Education*
>high school, 2 percent
>college, 86 percent
>graduate school, 12 percent

*Religion*
>Christian, 70 percent
>spiritual, 20 percent
>agnostic/atheist, 10 percent
>Jewish, 0 percent

*Political attitudes*
>liberal, 50 percent
>conservative, 50 percent

*Want children*, 74 percent

*Previous marital relationship*, 14 percent

*Highly valued traits*
>fun-loving, 96 percent
>long-term relationship, 65 percent
>honest, 65 percent
>open to new experience, 56 percent
>ambitious, 50 percent
>romantic disposition, 49 percent
>intelligent, 37 percent
>short-term relationship, 35 percent
>independent, 28 percent
>easygoing, 25 percent
>kind, 20 percent
>idealistic, 19 percent
>religious, 10 percent
>no identity problems, 9 percent

As before, a sampling of the open-ended individual messages provides qualitative information about the wishes and attitudes we seek to capture in their coded summary. Almost every individual wish list and self-presentation illuminates a larger cultural theme or preoccupation. Several of them illustrate a somewhat problematic confluence of traditional and modern attitudes.

A twenty-seven-year-old case manager for a nonprofit organization writes, "I am passionate about life and living every minute to the fullest. I enjoy trying new things." She is looking for someone who is "first and foremost genuine . . . and has a lot of [religious] faith." This writer, who repeatedly affirms her own strong religious disposition, is at the same time also a truly modern American who likes to try new things. The benefits of such an innovative lifestyle have for some time been taken for granted; few Americans ask why trying new things is self-evidently desirable. By contrast, a woman of twenty-eight in an undisclosed administrative position is "looking for someone who will complete me and make me a better person"—a truly romantic wish. But here's the catch: she also wants "someone who will accept me for who I am, and never judge, never force me to be someone I am not and never want me to change." Surely becoming "a better person" cannot occur without making some judgments about what needs improvement. It is a hallmark of modern American individualism that it recoils from being judgmental, a heritage of the relativistic-therapeutic beliefs of the 1960s.

A "very down-to-earth girl" (actually a thirty-six-year-old woman) is "looking for someone to go out and have fun with"—an uncomplicated desire. Her "ideal date" would include "flowers, dinner, and a carriage ride in the Old Market [of Omaha]." Her ideal man must also "enjoy being around family and have a strong love for kids, whether they are yours or someone else's." This woman has no children of her own.

A confident, energetic single mother, age twenty-five, who knows how to have a good time and has a passion for life, is looking for an "intelligent, responsible, and dependable man who is established and young at heart." "Established" presumably alludes to financially comfortable, but this must be balanced by being "young at heart"

An "assistant operations manager" at a construction company, aspiring to an MBA, describes herself as "extremely responsible and completely self-sufficient," a rare reference to being "responsible." A thirty-year-old pediatric nurse is "looking for a friend and possibly more." Her "absolute favorite thing is to laugh and make others laugh." A twenty-seven-year-old teacher "is very open-minded and willing to try anything"; thinks of herself as "smart, successful, clever, and independent." She is looking for a man "who is witty, motivated, and thoughtful." A twenty-six-year-old "competitive" woman in an administrative job, "almost always on the go," loves her work and wants "a man that makes me laugh and has ideas in his head." He "must also love dogs and like to be outdoors."

## Older Women, Nebraska

*Education*
> high school, 5 percent
> college, 68 percent
> graduate school, 27 percent

*Religion*
> Christian, 66 percent
> spiritual, 34 percent
> agnostic/atheist, 0 percent
> Jewish, 0 percent

*Political attitudes*
> liberal, 51 percent
> conservative, 49 percent

*Want children*, 7 percent

*Previous marital relationship*, 85 percent

*Highly valued traits*
> fun-loving, 100 percent
> romantic disposition, 87 percent
> long-term relationship, 77 percent
> open, 75 percent
> honest, 57 percent
> kind, 51 percent
> ambitious, 41 percent
> independent, 38 percent
> intelligent, 30 percent
> short-term relationship, 23 percent
> easygoing, 21 percent
> religious, 21 percent
> no identity problems, 12 percent
> idealistic, 0 percent

A forty-three-year-old woman who sees herself as "active, honest, and loyal," considers her "perfect match" a man who is "strong . . . family oriented, confident, easy to get along with." But for the time being she is not interested in love or marriage, only in "getting out and meeting new people." A woman of forty-five who teaches kindergarten in a Catholic school is "looking for a man who is giving . . . churchgoing and somewhat old-fashioned in terms of how he treats a lady." He should also have a sense of humor and must be Catholic. A forty-eight-year-old biologist (who has put her "life on hold" in order to raise her daughter) is "try[ing] to find humor in most things" and "enjoy[s] making people laugh." She "need[s] someone to share the rest of [her] life with."

For a forty-four-year-old woman working in "health promotion," "God and family are important"; she "needs a person who understands that my children come first." For a fifty-year-old in pharmaceutical sales, the perfect match happens "from the minute you lock eyes . . . everything else seems to fall into place" and "chemistry takes over." A real romantic, she is "always ready for something spontaneous!" and is looking for a man with "a great sense of humor." A forty-three-year-old "thrill seeker" with a lot of energy declares that "fun and laughter are mandatory . . . a sense of humor is a must." Otherwise she says little about the type of man she would like to meet but more about her own interests, which include "just hanging out," her iPod, art, history, movies, and good books.

A career and leadership coach, age fifty-seven, sees herself as "an aging optimist" who wants "to continue to learn, love and grow." She is once more "ready for a soul mate to share my deepest self with." She is a Christian, has a law degree, and would not "do well with someone who has no faith at all." A fifty-three-year-old registered nurse "love[s] horses and God" (in that order) and seeks a "loving man of Faith . . . a man who cares for others" and is also "financially secure and manages his money well"—and, of course, also has a sense of humor.

A fifty-year-old woman who works in a factory is "looking for someone who likes to do things on the spur of the moment" and "wants a serious relationship." Her favorite activities include mall shopping and watching a good movie while eating popcorn. A remarkable number of people include eating popcorn while watching a movie or television as a favored leisure-time activity.

The most striking attribute of this group is the strong preference for long-term relationships that have a romantic aspect or foundation.

## Younger Men, Nebraska

*Education*
    high school, 10 percent
    college, 77 percent
    graduate school, 13 percent

*Religion*
> Christian, 78 percent
> spiritual, 19 percent
> agnostic/atheist, 7 percent
> Jewish, 0 percent

*Political attitudes*
> conservative, 60 percent
> liberal, 40 percent

*Want children*, 83 percent

*Prior marital relationship*, 18 percent

*Highly valued traits*
> fun-loving, 83 percent
> long-term relationship, 50 percent
> short-term relationship, 50 percent
> easygoing, 48 percent
> honest, 43 percent
> romantic disposition, 40 percent
> open, 38 percent
> intelligent, 34 percent
> ambitious, 29 percent
> kind, 29 percent
> idealistic, 14 percent
> independent, 12 percent
> religious, 7 percent
> no identity problems, 7 percent

A thirty-four-year-old sales manager writes, "Most of all I enjoy being active: biking, golfing, snow skiing, hiking, camping, fishing, wakeboarding, or any other outdoor activity. . . . I love to go country dancing. I go to as many basketball games as I can." He says, "I believe in having fun no matter what." A twenty-seven-year-old graduate student in chemistry "enjoy[s] picnics and running through the sprinkler." His hobbies include "fishing, brewing beer, hunting, cooking, and reading." He's looking for someone who is "honest, faithful, responsible, mature, and fun . . . as open-minded as myself. Someone who has a great sense of humor and wouldn't mind kissing in the rain would be ideal." Nebraskans too invoke rain as part of romantic activities or situations.

A thirty-six-year-old poet and songwriter (owner of several roofing companies) describes himself as "a happy-go-lucky nice guy with a good sense of humor . . . upbeat and optimistic. . . . Very romantic . . . looking for a heart of gold and someone who wants to have fun." A "down-to-earth" young man who majored in livestock management is looking for a woman who "will accept me for who I am." An engineer with a master's degree describes himself as "an active individual who enjoys most forms of entertainment"—but he's also "laid back, so I can have fun doing almost anything." A self-described "Christian dude" (elementary school teacher and football coach) likes "to have a lot of fun" while "Christianity plays a major role in my life." He considers himself "a hopeless romantic . . . very relaxed and laid back." He hopes to be "on Amazing Race at some point in my life." A twenty-six-year-old manager of inventories for a hunting and fishing company "loves to laugh and joke around" and enjoys "having a good time."

## Older Men, Nebraska

Attitudes are significantly different in this older age group, as is shown below.

*Education*
> high school, 16 percent
> college, 49 percent
> graduate school, 20 percent

*Religion*
> Christian, 83 percent
> spiritual, 17 percent
> agnostic/atheist, 0 percent
> Jewish, 0 percent

*Political attitudes*
> conservative, 66 percent
> liberal, 34 percent

*Want children*, 10 percent

*Prior marital relationship*, 64 percent

*Highly valued traits*
> fun-loving, 84 percent
> long-term relationship, 75 percent
> romantic disposition, 73 percent
> open to new experience, 59 percent
> easygoing, 53 percent
> honest, 50 percent
> kind, 37 percent
> ambitious, 28 percent
> short-term relationship, 25 percent

> idealistic, 24 percent
> intelligent, 20 percent
> religious, 8 percent
> no identity problems, 8 percent
> independent, 7 percent

The older men, understandably enough, are more interested in long-term relationships than the younger ones (75 percent vs. 50 percent) and also more interested in romantic relationships (73 percent vs. 40 percent). Sixty-four percent of them have been married before, as opposed to only 18 percent of the younger men. The older men would prefer to settle down in a durable relationship held together by deep emotional and romantic ties rather than "play the field" or just find company for fun. More of these men have strong religious commitments. A mechanic, age forty-eight, who has held the same job for thirty years, is "a committed believer looking for a companion with like values to share life with." A self-described "very simple looking guy," age forty-nine, is "hoping for eternal love and something real." He neither drinks nor smokes and has "a large heart, huge passion and romantic . . . hoping to meet someone that can take me out of this loneliness and share with me an eternal happiness, joy, blessings, unconditional love." Such explicit admissions of loneliness are rare in these messages and especially among the younger people who often mention many friends with whom they share a wide range of leisure-time activities.

A fifty-one-year-old man in financial services has "been patiently waiting for that right person to come along." He sees himself as "a real romantic" who "enjoy[s] almost anything . . . with the right person." A forty-six-year-old man of Asian descent (working for a Fortune 500 company) is among the few who consider respect, honesty, good manners, and loyalty the most important qualities.

A "technical manager" at a large manufacturing company, age forty-six, provides a detailed inventory of the traits he is looking for:

> My Perfect Date: Honesty is most important . . . someone that really loves life, has a good sense of humor, is caring, active, confident, a great kisser, adventuresome, down to earth . . . loves having fun, likes music, is spontaneous, patient not needy, can dress up or just hang out in jeans, is creative, intelligent.

His ideal relationship is one "based on trust and respect." One may wonder if such an inventory of self-evidently desirable traits helps or hinders the search for the ideal partner. By contrast, a forty-nine-year-old truck driver is "looking for an honest woman" and sees himself as "just a happy guy and easygoing person looking for a fun woman." Readers are free to determine the attributes of the "fun woman."

A fifty-three-year-old schoolteacher is looking for someone "who is . . . secure, independent yet caring, sensitive and thoughtful." Of himself he writes, "I am very open to change and a new and more exciting way of doing things."

Such eager affirmation of "openness to change" is among the most obvious indicators of the congruence between American character and the culture that enshrines change. These attitudes may not be generalized in the population as a whole and are likely to be more widely held among those who seek to solve their most intimate personal problems with the help of the new methods the Internet provides.

A fifty-two-year-old "outdoorsman" working for a "corporate outfitter" wants a woman "who can joke and laugh at herself . . . [and] should be as comfortable and happy sitting around a campfire . . . as hitting the town for dining and dancing." Such a modified version of the Renaissance woman—simple and elegant, independent and dependent, a homebody and an avid consumer of worldly entertainments, and so forth—is a recurring fantasy among the men of different ages. A forty-nine-year-old self-employed man who is "hardworking, passionate, honest, trustworthy, loyal, respectful, active, fun-loving, and playful and believes in down-to-earth values" is looking "for a passionate, attractive woman . . . who is independent, nonsmoker, and Christian." He seems unaware of the potential tension between some of these attributes.

Table 7.1 shows the comparative preferences of Nebraska women and men, expressed in percentages seeking particular traits.

One of the unexpected findings is that preference for a romantic disposition and relationship is far more pronounced among older women and men than among their younger counterparts. We expect younger people to be more inclined to romance, but this is not so in these groups. The most plausible explanation may be that older people are more appreciative of a durable and committed relationship that they perceive as romantic and deeply emotional.

Another notable difference is the higher rating given to ambitiousness by the older age groups. This may be related to an unstated preference for a more stable and higher socioeconomic position associated with ambition.

Women in both age groups place a far greater value on religious attitudes than do men. This is likely to be the case in the general population, including

**Table 7.1. Comparative Preferences of Nebraska Women and Men**

|  | Male (20–39) | Male (40–60) | Female (20–39) | Female (40–60) |
|---|---|---|---|---|
| Fun-loving | 83 | 84 | 96 | 100 |
| Long-term | 50 | 75 | 65 | 77 |
| Romantic disposition | 40 | 73 | 49 | 87 |
| Open to new experience | 38 | 59 | 56 | 75 |
| Honest | 43 | 50 | 65 | 57 |
| Easygoing | 48 | 53 | 25 | 21 |
| Ambitious | 29 | 28 | 50 | 41 |
| Short-term | 50 | 25 | 35 | 23 |
| Kind | 20 | 37 | 20 | 51 |
| Intelligent | 34 | 20 | 37 | 30 |
| Independent | 12 | 8 | 41 | 38 |
| Idealistic | 14 | 24 | 19 | 0 |
| Religious | 7 | 8 | 15 | 21 |
| No identity problems | 7 | 8 | 9 | 12 |

all those who are not seeking a date or a more durable relationship online. Why women are more inclined to religious belief than men may be explained by the persistence of their less aggressive and more altruistic disposition, notwithstanding the rise of feminist values and attitudes. This more altruistic disposition may also explain why a higher proportion of women identify themselves as liberal, compared to men.

In this group as in the others, younger women are far more interested then older women and older men in short-term relationships. This is not hard to understand: they are not as ready for a settled, committed, long-term relationship.

If the Nebraska sample revealed considerable differences in the cultural values and beliefs among its respondents and those in Massachusetts, the Alabama sample is even more distinctive.

Alabama match.com users are far more traditional in both their political and religious attitudes and, in some instances, in their conception of the "perfect match" or ideal partner. The Alabama samples also offer the most lopsided ratio of conservative to liberal political self-identification.

Only in this group did I repeatedly come across the explicit requirement of Christian religious faith (rather than just a preference) as the cornerstone of compatibility. The Alabama group also has the highest proportion of those with only a high school education, though it is still a minority.

Similar attributes would likely be found in the population of Alabama as a whole. What bearing they have on highly valued personal traits, or qualities, is reflected to some degree in the information obtained from our sample.

## Younger Women, Alabama

*Education*
> high school, 21 percent
> college, 44 percent
> graduate school, 35 percent

*Religion*
> Christian, 87 percent
> spiritual, 8 percent
> agnostic/atheist, 5 percent
> Jewish, 0 percent

*Political attitudes*
> conservative, 70 percent
> liberal, 30 percent

*Want children*, 75 percent

*Previous marital relationship*, 26 percent

*Highly valued traits*
> fun-loving, 96 percent
> romantic disposition, 65 percent
> open, 59 percent
> short-term relationship, 51 percent
> long-term relationship, 49 percent
> ambitious, 41 percent
> honest, 33 percent
> intelligent, 31 percent
> kind, 31 percent
> religious, 20 percent
> independent, 18 percent
> easygoing, 15 percent
> idealistic, 14 percent
> no identity problems, 4 percent

Most noteworthy in this group is the high preference for a romantic disposition. The part played by religious and other traditional values is also apparent and reflected in many excerpts from the Internet messages quoted below.

A twenty-two-year-old college-educated woman (occupation undisclosed) describes herself as "a family person" looking for a man similarly inclined. "My relationship with God is very important for me," she writes. Somewhat incongruously, her "favorite things" are "pina coladas and getting caught in the rain"—the romantic notion shared by respondents in the other samples. In the same spirit, numerous respondents confessed to being "turned on" by thunderstorms; this was actually listed as one of the "turn-ons" provided by the questionnaire.

Even in Alabama, a fun orientation is common. A thirty-year-old special-education teacher is "always up for fun, new experience." Social drinking, usually of wine, is frequently mentioned by both sexes as part of, or central to, recreational activities.

A thirty-three-year-old woman working for an electric company "can have fun doing just about anything." Like the authors of many similar messages, she emphasizes her versatility, the capacity to enjoy a variety of recreational or leisure-time activities. She is looking for "a normal guy with a normal lifestyle" who is intelligent and has a sense of humor. A twenty-two-year-old graduate of poultry science loves "to laugh, sing, and dance . . . and to be out doing things." She is "a Christian and is looking for a Christian." She believes it is "important to connect spiritually as well as physically and emotionally." A thirty-two-year-old divorced mother of three believes she is "sweet, honest, and sincere" as well as "somewhat romantic." A secretary "admire[s] a man who works hard for a living." A thirty-one-year-old black woman is looking for "a good person, someone I can connect with on a deeper level . . . who is nice, loyal, a good listener" and trustworthy.

A thirty-nine-year-old woman with a graduate degree "love[s] to go to church and missions trips" and is looking for "someone who is solid and grounded and can have tons of fun, sit back and relax." She needs "a trustworthy man . . . a Southern gentleman who opens the door for me." Such an individual would find her "romantically and physically attractive."

A twenty-five-year-old graduate student is "looking for someone special in my life. I am striving daily to be pleasing in God's sight and embrace God's vision of a 'virtuous woman.'" For a thirty-two-year-old speech pathologist, "family is very important"; she would also "love to be with someone who can make me laugh." She is among many who emphasize their enjoyment of going out for various entertainments or watching a movie at home—"favorite thing to do when raining: curl up on the couch and listen to the rain."

The combination of the comfortable-domestic with the glamorous-worldly dimensions of life is another recurring theme in these self-presentations and presumably thought to be a major asset by many (especially women) who use match.com. It is reminiscent of the more sophisticated (or pretentious) self-presentations of the "Renaissance women" encountered in the personals of the *New York Review of Books*.

## Older Women, Alabama

*Education*
> high school, 16 percent
> college, 50 percent
> graduate school, 34 percent

*Religion*
> Christian, 84 percent
> spiritual, 16 percent
> agnostic/atheist, 0 percent
> Jewish, 0 percent

*Political attitudes*
> conservative, 75 percent
> liberal, 25 percent

*Want children*, 2 percent

*Previous marital relationship*, 86 percent

*Highly valued traits*
> fun-loving, 95 percent
> romantic disposition, 78 percent
> long-term relationship, 74 percent
> open, 56 percent
> honest, 46 percent
> ambitious, 38 percent
> intelligent, 33 percent
> kind, 31 percent
> religious, 31 percent
> short-term relationship, 26 percent
> easygoing, 21 percent
> independent, 20 percent
> idealistic, 16 percent
> no identity problems, 6 percent

Why do the middle-aged and older women in Alabama sampled here rate romantic love so high? Southern cultural influences may be the most plausible answer—some combination of traditional ideals and individualism, or a present-day expression of the affinity between religiosity and romanticism.

A forty-seven-year-old single mother and legal assistant at a law firm "enjoy[s] the simple things in life and appreciate[s] all that the Lord has blessed me with." She is "loyal, trustworthy, and has a great sense of humor." Her "perfect match would be a man that has a relationship with the Lord, his family, and friends. He knows who he is . . . he would be kind, gentle, and have a great sense of humor."

A fifty-eight-year-old widow (schoolteacher) is interested in a man who can respect her for what she is; she is "a romantic soul," and is "optimistic, fun-loving, and thoughtful." A forty-nine-year-old divorced, college-educated black woman, one of the few in these samples, "consider[s] herself to be a person that is homey, enjoys and loves God." She would "enjoy male company and conversation."

A forty-eight-year-old woman (business manager in a fast-food franchise) who has a daughter and grandson living with her would "like to find that one person I can't wait to come home to in the evening," a mature man with whom she hopes to have "that special chemistry." This phrase is invariably code for romantic attraction and a compatibility that cannot be fully explained but is deeply felt.

A fifty-eight-year-old reading coach and teacher describes herself as "outgoing, fun, great personality. Educated, romantic, affectionate, passionate, willing to try anything once as long as it is not dangerous." She is looking for someone "romantic, kind, loving" and "to have fun with." She concludes by repeating that she is "willing to try new things."

A forty-four-year-old African American widow, administrative assistant at a psychiatric institution, is "seeking someone who is Christian, mature, active, willing to travel and spend quality time exploring each other." He must also have "high moral standards" and "should treat women with the highest regard, as God does." She does volunteer work "to assist others in need."

A fifty-six-year-old "Christian woman looking for her 'soulmate'" describes herself as "old-fashioned . . . looking for an old-fashioned man" who still opens car doors for women. For fun, she loves to "cuddle in front of the fireplace" and "walk on the beach at sunset." (References to fireplaces recur probably because they are associated with a homey setting for intimate "quality time.") Faith is important for this writer who is "looking for someone to share our faith together."

A registered nurse of fifty-two is "looking for that special friend to share all the little things with . . . who accepts me just the way I am." Here we may pause once more to reflect on the frequency of this injunction: Why do so many of these people insist on being accepted as they are? Does it mean that they are content with themselves as they are, yet aware of some defect that should be accepted by their prospective partner? The most plausible explanation may be that the demand for acceptance (as one is) is an obvious expression of individualism, of being attached to what they see as their essential, unique personality, with no reason to change it. But this position contradicts the oft-expressed "openness to change" and new experience, the yearning for self-realization and the underlying desire to reinvent oneself. Cherishing oneself as is and a determination to reinvent oneself are mutually exclusive.

The most likely explanation of the wish to be accepted as one is, is that people do not like to be judged, or to undertake the difficult process of attempting to modify their personality in order to please another person. This resistance to change does not jibe with earlier observations about the supposed American readiness to reinvent oneself, with the belief in the possibilities of far-reaching change in one's life and personality. The two attitudes may be reconciled if the desire for reinvention originates with the self and not in outside pressures. In any event, it is noteworthy that so many of these writers are apprehensive about the possibility of being judged and found wanting. Their attitude reflects the cultural currents of the last several decades, when being "judgmental" has become subject to wide disapproval among educated and enlightened Americans. This disapproval expresses the ascendant—though selective—moral relativism of our times. I call it selective because such relativism has its familiar limitations, and its advocacy is compatible with a wide range of emphatic moral judgments rooted in political correctness. One ought not be judgmental about a common criminal or drug addict, or what some may consider sexual perversion, but it is necessary and proper to be judgmental about racism, sexism, "lookism," capitalistic greed, and other attitudes proscribed by political correctness. The latter amounts to a set of left-liberal political beliefs which have become entrenched since the late 1960s.

## Younger Men, Alabama

*Education*
> high school, 20 percent
> college, 58 percent
> graduate school, 22 percent

*Religion*
> Christian, 82 percent
> spiritual, 10 percent

agnostic/atheist, 8 percent
Jewish, 0 percent
*Political attitudes*
conservative, 80 percent
liberal, 20 percent
*Want children*, 72 percent
*Prior marital relationship*, 32 percent

*Highly valued traits*
fun-loving, 94 percent
short-term relationship, 56 percent
open, 49 percent
romantic disposition, 49 percent
easygoing, 48 percent
honest, 47 percent
intelligent, 45 percent
long-term relationship, 44 percent
ambitious, 36 percent
kind, 27 percent
religious, 15 percent
independent, 10 percent
idealist, 6 percent
no identity problems, 4 percent

A thirty-six-year-old rocket engineer describes himself as "an all-around great guy: thoughtful, mature, responsible, and somewhat shy" with "a good sense of humor." He does not "play impression games" and wants to meet "an intelligent woman who enjoys having fun together" and is able "to clearly communicate what she wants and likes so I can keep her happy."

"A Christian gentleman" of twenty-eight wants to meet a Christian woman who is "fun and interesting . . . in good shape . . . can and will support me in any decision . . . [and] loves to laugh." A computer technician, thirty-seven (who admits to being overweight but is on a diet), is "very open and honest . . . a dreamer" and has "a good imagination." Under "Favorite Things" he writes, "I am into anything romantic. I love thunderstorms and the rain."

One may wonder again where the numerous references to rain and thunderstorms in these communications come from. As we have seen earlier, *Werther* has some memorable passages about the emotions stimulated in the protagonists by thunderstorms but it is unlikely that the match.com correspondents were influenced by such romantic texts. More likely, romantics, then and now, associate thunderstorms with raging passions and the beauty of nature.

A twenty-nine-year-old man in the construction business likes to "ride 4-wheelers and play in the mud." He lives with what he calls "my baby boy Chance, a two-year-old bulldog," and is "looking for someone to spend time with and maybe even the rest of my life." A thirty-seven-year-old self-employed man in the communications industry "would like to find what most others want, honesty, sincerity, faithfulness." He sees himself as "very grounded and old fashioned . . . a God-fearing man and Christian." He cautions that he would not sacrifice his Christianity for a relationship.

A thirty-five-year-old diesel engine repair technician is interested in meeting "a girl with integrity, education, ambition, individuality . . . who doesn't have any mental disorders." He considers himself "a sophisticated gentleman with style and taste . . . extremely active and hardworking, creative, romantic, and a very good listener . . . clever and always willing to compromise."

The thirty-five-year-old co-owner of an executive recruiting firm is "independent, successful . . . knows what he wants and where he is going." He is also "easygoing, affable, and has a good sense of humor." A twenty-four-year-old man who works for a software company is looking for a friend, lover, or soul mate—or "something in between." Among his qualifications, he "love[s] to make other people happy," is a "wonderful listener," and tries his best "to look on the bright side of everything." He wants "to embrace change," whatever that it means.

A twenty-nine-year-old attorney (one of a very few encountered in these samples) writes, "I am very family-oriented and generally a nice, Christian, conservative person." He says nothing about the kind of woman he is looking for.

A thirty-four-year-old air force officer (one of a very few military personnel encountered on match.com) is quite specific both about himself and what he is looking for. "I am a fun, well-rounded guy who has his life in order and has a lot to offer. . . . I am driven in my professional life but . . . laid back outside of work. . . . I am positive, confident, and I like to set goals. I am down to earth and enjoy the simple things in life. . . . I think it's important to have a balance between achieving goals and staying close to family and friends." He would like to meet "an intelligent, attractive woman . . . who is comfortable with who she is . . . she should have a healthy sense of humor, an open mind to appreciate the absurdities of life."

## Older Men, Alabama

*Education*
>	high school, 24 percent
>	college, 64 percent
>	graduate school, 12 percent

*Religion*
>	Christian, 84 percent
>	spiritual, 16 percent
>	agnostic/atheist, 0 percent
>	Jewish, 0 percent

*Political attitudes*
>	conservative, 86 percent
>	liberal, 14 percent

*Want children*, 10 percent

*Prior marital relationship*, 90 percent


*Highly valued traits*
>	fun-loving, 92 percent
>	long-term relationship, 61 percent
>	romantic disposition, 57 percent
>	open, 49 percent
>	ambitious, 47 percent
>	intelligent, 41 percent
>	easygoing, 41 percent
>	short-term relationship, 39 percent
>	honest, 37 percent
>	kind, 21 percent
>	independent, 12 percent
>	religious, 12 percent
>	no identity problems, 6 percent
>	idealistic, 4 percent

A forty-seven-year-old divorced man in medical sales is looking "for that special person to share life with," including "love, fun, and passion." He is one among many who notes that he can have fun by going out or by staying at home, "watching a good movie or sporting event." He also stresses his interest in "hard work" and "fun." There are no specifics about the kind of person he would like to meet. In this respect his message resembles many others similarly unbalanced: many of these communications concentrate either on the qualities of the sender or on the qualities sought in another person, but not on both.

A "hardworking" forty-three-year-old man wants a woman who is honest, capable of good conversation, "down to earth and lives in reality." He would like "to walk the beach with someone other than myself and . . . watch the sun set." A forty-six-year-old man (looking like twenty-six or younger on the enclosed photo) also thinks of himself as a "hard worker," as many men do; he is in the "Mexican restaurant business." But he is also "easygoing, laid back, and happy-go-lucky." His "perfect match" "would have long straight brunette or blonde hair . . . around 5 and half feet tall [with] brown, blue, or hazel eyes. Her personality would be something like mine [of which he says little] or a little more outgoing." He names some places he hopes she would like to eat, presumably to complement his tastes.

A fifty-four-year-old man working in "technical support" at a university is "looking for someone interesting to go to dinner with and have a nice conversation with the hope of possibly more later. I am easygoing, well educated, enjoy traveling, and I'd love to meet someone . . . similar."

A fifty-eight-year-old widower, holder of an MBA and a CPA, considers retiring in two years and would like to meet someone to travel with, "that special someone that would like to see new places. . . . Every day should be lived to the fullest." A forty-four-year-old has been looking for "that one special person that truly touches our heart and soul." He would begin "as friends and let the romance completely take over." He plays in a local band of which he is the youngest member.

A fifty-three-year-old grandfather of four is "looking for a relationship full of honesty, openness, loyalty, lots of laughter." He says little about himself or the type of person he would like to meet except that he had once been married (for twelve years) and has had two serious relationships since his divorce in 1989. He is not interested in "playing the field"; he wants to find out "if the chemistry is there." A graduate teaching assistant at Auburn University wishes to meet "a multicultural person, preferably someone bilingual or with knowledge of other languages." Other requirements are honesty, faithfulness, and trustworthiness. He is "not into playing games."

"A Southern gentleman [of fifty-six], looking for someone to share life's adventures," describes himself as "easygoing, fun-loving, and warm." He seeks a "classy lady . . . who wants to be pampered." He "like[s] to laugh and make others smile/laugh too." He "love[s] adventure and romance." He has a good relationship with his former wife.

A forty-year-old man has set his goal as "to live at the beach," and has a career (not disclosed) that allows him to live there or nearby. He is "very caring, considerate, and honest" and is "looking to build a life with someone incredible." This woman should be "fun, intelligent, engaging, honest, goal oriented, loyal, athletic, and carefree."

Few of these notices say much about physical attractiveness. Would a person endowed with all the desired character traits be acceptable even if physically unattractive? We do not know. But many studies (quoted in chapter 1) indicate that looks matter, especially for men. In "real life" they play an important part in the relationships between men and women, including initial decisions to pursue a relationship. We cannot determine from these communications the importance of looks, compared with other attributes, nor do we know why relatively few men allude to them.

As table 7.2 makes clear, age and sex are important influences on numerous attitudes and preferences in this sample. Women, and especially older women, are more interested in long-term relationships than men. Older people of both sexes are more interested in such relationships.

It is not difficult to account for the part played by age in these preferences: middle-aged and older people prefer to settle down in a stable and durable relationship; they are less interested in experimentation, in "playing the field." Many of them have been married before. Women are more interested than men in durable and committed relationships—an expression of widely and conventionally recognized gender differences. Women of both age groups rate a romantic disposition higher than men do, overlooking the potential conflict between stability and a romantic disposition. Apparently

**Table 7.2. Highly Valued Traits by Age and Sex in Alabama Sample**

|  | Male (20–39) | Male (40–60) | Female (20–39) | Female (40–60) |
|---|---|---|---|---|
| Long-term | 44 | 61 | 49 | 74 |
| Short-term | 56 | 39 | 51 | 26 |
| Fun-loving | 94 | 92 | 96 | 95 |
| Easygoing | 48 | 41 | 15 | 21 |
| Open | 49 | 49 | 59 | 56 |
| Romantic disposition | 49 | 57 | 65 | 78 |
| Honest | 47 | 37 | 33 | 46 |
| Idealistic | 6 | 4 | 14 | 16 |
| Ambitious | 36 | 47 | 41 | 38 |
| Intelligent | 45 | 41 | 39 | 52 |
| Kind | 27 | 21 | 31 | 31 |
| Independent | 10 | 12 | 14 | 13 |

many Americans are unaware of, or unconcerned with, the disruptive aspects of romantic passion.

Two other notable gender differences confirm widely held stereotypes of women: they express stronger religious values and preferences than men, and their idealism or civic consciousness exceeds that of men by an even wider margin. Not surprisingly, religiosity increases with age for both sexes.

Far less obvious is why men of both age groups value more highly a "laid-back," "down-to-earth," or "easygoing" personality in women. These male preferences coincide with the persistence of more traditional attitudes among women: they are more willing to adapt, to accommodate, to please, to stabilize a relationship. In short, because such relationships may be more important for women, they are more willing to put up with a man who is not necessarily laid back or easygoing. This suggestion contradicts the well-established fact that women tolerate living by themselves better than men do, and men seem to derive greater benefits from marriage than women do.

# CHAPTER EIGHT

❧

# Looking for Love on
# the Internet: California

I am a fun and professional California girl that believes anything is possible. I'm living the dream . . . always looking for ways to improve myself. . . . I love to laugh and enjoy doing new things and going to new places.

Accountant, California

I own a sense of humor. Heart is full of interesting things. Feel and act like 30. . . . Inside being is renewing daily . . . obligated to nourish spiritual growth entrusted by the Lord . . . honest, God-fearing, faithful, spontaneous, affectionate, playful, passionate and romantic.

Self-employed entrepreneur, male, California

In selecting four major and culturally distinct regions of the United States, California was the logical choice to represent the West. It has the largest population of all Western states and, more important, is generally considered to be emblematic of prevailing American attitudes as well as a harbinger of emerging trends. It adds further interest to California that it has a politically and culturally polarized population: those who embrace what used to be called countercultural values as well as a sizable number of conservatives who elected Ronald Reagan governor and voted in referendums to prohibit "reverse discrimination" and to place a cap on property taxes, which has severely limited the state's capacity to fund many programs.

California's distinctiveness and importance as a cultural trendsetter is underscored by being the home of Hollywood and a high concentration of the celebrities of popular culture and entertainment. In all probability, popular and celebrity culture has had a greater impact in California than in any other part of the country.

In the popular imagination, California is a land of wild fantasies populated by a more rootless, restless, and unstable portion of the general population whose expectations are even higher, more colorful, and more outlandish than those of their fellow Americans in other parts of the country. The late George Kennan, the historian and diplomat, had this to say of Californians:

> Here it is easy to see that when man is given . . . freedom from both political restraint and want, the effect is to render him childlike . . . fun-loving, quick to laughter and enthusiasm, unanalytical, unintellectual . . . driven constantly to project his status . . . by an eager conformism. . . . Southern California, together with all that tendency of American life which it typifies, is childhood without the promise of maturity.[1]

One may object that these observations were limited to Southern Californians and that Kennan exaggerated their political freedom and even more their affluence—that his observations apply, at best, to the comfortable middle classes. Even so, his views, like many stereotypes, have a kernel of truth.

It is probably true that Californians more self-consciously and energetically pursue "the American dream" of boundless self-realization through elaborate consumption, the acquisition of status symbols, a wide range of recreational activities, and fulfilling (if rapidly changing) personal relationships than most other Americans.[2] Their restlessness is further evidenced by their mobility: a great many Californians were not born in the state, and an even larger portion of residents were not born in the United States.[3]

Differences between the California sample and those from other regions of the country are immediately apparent. Jews reappear in the California samples after their absence in those from Nebraska and Alabama; liberals are again the majority, though not as overwhelmingly as in Massachusetts; atheists and agnostics also reappear and, as one would expect, "spiritual but not religious" self-identification rises sharply to approximately one-third of the sample, a position more widely embraced by Californians than in any of the other three states considered earlier. Another unique feature of Californians' attitudes is their greater preference for short-term relationships. Somewhat unexpectedly, Californians sampled also rate the romantic disposition significantly lower.

Californians of both sexes and age groups (as those in the other states) rate a sense of humor (the capacity to laugh, a fun orientation) more highly than honesty, kindness, or intelligence as components of a romantic relationship and as a personality trait.

A noteworthy similarity among all samples, including California, is the frequent reference to eating, dining out, cooking, favorite foods, and types of restaurants among favorite or fun activities. Many of the same people also claim interest in outdoor activities and advocate a healthy lifestyle.

## Younger Women, California

*Education*
> high school, 15 percent
> college, 52 percent
> graduate school, 33 percent

*Religion*
> Christian, 54 percent
> spiritual, 34 percent
> agnostic/atheist, 6 percent
> Jewish, 6 percent

*Political attitudes*
> liberal, 80 percent
> conservative, 20 percent

*Want children*, 75 percent

*Previous marital relationship*, 18 percent

*Highly valued traits*
> fun-loving, 74 percent
> short-term relationship, 50 percent
> long-term relationship, 50 percent
> open, 44 percent
> kind, 39 percent
> romantic disposition, 31 percent
> intelligent, 31 percent
> honest, 25 percent
> easygoing, 22 percent
> ambitious, 22 percent
> independent, 18 percent
> no identity problems, 8 percent
> religious, 6 percent
> idealistic, 6 percent

Many Californian self-presentations confirm certain widely held stereotypes.

A thirty-four-year-old San Diego native (corporate meeting planner) sees herself as "relatively normal, genuinely genuine . . . fun, sensitive, thoughtful, artistic, love[s] going to the movies"; her "glass is half full"; she "appreciate[s] all kinds of humor . . . [and] outdoor adventures"; she loves her family and friends. Her fun activities include "hiking, running, snowboarding, hot yoga, films, surf fishing, ethnic food, live music, beer, weekend trips, dinner parties, laughing so hard I cry." Her ideal match would be "smart, funny . . . makes me feel good just by being in the same room . . . slightly introspective, open to new experience," and should appreciate "me for me."

A thirty-six-year-old woman in some undefined helping profession describes herself as "outgoing, friendly, smiley, silly, compassionate, courageous [and] creative"; she enjoys being around people who make her laugh; she loves learning and new adventures and professes to be "interested in all people"; she likes to make people smile. She values "humor, adventure. Intelligence, generosity, kindness, courage, creativity," and likes "people who can be spontaneous and laugh easily." Another thirty-five-year-old resident of San Diego (college educated, occupation undisclosed) writes, "I am an advocate for animals, children, and freedom & justice. I do not like to be categorized into boxes [sic] and do not categorize others. . . . Every day I awake, I put my best foot forward and do my best to emit peace and love into the world. . . . I always recycle . . . and will welcome most any person or animal into my life." A thirty-year-old accountant in Palm Desert is looking for someone "who has a passion for life and isn't afraid of being spontaneous."

A thirty-one-year-old woman offers a formidable inventory of her attributes: "articulate, brazen, charismatic, determined, exuberant, fun, gregarious, honest, intellectual, joyful, kind, loving, modest, naughty & nice, open, perceptive, quirky, resilient, sarcastic, tenacious, unique, vivacious, witty, xenial [?], yummy, zealous." She is also "passionate about the world and all that life has to offer." For fun she tries "to find new and exciting activities to keep me entertained."

A twenty-four-year-old graduate student at the University of Southern California "like[s] laughing and tr[ies] to do it as much as [she] can." She expects her ideal match to "like animals and naturey [sic] things, and coffee and crosswords." He should also be "smart, laid back, decisive, kind, and physically active."

A thrity-year-old woman who works for an institutional investment counseling firm is "looking for someone interesting that makes me excited to see what comes next." She also writes, "I am comfortable in my skin. . . . I just went skydiving for the first time and it was amazing! I am always up for a new challenge." She "loves to go to different places and meet new and interesting people. I am definitely a group person."

A twenty-seven-year-old woman from San Diego (occupation undisclosed but with a graduate degree) is "looking for an outdoor fellow who can wakeboard or snowboard during the day and then get dressed up to go to the theater at night." Many women in these notices claim to be capable of such rapid sartorial transformation (and many men expect them to do so). It is more unusual for a woman to have the same expectation regarding men. The writer describes herself as "very sociable, always busy and eternally optimistic."

## Older Women, California

*Education*
> high school, 16 percent
> college, 52 percent
> graduate school, 32 percent

*Religion*
> spiritual, 46 percent
> Christian, 41 percent
> agnostic/atheist, 6 percent
> Jewish, 6 percent

*Political attitudes*
> liberal, 72 percent
> conservative, 28 percent

*Want children*, 5 percent
*Previous marital relationship*, 79 percent

*Highly valued traits*
> fun-loving, 67 percent
> long-term relationship, 57 percent
> open, 45 percent
> short-term relationship, 43 percent
> romantic disposition, 36 percent
> kind, 35 percent
> intelligent, 30 percent
> honest, 25 percent
> easygoing, 22 percent
> no identity problems, 19 percent
> ambitious, 16 percent
> idealistic, 16 percent
> religious, 12 percent
> independent, 9 percent

A forty-seven-year-old "financial analyst" in Southern California is "a loving, affectionate, passionate woman with a big heart." Like so many others, she claims to be "the kind of woman who can quickly transform from sweats and a tank top to looking glamorous in heels and a dress." But she also enjoys "staying home for a nice dinner with wine, watching a movie and cuddling up in front of a fire." The reference to cuddling in front of a fire is all the more noteworthy since fireplaces are not common in Southern California. It suggests the influence of television commercials in which loving couples are entwined in front of a fire. This woman wishes to meet a man who is "honest, kind, loyal, intelligent, mature, and emotionally secure . . . passionate about life and love."

A woman in Newport Beach, forty-seven, is seeking "someone respectable, responsible, dependable, honest, loving and caring, romantic and active." Again, she is "someone who can dress up and also dress down." Her men should be "secure with themselves." A fifty-two-year-old widow, physical education teacher of students with special needs, sees herself as "an active outdoor person who is casual and easygoing." She has "faith in God, and having religious beliefs is very important for me." She hopes to find someone "who fills your heart with a complete love." Among "favorite things" she mentions "enjoying most foods," reading, and numerous outdoor activities.

A woman of fifty-one "like[s] variety and will try just about anything. The man I am looking for needs to maintain a healthy lifestyle and enjoys the outdoors." He should also be "self-assured and honest. I am not into playing dating games." Favored travel destinations should have "lots of pure nature." We do not learn of her occupation. She will "try just about anything"—another recurring phrase.

A fifty-six-year-old woman from San Diego advises, "Life is too short to be so serious. I am fun-loving, positive, flexible, spontaneous, a people person, persistent, warm, engaging." She loves to travel, "try new foods, new adventures." Her ideal match would be "free to be himself" as well as a "strong Christian, remaining sexually pure until marriage. I will only consider men who attend church regularly." Her favorite activities include "sitting on the couch with popcorn on a rainy day" as well as "exploring Home Depot or Costco."

A fifty-year-old executive assistant is "a happy and confident woman with a positive attitude towards life!" She also describes herself as "fun, sweet, outgoing, genuine, very affectionate, compassionate and [one who] loves to laugh . . . caring, loving, kind, passionate, and romantic." She is "comfortable in jeans" and of course "loves to dress for that special occasion. . . . Making others smile and laugh is something I do easily." She provides a long list of activities she enjoys but hastens to add that she also loves "relaxing or just laying low at home." A forty-nine-year-old from La Mesa "love[s] her job—I've worked for the same company over 15 years." (She doesn't say what she does.) She also writes, "I have a great life that is filled with friends, family, and my wonderful 15-year-old son." She loves "informal dinners, scary movies, refinishing furniture, swimming at night . . . warm nights in the desert." She would like to find "a man who has good balance in his life. The fun factor is really important," but she also wants someone "who approaches life with passion and sincerity."

A forty-seven-year-old woman from Escondido believes that "with the right company most anywhere can be fun . . . hiking, enjoying nature, a spontaneous road trip, a great dinner, with conversation to match. Animal activism and environmental awareness are my passion." A fifty-three-year-old woman loves to laugh and likes "being casual most of the time." She would like to meet "someone who is intelligent, warm, compassionate, affectionate, and a gentleman, with a great sense of humor. He should smile easily . . . and like holding my hand." She does not reveal her line of work.

## Younger Men, California

*Education*
>high school, 7 percent
>college, 62 percent
>graduate school, 31 percent

*Religion*
>Christian, 49 percent
>spiritual, 31 percent
>agnostic/atheist, 16 percent
>Jewish, 4 percent

*Political attitudes*
>liberal, 67 percent
>conservative, 33 percent

*Want children*, 82 percent

*Previous marital relationship*, 9 percent

*Highly valued traits*
>short-term relationship, 84 percent
>fun-loving, 71 percent
>intelligent, 41 percent
>open, 33 percent
>ambitious, 30 percent

easygoing, 27 percent
kind, 22 percent
honest, 20 percent
romantic disposition, 19 percent
long-term relationship, 16 percent
no identity problems, 13 percent
religious, 6 percent
idealistic, 6 percent

This group of young men has the least interest in a long-term relationship of all those sampled in all four states. Correspondingly, the value placed on a romantic disposition (usually associated with interest in a long-term relationship) is also low, as are the rankings of honesty and warmth; religiosity and idealism also get short shrift. This seems to be a group most of whom are interested only in fun, probably in what has come to be known as "hooking up."

A thirty-one-year-old man soon to be lawyer is "a big fan of trying new things. . . . I am really into anything that will involve people and the outdoors." He is "adventurous" but in the process of settling down and "settled in who I am." A twenty-nine-year-old "localization producer" [?] in Costa Mesa, working for a "software developer," started out in computer science but instead got a BA in English and creative writing at Stanford. He watches at least two movies a week, and loves to cook and bake. His "favorite things" include "potato-filled buritos. Subtitled movies . . . spicy curry . . . cold barley tea. Listening to the same song for an hour. . . . The thrill of something new."

A thirty-three-year-old project manager for a resort, from San Diego, describes himself as "a true English gentleman," "funny" and "really ambitious in my career," who "enjoys living in California." He is looking for someone who can "challenge" him and "has a lot to say for herself . . . and can make me laugh. The biggest attraction for me is women who are just totally honest, frank, and sarcastic."[4] His "favorite things" include Indian, Italian, Korean, and English cuisine. He "adore[s] his iPod and road trips with the music blaring."

A more unusual respondent is a self-described Korean American "geek" with a degree in electrical/computer engineering and rather atypical interests. Unlike the vast majority of his fellow seekers, "the number one thing [he is] . . . looking for is intelligence." He reveals that he has difficulty finding someone as smart as he considers himself. His "typical geeky interests" include "gadgets, science, technology." He confesses that "I would really rather curl up with a good book than hike up a mountain." He has never had the "travel bug."

A twenty-two-year-old man from San Clemente who has just graduated from college and intends to go to law school is "looking for a sweet girl who likes to have fun" and will tolerate his watching basketball games (he is a Lakers fan). He further writes, "I like to be romantic and have fun at the same time! . . . I love to make people laugh! I love sports and play basketball whenever I have a chance."

A twenty-eight-year-old man in Newport Beach who works in the landscape renovation of athletic fields is "not looking for a hook-up or a dating situation . . . but a mature relationship." He "love[s] to go out to eat, good wine and good conversation." A twenty-five-year-old San Diego man, more inclined to personal revelation, believes that "I am a pretty unique guy . . . but with a twist. I love sports, beer, being outside, working out . . . not afraid to get dirty." As for the "twist," he has "a love for all things aesthetic . . . for art, fashion, architecture, and music." He is looking for someone similarly inclined, and again, "someone who is as comfortable in heels as she is in running shoes."

The widespread insistence on this capacity to change from formal to informal (footwear or clothing) may also be interpreted as a version of the American aspiration "to have it all," a diluted version of the Renaissance man (or woman) as defined by a typically American emphasis on physical appearance.

## Older Men, California

*Education*
> high school, 11 percent
> college, 54 percent
> graduate school, 34 percent

*Religion*
> Christian, 54 percent
> spiritual, 35 percent
> Jewish, 6 percent
> agnostic/atheist, 4 percent

*Political attitudes*
> liberal, 55 percent
> conservative, 45 percent

*Want children*, 30 percent

*Previous marital relationship*, 62 percent

*Highly valued traits*
> fun-loving, 65 percent
> short-term relationship, 56 percent

long-term relationship, 44 percent
kind, 44 percent
romantic disposition, 42 percent
intelligent, 37 percent
open, 31 percent
honest, 30 percent
easygoing, 28 percent
ambitious, 27 percent
independent, 19 percent
no identity problems, 10 percent
religious, 2 percent
idealistic, 2 percent

Of the four California groups, the older men are the most conservative. As will be discussed further in the comparison of samples from the four states, age and sex correlates with political attitudes: men are more conservative than women, older men are more conservative than younger ones. Insofar as being liberal in American society is associated with greater idealism and more compassionate attitudes (concern for the poor, animal rights, peaceful foreign policies, etc.), women's greater, seemingly innate idealism predisposes them to more liberal attitudes. These female dispositions confirm the time-honored, biologically derived stereotypes of women as being more compassionate, more nurturing, warmer, and kinder.

It is noteworthy and somewhat puzzling that more than half of even older California men prefer short-term relationships, more than men in any of the other states. Why are the men sampled in California less interested in long-term, committed relationships than their counterparts in the other three states sampled? Has there been a selective migration of this type of men to California, or is there something in the California way of life or its sociocultural environment that shapes these preferences? Or are the samples unrepresentative of broader attitudes in these states? One may also wonder why the California men sampled are among the least idealistic, as indicated in the low ratings for religiosity and "idealism."

A fifty-two-year-old man from Newport Beach with a lucrative job in executive management (he owns a vacation home and a boat) will give "extra bonus points" to a woman who can help him launch his boat. His ideal woman "is truly happy inside . . . had a loving upbringing as a child, knows how to show love to her man, is always playful and always looks for the positive side of life . . . and is fun to be around. . . . [She] is active, healthy, happy, and has a good soul. She is comfortable . . . wearing jeans or elegantly dressed in an evening gown dancing with me during a classy night on the town. She is unpretentious, warm, loving, caring, unconditional." He says little about his own personality other than being a "romantic classy man" who knows "how to treat a lady," likes to have fun and to be "creative in all aspects of life," and is "confident, genuine, generous, and humorous."

A forty-three-year-old "managing partner from a small law firm" in San Diego would like to meet someone "to share great conversation, laughter, nature, hiking, art, travel music, romance." He is characterized by others as "giving, intelligent, sensitive, adventurous, respectful, philosophical, loyal, dependable, caring, politically aware, and down to earth"—and has a "strong sense of humor." He is widely traveled and an outdoors person; his "favorite things" are "hikes with a special person, sunsets, full moons, stormy days at Torrey Pines, shooting stars, listening to the rain . . . chocolate, music, great art, visiting remote places." He hopes to meet "a woman who is bright, strong, sensitive, loyal, independent, successful, curious, and attractive . . . with a global perspective. . . . Ideally we should complement each other."

A fifty-five-year-old man (with degrees in engineering and computer science) is "chief technology officer" at a software company he founded. He loves his work, but his "real love" is "music, writing, travel, hiking . . . anything that takes me to new places and adventures." He wants to meet a woman who is "independent, self-motivated, enjoys life, and is essentially happy."

A forty-eight-year-old retired Air Force officer and current airline pilot is a Mormon with a degree in political science and an MBA in aviation management. He sees himself as "an optimistic and happy person . . . who loves to laugh . . . but also relishes quiet intimate moments with a woman." He enjoys "making people smile and laugh." Widely traveled, his favorite places include the Dolomites and Lake Garda in Italy.

A fifty-year-old man with a bachelor's degree has "a great sense of humor and enjoy[s] making people laugh." He further writes, "I am an interesting man with nothing to prove, an ego well in check, and honest to a fault. Not into chest beating." He is looking for a woman "who knows who she is . . . [and] wants a shoulder to cry on and a person to trust."

A high school special education teacher, fifty-five, never married, loves his job, enjoys the outdoors, music, and travel but misses "the warmth, intimacy, laughing, sharing, and togetherness of a committed relationship." He is a "decent, down-to-earth guy who enjoys trying many things." Most of all, he likes "a good sense of humor."

Table 8.1 shows the preferences of the California samples, whereas table 8.2 is a comparison of all four states. As these tables indicate, the California sample

**Table 8.1. Highly Valued Traits by Age and Sex in California Sample**

| | Women (20–39) | Women (40–60) | Men (20–39) | Men (40–60) |
|---|---|---|---|---|
| Fun-loving | 74 | 67 | 71 | 65 |
| Open to new experience | 44 | 45 | 33 | 31 |
| Intelligent | 31 | 30 | 41 | 37 |
| Long-term | 50 | 57 | 16 | 44 |
| Short-term | 50 | 43 | 84 | 56 |
| Honest | 25 | 25 | 20 | 30 |
| Ambitious | 22 | 16 | 30 | 27 |
| Kind | 39 | 35 | 22 | 44 |
| Easygoing | 22 | 22 | 27 | 28 |
| Romantic | 31 | 36 | 19 | 42 |
| Independent | 18 | 9 | 22 | 19 |
| Idealistic | 6 | 16 | 6 | 2 |
| No identity problems | 8 | 19 | 13 | 10 |
| Religious | 6 | 12 | 6 | 2 |

has a number of distinctive features. Among all groups, Californians register the highest preference for short-term relationships and give the lowest priority to a romantic disposition. In turn they rate short-term relationships highest. The Californians sampled also give the lowest ratings to honesty, ambition, independence, and idealism as valued personality traits. Such preferences suggest high levels of self-absorption and an overall short-term orientation, not limited to romantic relationships.

**Table 8.2. Four-State/Regional Comparison of Highly Valued Traits**

| | Massachusetts | Alabama | Nebraska | California |
|---|---|---|---|---|
| Fun-loving | 88 | 94 | 91 | 69 |
| Open to new experience | 63 | 45 | 57 | 38 |
| Intelligent | 52 | 32 | 30 | 35 |
| Long-term | 60 | 56 | 67 | 42 |
| Short-term | 40 | 44 | 33 | 58 |
| Honest | 47 | 41 | 54 | 25 |
| Ambitious | 43 | 41 | 54 | 25 |
| Kind | 46 | 28 | 32 | 35 |
| Easygoing | 59 | 31 | 34 | 25 |
| Romantic | 45 | 62 | 62 | 32 |
| Independent | 27 | 15 | 25 | 17 |
| Idealistic | 27 | 10 | 14 | 8 |
| No identity problems | 17 | 5 | 9 | 13 |
| Religious | 3 | 18 | 13 | 7 |

## Comparative Findings, Their Likely Sources and Meanings

The most striking and unexpected of all findings is the predominance of a fun orientation (sense of humor, good cheer, etc.) as the most highly rated quality in each group sampled. It would have been more plausible to anticipate that kindness, warmth, honesty, or empathy would emerge as the most highly rated quality, but this is not the case. The high value placed on fun is reflected not only in explicit statements indicating preferences but also in descriptions at great length of various leisure-time activities considered to be entertaining. Prominent among them is watching television or DVDs at home, going out to eat and drink and shop, and watching sporting events. Leisure-time, or recreational activities, turned out to be a major basis of self-definition in all groups.

A recent *New York Times* article about current dating customs in New York City supports the centrality of active recreation in the process of self-definition. For these young daters it is extremely important to find specific and preferably novel activities, or "themes," for first dates. Many of them center on different foods. In March 2010, "New Yorkers opted to have their first dates over tacos . . . by the month end tacos went out of vogue and fondue became the fare of choice for first dates. . . . A few weeks later, outings for lobster rolls were all the rage." Owners of a new dating website "wanted to create a new kind of dating site where members could demonstrate who they are, not with personal essays and awkward messages, but by proposing dates that begin with the words 'How about we . . .'" (referring to proposed activities). Analysis of thousands of dates arranged on this dating site identified the most popular categories as "foodie, dance, games, make-believe and prankster dates." A psychologist at the University of California, Berkeley, studying such matters, observed, "What's interesting about it is the way we try to show that we're special and unique is that we like to do things like everybody else." The author of the *Times* article seconded the point: "New data from a Web site suggests that not only do many people plan similar dates, but like lemmings, they collectively migrate from one theme to the next."[5]

Needless to say, this emphasis on self-definition by what one does, and especially on a date, is not the most helpful in laying the foundation of a long-term relationship that does not center on "fun" activities. These dating aspirations also reflect the ultimate paradox of American individualism, namely that the striving for uniqueness and originality is conditioned by the simultaneous compulsion to be "trendy" or "with it."

While being cheerful and having a sense of humor are highly valued in most societies, they clearly are more so in America, as indicated by a great deal of anecdotal, experiential, and probably social scientific evidence as well. Americans are inclined to avoid or suppress whatever is sad, troubling, tragic, or depressing and are drawn to whatever is funny, cheerful, optimistic, diverting, or uplifting. They are also distinguished by a belief in the solubility of most personal, social, political, and economic problems.

How to account for this phenomenon? What drives this attitude? How far back in social history does this predisposition reach? Presumably the American national character has benefited from the relatively benign circumstances of the evolution of American society: material abundance, physical space, freedom of choice, economic opportunity, and the belief of immigrants in the possibility of substantially improving their lives. Nonetheless it seems that the conspicuous cheerfulness of Americans is a relatively recent phenomenon that emerged in the twentieth century. The observations of some early distinguished visitors to the United States lend support to this proposition. In his *American Notes* (1842), Charles Dickens observed that "the American people certainly are not a humorous people, and their temperament always impressed me as being of dull and gloomy character." Mrs. Frances Trollope, in the first edition of her *Domestic Manners of Americans* (1832), also asserted that Americans "lacked humor."[6] Tocqueville also commented on the "seriousness" and "astonishing gravity" of Americans and came to the conclusion that the United States was "the most serious nation on earth."[7]

The social and geographic mobility of Americans has probably encouraged the development of a cheerful attitude: there is a greater urgency to make a good impression when less time is available to do so, less time for people to get to know one another. And the best way to make a good impression is to appear cheerful, good-natured, and ready to laugh and joke. In the more stable and less dynamic societies of the past, relationships evolved more slowly and over a much longer period of time; people lived in long-standing communities and had ample opportunity to observe one another and draw appropriate conclusions.

The wish to be popular is another stereotypical American attitude and another reason why Americans are anxious to make a good impression. Competitiveness further stimulates this desire.

The preoccupation with good cheer has probably been at least in part a by-product of modern techniques of marketing and salesmanship: it is easier to sell anything when the salesman (or advertiser) displays a good-natured, cheerful disposition. As the notion of "salesmanship" has spread to the non-commercial realm, it has become common to refer to "selling" ideas, policies, and beliefs of all kinds. Increasingly Americans have come to think of themselves, of their personality, as something to "sell," not only when looking for a job or running for office but in personal relationships as well. The best way to sell oneself, for whatever purpose, is to appear cheerful, good-natured, ready to laugh and joke.

Omnipresent advertising has made an important contribution to this attitude as its role models are almost invariably cheerful beings, uplifted by the benefits of consuming whatever is advertised. It is not easy to find an advertisement in which people don't smile, laugh, or joke. Almost everything advertised is associated with good humor, and whatever is advertised promises to make us laugh or smile. Smiling and laughing consumers testify to their satisfaction with whatever they buy and consume. Their laughter and good cheer indicate that they are generally good natured, sociable, trustworthy, and easy to get along with.

While advertising certainly reinforces and perpetuates the veneration of good cheer, it is hard to determine if this merely reflects existing cultural values or more actively creates and shapes them.

The high value placed on laughter and good cheer is also linked to the overarching entertainment orientation of American society, though here again it is not easy to separate cause and effect. People who make us laugh are, of course, entertaining. Americans energetically seek entertainment and can get it twenty-four hours a day via a wide range of technological devices and services. Even the TV weather forecast must be made, if at all possible, humorous and interspersed with jokes. Does being entertained make people more entertainment oriented, that is, more desirous of entertainment, or are these entertainments provided in response to what people demand and desire?

Modernity and entertainment orientation are connected: modern technology makes it possible to access a bounty of nonstop sources of entertainment—television, radio, movie theaters, electronic devices, etc. More important, modern Americans seem to need more diversion to escape boredom and the unrewarding routines of their lives. Modernity also brings loneliness: tens of millions live by themselves and find comfort in hearing human voices on the radio and seeing human faces on television. Modernity has also brought us a great increase in leisure time and the discretionary income that pays for many of the entertainments.

The wish to be entertained also has a pragmatic, interpersonal dimension. Humor is a lubricant of human interaction and as such is a justifiably valued component of personal relationships. A person possessed of a sense of humor is easier to get along with; humor helps minimize conflict. Americans are anxious to avoid conflict in personal relationships, though they don't necessarily succeed.

Growing familiarity with pop psychology also helps explain fun-loving attitudes. Therapeutic perspectives seek to create greater awareness of attributes believed to be useful for establishing and maintaining satisfactory personal relationships, and cultivating a sense of humor and cheerfulness is highly recommended as a means toward this end.

Finally, this preoccupation with laughter and good cheer may be an effort to overcome, diminish, or compensate for a deeper insecurity and anxiety among Americans.[8] The highly competitive nature of American society is an obvious source of this anxiety and insecurity since competitors never know who will win—unless the competition is rigged.

A survey by the American Association of Retired Persons (AARP) of a national sample of 3,501 individuals echoes our findings about the popularity of good cheer. Those surveyed by AARP were singles aged forty through sixty-nine. The leading qualities both men and women were seeking in a new partner were "Pleasing Personality/Sense of Humor, 67 percent; Common Interests and Activities, 49 percent." Other highly rated qualities diverged: 39 percent of women were looking for men with "similar moral or religious values" while 40 percent of men were looking for "great-looking" women.[9] Only half the sample rated highly a "romantic disposition."

Only half of the aggregated sample rated a "romantic disposition" highly. I expected romantic attitudes and expectations to be more prominent and highly rated. Instead the match.com communications reflected, for the most part, what I take to be the typically American blend of romanticism and pragmatism. Unlike the older, archetypical holders of romantic beliefs (as portrayed in the nineteenth-century novels), few modern Americans are convinced that they are predestined to meet someone who is uniquely compatible and will meet all their emotional needs. They correctly believe that there are many potential candidates for such roles and relationships and that suitably compatible human beings are, within certain limits, interchangeable. This is not to say that pragmatic considerations invariably dominate. An observer of the dating scene writes, "Ask most young singles about the idea that there is a socioeconomic underpinning to modern love and they are offended. They will insist that economics in mate selection is a thing of the past, a primitive relic."[10] In our samples, material considerations such as income and occupation received little attention, though frequent references to the desirability of comparable levels of education reflect an understated status consciousness.

The relative scarcity of romantic statements may also be attributed to the nature of these electronic communications. Condensing a message of availability and needs into a highly structured written message leaves little room for romantic self-revelation. Instead, online communications predispose someone looking for a partner to convey an impression of a ready compatibility with a variety of individuals, flexibility, and openness to a wide range of new experiences. The greater the urge to maximize compatibility, the less distinctive the individual self-presentation becomes. Advertising on the Internet is an attempt to make rational choices, leaving little room for the spontaneity that is a key ingredient of the romantic personality as conventionally understood. A similar observation has been made about the paradoxical message of self-help books.[11]

Several aspects of what one author has called our "therapy culture" are also reflected in many of the messages. One is an awareness of and apprehension about the identity problems of potential partners and their impact on a committed relationship. Such an awareness of risk is associated with a culture in which "so much of life and everyday human encounters [are] interpreted as risky and potentially victimizing," and in which "perceptions of vulnerability" have greatly increased "in sharp contrast to the way people viewed their engagement with adversity in previous decades," Frank Furedi, a British sociologist, writes. What he calls "the emotional orientation towards the self," or a preoccupation with personal attributes and subjective feelings, is also evident in the messages examined. It is an orientation that has largely replaced an interest in objective characteristics such as occupation, income, and socioeconomic background. As Furedi points out, "the emotional needs of the self most often cited are, first, the need to feel good about oneself and, second, the need to be affirmed by others." This therapeutic culture "takes emotions very seriously. . . . The language of emotionalism pervades popular culture . . . politics, then workplace, school and universities, and everyday life."[12]

Highly valued traits found in these (and other) Internet communications differ in various ways from findings in studies based on other sources and populations. Thus a study of happily married couples found that "a partner was admired and loved for his or her honesty, compassion, generosity of spirit . . . and fairness. . . . The value these couples placed on the partner's moral qualities was an unexpected finding."[13] These responses suggest that people in a long-term relationship develop different values than those seeking to initiate one.

Another study of American married couples made more than a quarter-century ago also shows different highly valued (and devalued) traits. The ten most valued characteristics in a partner were "good companion, considerate, honest, affectionate, dependable, intelligent, kind, understanding, interesting to talk to, and loyal." Characteristics not viewed as highly desirable were "wants a large family, dominant, agnostic in religious matters, night owl, early riser, tall, and wealthy."[14]

There remain important unresolved questions about our findings. Among them, how much difference has the Internet made in meeting potential partners and initiating romantic relationships? It is indisputable that the Internet has provided new opportunities for communications that promote meetings by potentially compatible people; it also encourages the specification of individual needs for both short- and long-term relationships. But we know little about what proportion of these electronic communications lead to actual meetings and, more important, to subsequent relationships, cohabitation, or marriage.[15] Nor do we know how the number of relationships originating in Internet communications compares to those resulting from meetings not initiated on the Internet. It would be of special interest to know whether or to what extent online communications are more or less suitable vehicles for the development of romantic relationships, compared with printed notices or face-to-face contacts initiated in conventional settings.

Another important and unknown matter is how often disappointment follows meetings arranged on the Internet, based on unrealistic self-presentations that are refuted by experiences during actual meetings.

One study of such matters proposes that "people who develop *strong ties* on the net in the forms of friendships or romantic relationships represent a minority of the online population. A minority which nevertheless might, in absolute numbers, include several million worldwide."[16]

The Internet exchanges have some undeniable advantages: they provide a huge database from which to select potential partners and make it easy to establish communications with them. The information provided, even if not entirely trustworthy, helps eliminate flagrantly unsuitable candidates. But there remain two important drawbacks. First, Internet communications (like printed messages) encourage an initial misrepresentation of the self that can only be checked or dispelled after face-to-face meetings. Second, these communications exclude a social context that helps evaluate the potential partner. Such contexts are available when we meet in college, at work, in a group or association of specific purpose, at a social gathering, or through the introduction by friends. All these settings or connections provide real-life reference points that are absent when Internet or printed personals are used.

We can only speculate about whether Internet communications alter the quality of personal relationships and the expectations preceding them. At least one expert on such matters, Aaron Ben-Ze'ev, believes they do:

> The Internet has dramatically changed the romantic domain; this process will accelerate. . . . Such changes will inevitably modify present social forms such as marriage and cohabitation and current romantic practices relating to courtship. . . . We can expect further relaxation of social and moral norms. . . . The relaxation of such norms will be particularly evident in matters pertaining to romantic exclusivity. It will be difficult to avoid the vast amount of available tempting alternatives. . . . The notion of "betrayal" will become less common in connection with romantic affairs. . . . The romantic realm will become more dynamic, and it will be more difficult to achieve the emotional advantages of a stable romantic framework.
>
> The test of the Internet will be whether it can complement ordinary romantic activities, just as the telephone complements ordinary social activities, or whether it will replace them with less valuable activities, as the television frequently does. Society faces a great challenge if it is to integrate cyberspace successfully into our romantic relationships.[17]

It is difficult to evaluate these speculative propositions since evidence is limited either to confirm or refute them. Insofar as Internet dating implies that human beings are virtually interchangeable—including those with whom we can establish a close relationship—it undermines and demystifies romantic notions about the uniqueness of such compatibilities and resulting attachments. The apparent abundance of potential partners to be found online may also undermine existing relationships by suggesting that superior alternatives may be readily found, supporting notions of the endless interchangeability of partners.

According to Zygmunt Bauman, "One expert counsellor informs readers that 'when committing yourself, however half-heartedly, remember that you are likely to be closing the door to other romantic possibilities which may be more satisfying and fulfilling.'" Bauman links the superficiality of what he calls "virtual relations" to consumer culture. These relations "seem to be made to the measure of a liquid modern life setting where 'romantic possibilities' . . . are supposed and hoped to come and go with ever greater speed and in never thinking crowds . . . out-shouting each other with promises 'to be more satisfying and fulfilling.' Unlike 'real relationships,' 'virtual relationships' are easy to enter and exit. . . . The advent of virtual proximity renders human connections simultaneously more frequent and more shallow."

"In a consumer culture like ours," Bauman observes, "which favors products ready for instant use, quick fixes, instantaneous satisfaction, results calling for no protracted effort . . . The promise to learn the art of loving is a promise to make 'love experience' in the likeness of other commodities."[18]

Electronic communications may also become a substitute for meeting and interacting with flesh-and-blood human beings. Studies and anecdotal evidence indicate that people spend enormous amounts of time online looking through the profiles of potential partners and vetting the candidates. Reportedly some people conduct imaginary affairs in cyberspace, and these flights of fantasy become substitutes for real relationships. People are even said to engage in online sex, that is, masturbation assisted by online communications.[19] It seems plausible that these fantasy (or "virtual") relationships may undermine existing ones or become substitutes for them. Such electronic fantasy relationships may also help maintain emotionally or sexually unsatisfactory relationships in the way an occasional visit to a prostitute might at other times have alleviated the hunger for sexual variety.

Internet communications may also contribute to the romantic idealization of poorly known potential partners, a result of unrealistically positive self-presentation. As Ben-Ze'ev puts it, "The apparent ease of finding true and everlasting love in cyberspace creates the need to have such a 'perfect' love." More generally, "the major features responsible for the great romantic seductiveness of cyberspace are imagination, interactivity, availability, and anonymity."[20]

Perhaps the key problem of both online and printed personals (even if serious misrepresentations are minimal) is that the information exchanged and the details provided don't add up. There remains a disjunction, a gap, between the parts and the whole: "Despite the level of detail in these profiles, it is very hard to tell what a person is like from what is essentially a catalogue."[21] Written listings or summaries of human traits have an abstract quality that is no match for the vividness and authenticity integral to personal contact. Certainly people can convey misleading impressions—deliberately or unwittingly—even when they interact face-to-face. Dating relationships too are marked by the concentrated efforts of the participants to make the best possible impression on each other. However, such tactics and simulation during actual dating cannot be sustained over a long period. Under conditions of physical proximity, individuals gain insights that are incomparably more valuable and illuminating than what can be learned from the written messages of self-promotion.

CHAPTER NINE

# Conclusion: The Entitlement to Happiness

Of all animals, with which this globe is peopled, there is none towards whom nature seems . . . to have exercised more cruelty than towards man, in the numberless wants and necessities, with which she has loaded him, and in the slender means, which she affords to the relieving these necessities.

David Hume[1]

Divorce . . . did begin to increase . . . almost as soon as people began choosing their own partners for reasons of mere love. . . . All across the world, all across time, whenever a conservative culture of arranged marriage is replaced by an expressive culture of people choosing their own partners based on love, divorce rates will immediately skyrocket.

Elizabeth Gilbert[2]

The persistence of romanticism (like that of religion) suggests that people do not wish to live in a wholly rational world in which everything can be explained and understood, a world from which, as Max Weber put it, the gods have retreated. The appeal and pursuit of romantic love, even in its modified form, is part of a broader and deeper resistance to modernity and rationality. At the same time, it may be argued that while romanticism was in part a rebellion against modernity, the latter created the conditions and opportunities for an increasing number of people to indulge in romantic longings and fantasies. Only people who can take for granted the gratification of basic material needs,

199

who have plenty of personal freedom and free time, will develop romantic conceptions of the self and personal relationships. Such relationships will not flourish in societies of scarcity or authoritarian regimentation, or those in which social roles are fixed by tradition. Modern, democratic, commercial, mass societies have further encouraged a shallow romanticism in the context of advertising, consumption, and popular entertainment. Finally, the widespread search for a romantic partner in modern societies may also reflect not only loneliness—fear of it or actual experience—but boredom. Modernity and boredom are linked by the excess of free time and the decline of social obligations and routinized activities that are part of making a living.

The pursuit of romantic love, whatever its sources, is also an essential part of the self-conscious pursuit of happiness—the "unquenchable human need to feel connected to something larger than the insular self." It is a pursuit spurred and intensified by "the melancholy suspicion that we live in a world without meaning."[3] In the past such needs were satisfied by religious beliefs and practices. Religious activities were, for the most part, communal, and as such they helped guard against social isolation and an uncertain sense of identity. These publicly shared religious beliefs also gave meaning to the world. Not surprisingly, recent movements of religious revival in the United States and elsewhere have been motivated chiefly by the widely felt need to combat social isolation and the loss of meaning.

From its very beginnings, as noted earlier, romantic love has had distinctly religious undertones and provided a measure of self-transcendence through the idealization and quasi-worship of the love object. Darrin McMahon writes, "For what is Romantic joy if not a partially secularized dream of experiencing heaven on earth: the dream of recovering the lost child within."[4] The ecstatic intensity and intimacy of the romantic relationship is, to a large degree, a reaction against and compensation for the coldness and impersonality of much of the modern world and its increasingly inadequate, impoverished social bonds. Although in its origins romanticism was, for the most part, a compensatory response to the Enlightenment and modernity, it could not repair the psychic damage those forces inflicted. Nor could it remedy the decline of community or become a substitute for it. As Andrew Delbanco notes, "We live with undiminished need, but without adequate means, for attaining what William James called the feeling of 'elation and freedom' that comes only when the outlines of confining selfhood melt down."[5]

While attempting to remedy the impersonality and social isolation of the modern world, romanticism inadvertently created a new set of anti-social attitudes which fortified and glorified that "confining selfhood." These anti-social aspects of romanticism derive from its focus on the single individual and the corresponding exclusion and devaluation of the social world. The idealized individual became the centerpiece of the romantic relationship, the singular source of meaning, self-fulfillment, and emotional sustenance. The romantic love object towered above all other connections and relationships, which became matters of indifference.

For all these reasons, at the present time "[r]omantic love is under siege, both from within marriage and from outside it, but neither have we yet come up with a new ideal to replace it. . . . The decline of romance has left us feeling abandoned, with nothing much to substitute for it."[6]

This brings us once more to what might be called the darker side of individualism. While its rise was liberating in many ways, this liberation has also brought about a vacuum of meaning and a weakening of social bonds and a sense of community. As Delbanco further observes, "The modern self tries to compensate with posturing and competitive display as it feels itself more and more cut off from anything substantial and enduring."[7] The liberating thrust of individualism has increasingly given rise to and merged with self-centeredness, narcissism, or just plain selfishness—qualities displayed in abundance in American society. They find a most extreme and unappealing expression in the posturing and cult of celebrities.[8]

Individualism is the most obvious link between modernity and romantic love, and it offers the most persuasive explanation of its persistence. As Michael Miller observes, "Romantic love is the perfect ideal of intimacy for the individualist, since it promises togetherness without giving up anything or self-realization."[9] Even more compelling is that the autonomous individual cannot accept the familial or communal determination of his love life and marital choices. His personal needs and preferences dictate his associations and relationships, including those culminating in marriage.

Romantic self-fulfillment, individualism, and concern with one's sense of identity are thus linked. In a romantic relationship, "the flawed individual is made whole," as Anthony Giddens puts it.[10] Laura Kipnis makes the obvious but still important point that "the emphasis on love as a unique individual experience presupposes the existence of the modern individual." Intimate and supposedly unique personal needs are essential building blocks of our sense of identity: "We love our needs because they make us the individuals we are, and the individual is much vaunted in our time."[11]

Romantic love has further attractions for the modern, nonconformist individual. As Ethel Person notes:

> Romantic love . . . is an emotion of extraordinary intensity. . . . Love may also enable lovers to break through the stifling limits of self. Hence, it is a mode

of transcendence. . . . Because of its intensity, love has the capacity to disrupt social norms and conventions, giving lovers both cause and sanction to escape the established order. In this sense romantic love is the expression of individuality . . . the celebration of the individual and the pair.[12]

Insofar as modern societies create social isolation, undermine traditional beliefs, and generally "disenchant" life (as Max Weber put it), *in the short run* romantic love overcomes such isolation as well as the modern loss of meaning and the more profound existential isolation of human beings:

> Love is an antidote not just to personal neediness but to those existential anxieties that encompass our sense of frailty and brevity of our life. . . . The aim of romantic love is union, or merger with the Other. . . . Passionate love attempts to overcome the pain of separation, separateness, and the felt inadequacies of the solitary self through merger with the Other.[13]

Self-indulgence and the urge for instant gratification are familiar excrescences of individualism, by-products of the drive for self-realization through consumption and the pursuit of attention and popularity. This darker side of individualism at once stimulates and compromises the ideals and pursuit of romantic love. It produces heightened expectations and their unanticipated consequences. These expectations indisputably contribute to the difficulties of maintaining close, intimate, and durable personal relationships, marital or otherwise. The contemporary expectations brought to marriage include the following:

> Their partners are going to do it all—satisfy unmet childhood needs, complement lost self-parts, nurture them in a consistent and loving way, and be eternally available to them. These are the same expectations that fueled the excitement of romantic love, but now there is less of a desire to reciprocate. After all people . . . get married to further their own psychological and emotional growth.[14]

This is the kind of individualism that may also lead to viewing divorce as an opportunity for personal growth,[15] a position embraced in a recent *New York Times* op-ed piece which warmly commended divorce among the middle-aged and elderly. For these people, Deirdre Bair wrote, "divorce meant not failure and shame but opportunity. . . . They divorce because they cannot go on living in the same old rut with the same old person." She also wrote:

> Men and women I interviewed [126 men and 184 women married 20 to 60-plus years] insisted they did not divorce foolishly or impulsively. Most of them

mentioned "freedom." . . . Women and men alike wanted time to find out who they were. . . . One grew disenchanted with the wrinkled person across the dinner table and wanted someone new and exciting.[16]

Hopefully, the individual described above as growing "disenchanted" was herself exciting and free of wrinkles.

The attitudes Ms. Bair so heartily endorses—and we do not know how representative they are given her small sample and the undisclosed method of its selection—suggest that radical individualism has penetrated the ranks of the elderly, or at any rate those among them chosen for her study. Apparently her elderly subjects continue wrestling with an unresolved quest for their true identity, not knowing who they are but expecting to find out in the wake of their liberating divorce. Evidently it did not occur to her that human beings, including those who succeed in persuading themselves about the wisdom of divorce at an advanced age, are generally disinclined to admit making foolish or impulsive decisions which might have dire consequences. In the Pollyannaish world of self-vindication that Bair describes approvingly, "few had regrets. Men who wanted new companionship easily found it and women who wanted new partners had them within two years."[17] While there is little evidence outside this study of such delightful outcomes—including breakthroughs in self-discovery and personality growth awaiting people who divorce late in life—American popular culture tirelessly encourages such hopes.

Readers in the *Times* were critical of the argument for the joys of late-life divorce: "The assumption here is that one comes to self-discovery only in something approaching a vacuum; free of responsibility we finally manage to understand ourselves." Another reader wrote, "[T]here is the clear implication that those who remain married for life are benighted, craven losers without the guts to pursue their zen." According to a third reader, "Divorce is failure. It makes people feel disposable. It is no fun for kids or grandkids. . . . Ms Bair's convenient untruths trivialize the promises we make. And in genuflecting before the altar of personal freedom, she epitomizes our culture's free fall into the vast supermarket of undisciplined desire."[18]

"The vast supermarket of undisciplined desire" aptly captures the conditions that underlie much of the marital instability, and more generally, the difficulties of all age groups in finding durable, emotionally fulfilling relationships. Also noteworthy, as one of the correspondents pointed out, is that Ms. Bair overlooks the impact of these divorces on children and grandchildren, given her preoccupation with the great rewards of late divorce.

I am not opposed to late divorce or divorce in general. What I reject—as did the *Times* correspondents—is the notion that divorce (or late divorce) is a painless, liberating experience and that regardless of age there are endless opportunities for new beginnings and relationships. I am also dubious about the inexhaustible potential for personal growth possessed by each and every human being. At last I doubt that people who have gone through much of their life unable to find a satisfactory sense of identity will accomplish this in ripe old (or ripe middle) age if only they discard an unsatisfactory spouse.

Belief in an entitlement to happiness—a preeminently American disposition—is closely related to the pursuit of romantic love, which is widely considered a shortcut to happiness.[19] Such a sense of entitlement to happiness is the highest expectation a person can have, other than everlasting bliss in an afterlife. Arguably the American national character is both a reflection and a determinant of the high expectations that include romantic love. The source of these expectations may be found at the convergence of optimism, egalitarianism, belief in progress, and problem solving as well as in the actual opportunities that have existed in American society.

The Founding Fathers were imbued with Enlightenment beliefs and interpreted them as amounting to an endorsement of the pursuit of happiness. This idea has doubtless made an important contribution to the United States becoming the only society designed to accommodate and encourage, over a long period of time, a huge influx of immigrants eager to embark on the wholesale transformation and improvement of their lives.

The intensification of the belief in an entitlement to happiness in our times is further illustrated by American attitudes toward death and old age. While the awareness of death has been generally repressed, in recent times old age has been transformed, quite unrealistically, from a condition of decline and deprivation (physical, mental, and social) to a state of veritable bliss and fulfillment, redolent with new opportunities for self-expression—a new golden age. Even the terminology of aging has been altered to divert attention from the less than uplifting aspects of aging as "old" has been replaced by the euphemism of "senior" or "senior citizen." Instead of referring to someone as seventy years old, we often say "seventy years young." In the same spirit, it is often wishfully suggested that advancing age can be ignored, that the old do not differ significantly from the young, and that given positive attitudes we can keep ourselves healthy, happy, and fulfilled indefinitely, regardless of age. Being old need not lead to reduced expectations and contentment.

Another remarkable illustration of the hypertrophy of such expectations and the denial of limits (inherent in high expectations and romanticism) has recently been provided by the best-selling author Gail Sheehy, rhapsodizing about the wonders of carnal passion in old age and insisting that it is "never too late." She writes, "Romantic passion offers the opportunity to live completely in the present. . . . While it is often short-lived, it is an exhilarating send-off to the journey of the Second Adulthood"—her new euphemism for old age. In her imagined pleasures of being old, senior "seductresses" offer "enchantments [that] combine a fully enriched character, a sharp mind, endlessly rechargeable vitality, status, glamour, and contagious spirit." Sheehy suggests, "Both midlife men and women love the freedom that being single brings"—another dubious claim.[20]

More realistically, a survey undertaken by AARP found that "Americans 45 and older are far more open to sex outside marriage than they were 10 years ago, but *they are engaging in sex less often and with less satisfaction*" (my italics). In the sample, 43 percent were satisfied with their sex life, down from 51 percent in 2004. The frequency of sexual activity dropped by 10 percent. In all probability, for those over sixty-five there was a substantially larger drop in sexual activity and satisfaction that the survey did not reflect since it did not distinguish between different age groups over forty-five.[21]

High expectations have lately come under attack by an author who considers herself a victim of them.[22] Lori Gottlieb's widely reviewed autobiographical narrative is an unusually candid critique of the culture of high expectations that in her view prevails among women and results in collapsed relationships and loneliness:

> In my mother's generation, you were "happy" in your marriage because you had a family together, you had companionship, you had a teammate, you had stability and security. Now women say they also need all-consuming passion, stimulation, excitement, and fifty other things our mothers never had on their checklist. . . .
>
> Our generation of women is constantly told to have high self-esteem, but it seems that the women who think the most highly of themselves are at risk of ego-tripping themselves out of romantic connections.

Paul Amato, a sociologist whom Gottlieb quotes, believes that "our culture became more individualistic and our expectations of marriage changed—it became a therapeutic relationship instead of a practical relationship." He observes that "the 'soul mate' concept has done a lot of harm because it sets the bar extremely high for a 'successful' marriage." Another specialist Gottlieb consulted (Michael Broder, a psychologist) "thinks that many single women today bring a dangerous sense of entitlement to dating." Gottlieb is also critical of the ideals of self-realization through marriage—or marriage as an avenue to "personal growth." What she calls "the online dating mentality" feeds these expectations by suggesting that "there is a seemingly infinite supply of new dating candidates lined up."[23]

It remains to reconsider the question—especially in light of the debate over the role of expectations in the success or failure of committed personal relationships: in what ways does the search for romantic love persist in American society despite the familiar obstacles to its successful pursuit, including the contradictory and often self-defeating human desires and the specific difficulties of the modern social setting? Are we justified in designating the beliefs and attitudes discussed in this study as "extravagant expectations"? And if they are, should we consider them an integral part of American cultural values or a fringe phenomenon? Are they rooted in the national character or are they by-products of popular culture? Of further importance is to reconsider once more the question of what ways American popular romanticism resembles or differs from its European antecedents.

The persistence of attitudes that approximate the romantic mind-set is reflected in the findings of survey research indicating that "most twenty somethings see marriage as centered on intimacy and love rather than on practical matters such as finances and children: 94 percent of those who had never married agreed that 'when you marry you want your spouse to be your soul mate, first and foremost.'"[24] According to another study, "Surveys from the late 1950s to the end of the 1970s found a huge drop in support for conformity to social roles and a much greater focus on self-fulfillment, intimacy, fairness, and emotional gratification." By the same token, "Increasingly people filed for divorce because their marriage did not provide love, companionship and emotional intimacy, rather than because the partners were cruel or failed to perform their marital roles as housekeeper or provider."[25]

The two strains of romanticism discussed in this study share the belief in the uniqueness of the individual and his or her needs. There is a corresponding shared belief in the possibility of finding a soul mate capable of

satisfying all such needs and expectations. American and old-style romantics further have in common a pervasive preoccupation with authenticity
concerning both individual character and social arrangements and institutions. Strong and pure feelings, untainted by material interests and status
seeking, are likewise highly valued, as are a veneration of nature and all
things natural.

But there are also differences between the two strains. American popular
romanticism does not follow the European idea that finding the perfect soul
mate is outside the control of the individual, that it is something mysteriously preordained, a matter of fate or providence, and that only one or a
very small number of select individuals may qualify for such a role. Modern
Americans are convinced—given their optimistic, egalitarian, and practical disposition—that people are largely interchangeable, and that there are
many individuals out in the world who may be ideal long-term partners,
provided that appropriate methods are used to locate them. Americans believe in planning, calculation, and conscious effort, even in matters of the
heart—hence the proliferation of matchmaking services. This modern romanticism incorporates a rational component that was absent, or sometimes
even abhorred, among the European romantics of the past. Likewise, the
religious element of worship of an individual is absent in our times, and passion is more subdued as irrational impulses are held in check to a far greater
degree by pragmatism and common sense.

Among the sources used to sample American beliefs and attitudes relevant to these questions were printed personals, self-help or "relationship"
books, and the online dating service, match.com. The printed personals in
the *New York Review of Books* and the Harvard and Yale alumni publications
reflect the highest and most unrealistic expectations and self-presentations.
They express, for the most part, truly extravagant expectations comple-
mented by implausible self-portraits. These advertisements—whatever their
basis in reality—are highly informative and relevant to this study, but their
messages cannot be generalized. They are posted by highly educated, middle-
or upper-middle-class individuals, middle-aged or older. Their attitudes and
preferences are clearly different from the rest of the American population.
At the same time these advertisements do reflect (perhaps in a caricatured
form) broader trends among the more liberal, better-educated segments of
the general population. They include high expectations and the continued
influence of the residual countercultural values of the 1960s and 1970s, foremost among them a pervasive and heightened individualism and a sense of
entitlement.

The self-help/relationship books embody and encourage high expectations by the truly extravagant promises and claims of their authors. They are less informative of specific human qualities to be desired for good relationships, given their overriding preoccupation with methods, techniques, and practical matters. Like the online messages, these books are divided between those advocating and promising deeply romantic relationships and others of a more sober and calculating persuasion, which seek to blend extravagant, romantic expectations with a more hard-nosed, market-oriented approach.

The online personals sampled are probably the most representative and informative of the preferences and values that influence mate selection among middle-class Americans. These messages frequently incorporate elements of what I have earlier called popular or American-style romanticism.

In all three sources of data we can discern the influence of larger cultural currents and social forces on individual attitudes toward mate selection. One of them is the widely held belief in the benefits of communication— a by-product of the combination of individualism and egalitarianism. This conviction rests on the assumption that everyone has something of value and interest to communicate. Experts and ordinary Americans alike believe that good communication is the key to good relationships. This fetish of communication may be another by-product of modernity and individualism. It has also been encouraged by the influence and popularization of pop psychology and psychotherapy. Because psychotherapy rests on communication, it is a major proponent of its benefits in improving close personal relations and various kinds of conflict resolution. Mass media relentlessly disseminate the messages of pop psychologists, experts on physical and mental health, and lately even of "happiness studies." The vast number of talk shows, call-in programs, and presentations of assorted gurus further testify to the omnivorous interest in this kind of communication.

Another major cultural current that helps explain some findings and propositions of this study is the powerful American tradition of positive thinking, and the belief that such thinking is the single major determinant of the direction and quality of one's life. The advocacy of positive thinking—a major industry of our times—is particularly useful in understanding the overwhelming preference found in the online samples for good cheer, a sense of humor, and a fun orientation—what Barbara Ehrenreich calls "the cult of cheerfulness." She writes:

Nothing is more attractive to potential suitors than a positive attitude. . . . Women in particular should radiate positivity. . . . "You should remain positive at all times" counsels yet another site. "You should avoid complaining . . . [avoid] seeing the negative in things and allowing this negativity to show. . . . Being negative is never a way to go when it comes socialization."

. . . In the world of positive thinking, the challenges are all interior and easily overcome through an effort of the will. . . . In the world of positive thinking, other people . . . are there only to nourish, praise, and affirm.[26]

Positive thinking is clearly linked to individualism, to the relentless effort at self-improvement and the intended reinvention of the self. It assumes that all obstacles to happiness, success (however defined), and self-fulfillment can be overcome by the self-reliant, positive-thinking individual engaged in what a sociologist has called the "continuous and never-ending work on the self . . . offered not only as a road to success but also to a kind of secular salvation."[27]

The conviction that everything may be achieved by individual will and effort, and the positive thinking that underlies them, is as delusional as the romantic lovers' belief that pure and impassioned love transcends all obstacles. The cult of positive thinking and the popular romantic view of personal relationships share a wishful and highly optimistic disposition, projections of individual emotions upon the world. "Positive psychology" (or happiness studies) has recently emerged as a new academic subdiscipline, a descendant of the self-help tradition in American culture that exaggerates the internal, individual sources of happiness and slights the impact of circumstances, social forces, or the environment. As Ehrenreich sums it up, "Positive thinking seeks to convince us that . . . external factors are incidental compared with one's internal state or attitude or mood."[28]

The ardent belief in the benefits of positive thinking, Elizabeth Long has suggested, may also be related to a lurking realization that affluence and the associated ways of life fail "to engender individual happiness. . . . Large-scale impersonal bureaucracies, meaningless corporate work, stereotypic suburban family roles, the commodification of leisure, sexuality, and even 'meaningful experience'—all are social contributions to the individually experienced malaise that increasingly pervades best-selling novels and sociological descriptions of modern America."[29] If so, enthusing about the blessings of positive thinking may be a last resort born out of a resigned recognition that social forces and the environment are largely responsible for many personal problems and that individual attempts to change the social setting are futile. Hence, it may be more useful and feasible to try to change oneself and redefine or ignore the social setting.

In the personals, positive thinking finds prominent and obvious expression. It looms large in the cheery and favorable self-presentations, the optimistic expectations of finding a partner, the advocacy of wholesome activism, and the listing of all the rewarding activities and hobbies of the respondents, which suggest a seemingly inexhaustible capacity for pleasure and enjoyment.

Although rarely admitted, the part played by fear or the experience of social isolation in the pursuit of romance cannot be overestimated. As one study has observed, "Manifestations of loneliness . . . [have] permeated the modern world. . . . We imagine that to be alone is the worst we can experience."[30] Numerous sociological studies confirm that loneliness haunts the American social landscape even as it gives rise to a multitude of shallow group ties and superficial socializing. A national survey has found that between 1985 and 2004 "the number of people saying that there is no one with whom they can discuss important matters nearly tripled."[31]

High expectations, the discontents of modernity, and popular romanticism thus remain intertwined. Contemporary American society is permeated by a multitude of conflicting desires and values that make it difficult to establish and maintain emotionally gratifying long-term relationships, including marriage. We want both security and adventure, stability and intensity, intimate companionship and "personal space," a high degree of autonomy and intimacy, "status matching" and no-holds-barred passion. As Daniel Boorstin wrote almost half a century ago:

> We expect anything and everything. We expect the contradictory and the impossible. We expect compact cars which are spacious; luxury cars which are economical. We expect to be rich and charitable, powerful and merciful, active and reflective, kind and competitive. . . . We expect to eat and stay thin, to be constantly on the move and ever more neighborly. . . . Never have people been more the masters of their environment. Yet never has a people felt more deceived and disappointed. For never has a people expected so much more than the world could offer.[32]

Earlier, at the end of the nineteenth century, Emile Durkheim, a pioneering explorer of the problems of modernity, noted the connection between modernity, social disorganization, and the rise and multiplication of expectations. His observations help to better understand the problems explored in this study:

> The standard according to which needs were regulated no longer remain the same . . . the social forces thus freed have not regained equilibrium. . . . The limits are unknown between the possible and the impossible, what is just and

what is unjust, legitimate claims and hopes and those which are immoderate. Consequently *there is no restraint on aspiration* [my emphasis]. . . . Appetites not being controlled by public opinion become disoriented and no longer recognize the limits proper to them.[33]

There is another, deeper connection between modernity and the current difficulties in establishing and maintaining close and committed personal relationships. An essential feature of Western-style modernity is that it expands choice.[34] But conditions in American society suggest that the expansion and multiplication of choice, unguided by widely shared and thoroughly internalized values, presents difficulties for people. It is not merely the opportunity to make bad choices that is part of this predicament. As Durkheim observed, the rise of expectations is integral to having choices and options. A wide range of choices, whether on the supermarket shelves or in the Internet-driven mating market, creates unforeseen dilemmas and difficulties. At what point should one feel assured that his or her romantic choices are correct when it seems that there are endless opportunities to improve on them? And what criteria should guide these choices to begin with, at a time when individual needs are felt to be both unique and endlessly expanding? How can one tell which of his or her apparent personal needs are authentic and worth the efforts to gratify them? Which human qualities should be more highly valued—intelligence or the capacity to laugh? Openness to new experience or being responsible? Her wanderings in the Third World prompted Elizabeth Gilbert to reflect on the Western dilemmas of choice:

> Our choice-rich lives have the potential to breed their own brand of trouble. We are susceptible to emotional uncertainties and neuroses that are probably not very common among the Hmong [in Laos] but that run rampant these days among my contemporaries in, say, Baltimore.
>
> . . . We live in danger of becoming paralyzed by indecision, terrified that every choice might be the wrong choice. . . . The modern world has become . . . a neurosis-generating machine of the highest order. In a world of such abundant possibility, many of us simply go limp from indecision. . . . Or we become compulsive comparers—always measuring our lives against some other person's life.[35]

Moral relativism, another by-product of modernity and individualism, makes matters still more difficult. How should two individuals reconcile their divergent but supposedly equally authentic needs? Clearly, free and free-floating individuals are incapable of producing binding moral guidelines for their behavior and aspirations that can be shared by other equally free and autonomous individuals in search of a committed personal relationship.

At last, the importance of choice has increased because, as Andrew Cherlin argues, it has come to be associated with self-development:

> Your task as an adult today is to develop your sense of self by making choices that let you grow and change as a person. . . . Your friends will understand and even sympathize if you tell them that you are getting a divorce because your marriage isn't providing you with the personal growth you need. . . . Americans value the quest for personal fulfillment—the core of the newer, expressive individualism.[36]

The reader may justifiably leave this study with the melancholy conclusion that it is difficult, if not altogether impossible, to find a satisfactory balance between high expectations and a sober, even resigned acceptance of life constrained by the limitations imposed by our mortality, genes, social and physical environment, and chance. Perhaps inevitably the overreaching pursuit of high expectations—including romantic love—is bound to be undermined by more mundane and less uplifting desires and aspirations that also abound in American society.

~⍥

# Notes

## Preface

1. "Socialist realism" was invented in the Soviet Union in the early 1930s. It amounted to a "theory" or scheme for deliberately, openly, and coercively subordinating the arts, and especially literature, to political objectives; it represented another effort at political persuasion. Officials and cultural functionaries regularly instructed writers how to accomplish these goals. Those unwilling to comply could not publish.

2. Paul Hollander, "The Counterculture of the Heart," *Society*, January–February 2004.

3. David Rose, ed., *"They Call Me Naughty Lola": Personal Ads from the London Review of Books* (New York: Scribner, 2006).

4. Michael Vincent Miller, an American psychiatrist, wrote, "Couples don't exist in a vacuum. . . . How we love and make love are shaped by history. The most tender, private, and passionate . . . feelings are embedded in a social milieu made up of beliefs and expectations, myths and values that shape intimate conduct in fundamental ways." *Intimate Terrorism: The Deterioration of Erotic Life* (New York: Norton, 1995), 15–16.

## Chapter 1:
## Introduction: From Arranged Marriage to Social Isolation

1. Stephanie Coontz, *Marriage, a History: How Love Conquered Marriage* (New York: Viking, 2005), 15.

2. Robert Nisbet, *Community and Power* (New York: Oxford University Press, 1962), 30, 31.

3. David M. Buss et al., "International Preferences in Selecting Mates: A Study of 37 Cultures," *Journal of Cross-Cultural Psychology*, March 1990, 45.

4. David M. Buss, *The Evolution of Desire: Strategies of Human Mating* (New York: BasicBooks, 1994), 39. On the appeals of tallness in men, see also Michael Lynn and Rosemary Bolig, "Personal Advertisements: Sources of Data About Relationships," *Journal of Social and Personal Relationships*, 2 (1985), 377–383, esp. 381.

5. Buss, *Desire*, 99.

6. Buss, "Selecting Mates," 37.

7. John M. Townsend and Gary D. Levy, "Effects of Potential Partners' Costume and Physical Attractiveness on Sexuality and Partner Selection," *Journal of Psychology*, 124:4 (2001), 371, 387.

8. Quoted in Barbara Dafoe Whitehead, *Why There Are No Good Men Left: The Romantic Plight of the New Single Woman* (New York: Broadway Books, 2003), 112. The survey referred to was carried out by Edward O. Laumann et al., *The Social Organization of Sexuality: Sexual Practices in the United States* (Chicago: University of Chicago Press, 1994).

9. Helen Fisher, *Why We Love: The Nature and Chemistry of Romantic Love* (New York: H. Holt, 2004), 109.

10. Cited in ibid., 114.

11. A. Cierello, "Personal Advertisements: A Content Analysis," *Journal of Social Behavior and Personality*, 10:4 (1995), 756, 753.

12. David M. Buss et al., "A Half Century of Mate Preferences: The Cultural Evolution of Values," *Journal of Marriage and the Family*, May 2001, 492, 500.

13. Whitehead, *No Good Men Left*, 36.

14. Max Gluckman, *Custom and Conflict in Africa* (Oxford: Blackwell, 1955), 54–55, 77–78.

15. E. E. Evans-Pritchard, *Kinship and Marriage among the Nuer* (Oxford: Clarendon, 1951), 49, 52, 53.

16. M. F. Nimkoff, ed., *Comparative Family Systems* (Boston: Houghton Mifflin, 1965), 83, 86–87, 107, 109, 150, 151, 206, 219, 292.

17. Walter Edwards, *Modern Japan through Its Weddings* (Stanford, Calif.: Stanford University Press, 1989), 53–54.

18. Laurel Kendall, *Getting Married in Korea* (Berkeley: University of California Press, 1996), 89, 95–96, 104.

19. Ken Johnson, "Not in the Name of Love: Allegorical Imagery for Newlyweds," *New York Times*, January 6, 2009.

20. *International Encyclopedia of the Social Sciences* (New York: Macmillan, 1968), vol. 10, 4.

21. William J. Fielding, *Strange Customs of Courtship and Marriage* (New York: The New Home Library, 1942), 311–312, 23–25.

22. Coontz, *Marriage*, 5. See also 306.

23. Coontz quoted in *New Yorker*, January 11, 2010, 76.

24. David Reuben, MD, *Any Woman Can! Love and Sexual Fulfillment for the Single, Widowed, Divorced and Married* (New York: Bantam, 1971), 2.

25. Suzanne G. Frayser, *Varieties of Sexual Experience: An Anthropological Perspective on Human Sexuality* (New Haven, Conn.: HRAF Press, 1985), 209.

26. I refer here to marriages arranged not by family but by professional matchmakers. See, for example, Marcelle S. Fischler, "Online Dating Putting You Off? Try a Matchmaker," *New York Times*, September 30, 2007. According to the article there are now sixteen hundred such businesses which "prescreen potential matches, focusing on long-term compatibility."

27. Joshua Muravchik, "My Saudi Sojourn," *Commentary*, June 2007, 38.

28. Choe Sang-Hun, "Traditional Korean Marriage Meets Match on the Internet," *New York Times*, June 6, 2007.

29. Saher Mahmood and Somini Sengupta, "As Mores Evolve, India's Divorced Seek Second Chance," *New York Times*, February 14, 2008.

30. Anita Jain, "Is Arranged Marriage Really Any Worse Than Craigslist?" *New York Magazine*, March 28, 2005, 6.

31. See Jane Juska, *A Round-Heeled Woman: My Late-Life Adventures in Sex and Romance* (New York: Villard, 2003).

32. Gail Sheehy, *Sex and the Seasoned Woman* (New York: Random House, 2006), 243, 12. More realistically, another author wrote that "the middle-aged dating scene . . . isn't for the weak of heart. . . . For those looking for love with the like-minded and like-aged people, it's a brave new world often complicated by love-gone-wrong histories with ex-spouses or lovers, and by children and grandchildren, dependent elderly parents, careers, health problems and emotional baggage." Stacey Chase, "Older, Wiser and Available," *Boston Globe*, July 27, 2008.

33. Christopher Lasch, *The Culture of Narcissism* (New York: Norton, 1978), 41.

34. Andrea Orr, *Meeting, Mating and Cheating: Sex, Love and the New World of Online Dating* (Upper Saddle River, N.J.: Reuters, 2004), 16.

35. An American psychiatrist quoted earlier took an unusually dim view of some of these undertakings: "Dating bureaus . . . are magnets for those who are socially paralyzed. The man who is too passive to interact with the . . . females around him feeds his mind and body into the computer. Women who seek a man by this route find that the wonders of the electronic age have assembled a large proportion of cultural rejects. . . . The basic fallacy of dating bureaus, computerized or otherwise, is the assumption that someone else can choose the right man for a girl better than she can." Reuben, *Any Woman Can!*, 275. Of course arranged marriages rested exactly on this assumption, but they were not intended to create romantic fulfillment.

36. David Brooks, "Cellphones, Texts and Lovers," Op-ed, *New York Times*, November 3, 2009.

37. Melanie Thernstrom, "The New Arranged Marriage," *New York Times Magazine*, February 13, 2005, 5. A less upscale business called "Just Lunch," with 150 offices in the United States, promises to save time for its clients. It "skips online

profiles and hand-selects matches. . . . We believe that nothing replaces the human touch and we don't believe in 'computer matches' . . . you can like all the same things and still don't like each other. . . . We introduce our clients to real people—not online profiles." Advertisement in the *American Way* (a free airline magazine), January 1, 2010.

38. Abby Ellin, "The Dating Coach Is In ($125/Hour)," *New York Times*, September 27, 2007.

39. Ruth Padawer, "Keeping Up with Being Kept," *New York Times Magazine*, April 12, 2009.

40. The last three notices cited are from *New York Review of Books*, May 1, 2008.

41. Buss, *Desire*, 70, 4, 23–24. For other findings of the highly patterned differences (or "traditional sex role expectations") between the preferences of men and women, see Kay Deaux and Randel Hanna, "Courtship in the Personal Column: The Influence of Gender and Sexual Orientation," *Sex Roles*, 2:5/6 (1984), esp. 364, 374; and Simon Davis, "Men as Success Objects and Women as Sex Objects: A Study of Personal Advertisements," *Sex Roles*, July 1990. It is of course possible that more recent studies would find a decline of such gender-based expectations.

42. Albert A. Harrison and Laila Saced, "Let's Make a Deal: An Analysis of Revelations and Stipulations in Lonely Hearts Advertisements," *Journal of Personality and Social Psychology*, 35:4 (1977), 264.

43. Martin Whyte, *Dating, Mating and Marriage* (New York: Aldine de Gruyter, 1990), 100–101, 111.

44. Nisbet, *Community and Power*, 10.

45. See also Jean M. Twenge and W. Keith Campbell, *The Narcissism Epidemic: Living in the Age of Entitlement* (New York: Free Press, 2009).

46. David M. Potter, *History and American Society* (New York: Oxford University Press, 1973), 363–365, 387, 389.

47. Quoted in Nisbet, *Community and Power*, 66.

48. Richard Todd, *The Thing Itself: On the Search for Authenticity* (New York: Riverhead Books, 2008), 213.

49. James Q. Wilson, *The Marriage Problem: How Our Culture Has Weakened Families* (New York: HarperCollins, 2002), 105.

50. Nisbet, *Community and Power*, 66.

51. David Popenoe, *The State of Our Union: The Social Health of Marriage in America* (Piscataway, N.J.: National Marriage Project, 2006), 9, 11.

52. Andrew J. Cherlin, *The Marriage Go-Round: The State of Marriage and the Family in America Today* (New York: Vintage, 2010), 29.

53. Traditional collectivism is to be distinguished from the politicized collectivism of modern totalitarian states—such as Nazi Germany, the Soviet Union under Stalin, and Mao's China, among others—which sought to impose it by political means on their citizens.

54. David Popenoe, *War Over the Family* (New Brunswick, N.J.: Transaction, 2008), 46–47.

55. Ibid., 51.

56. The search for a more distinctive sense of identity probably contributes to the proliferation of hobbies in America. They include collecting worthless and aesthetically unappealing objects ("collectibles") such as bottle tops, matchboxes, beer bottles, old toys, and so on.

57. Eva Moskowitz, *In Therapy We Trust: America's Obsession with Self-fulfillment* (Baltimore: Johns Hopkins University Press, 2001), 219.

58. The late Norman Mailer was among those who admired violent criminals, erroneously associating their violence with a defiant authenticity and courage, as in his infamous short story "The White Negro," which glorified a murderer. Mailer also championed Jack Henry Abbott, a convicted murderer, and won him early release—which he used to commit yet another murder. Conflating violence with authenticity is not limited to American intellectuals; Franz Fanon and Sartre also embraced the idea.

59. For a rare critique of these beliefs, see Robert Weissberg, *Bad Students, Not Bad Schools* (New Brunswick, N.J.: Transaction, 2010).

60. "A recent study . . . at the University of California at Irvine found that a third of students surveyed . . . expected B's just for attending lectures and 40% said they deserved a B for completing the required reading list." Max Roosevelt, "Student Expectations Seen as Causing Grade Disputes," *New York Times*, February 18, 2009.

61. Potter, *History and American Society*, 332.

62. Advertising also extols the rewards of being part of a group. Various products are often depicted as being enjoyed in group settings, suggesting that such shared consumption contributes to a sense of community. In these commercials joyous, liberating consumption is typically shared by members of the same family and friends.

63. Popenoe, *War Over the Family*, 48.

64. Lasch, *Culture of Narcissism*, 34–40, 72.

65. Christopher Lasch, *Haven in a Heartless World: The Family Besieged* (New York: Basic Books, 1977), 140.

66. Ibid., xii, 5.

67. Judith S. Wallerstein and Sandra Blakeslee, *The Good Marriage: How and Why Love Lasts* (Boston: Houghton Mifflin, 1995), 7–8, 336, 5.

68. Whyte, *Dating, Mating and Marriage*, 17, 179.

69. Norval Glenn and Elizabeth Marquardt, *Hooking Up, Hanging Out and Hoping for Mr. Right: College Women and Dating and Mating* (New York: Institute for American Values, 2001), 24, 59. See also Charles M. Blow, "The Demise of Dating," *New York Times*, Op-ed, December 13, 2008.

70. Dinitia Smith, "Slippery Hitching Posts" (review of Cherlin, *The State of the Marriage and the Family Today*), *New York Times*, April 20, 2008.

71. Glenn and Marquardt, *Hooking Up*, 4, 42.

## Chapter 2:
## Modernity, Romantic Love,
## and the Rise of Expectations

1. Miller, *Intimate Terrorism*, 148.

2. Robert James Waller, *The Bridges of Madison County* (New York: Warner Books, 1992), 154.

3. Kenneth J. Gergen, *The Saturated Self: Dilemmas of Identity in Contemporary Life* (New York: Basic Books, 1991), 9.

4. Lasch, *Culture of Narcissism*, 188.

5. Isaiah Berlin, *The Roots of Romanticism* (London: Chatto and Windus, 1999), 8–9, 138–139, 141, 14, 15, 50.

6. Denis de Rougemont, *Love in the Western World* (Princeton, N.J.: Princeton University Press, 1983), 5. All other references to Rougemont are from the 1957 Garden City edition.

7. Rougemont, *Love in the Western World*, 51, 2, 212.

8. Alain de Botton, *On Love* (New York: Grove Press, 2006), 48.

9. Bertrand Russell, *Marriage and Morals* (New York: Liveright, 1929), 73.

10. Ibid., 76.

11. Botton, *On Love*, 40, 99–100.

12. Rougemont, *Love in the Western World*, 176, 291.

13. Ibid., 297, 223, 292.

14. Russell, *Marriage and Morals*, 75.

15. Sandra Tsing Loh, "Let's Call the Whole Thing Off," *Atlantic*, July–August 2009, 118.

16. Bertrand Russell, *History of Western Philosophy* (London: Allen and Unwin, 1946), 709, 701, 702, 707–708.

17. Stephen Vizinczey, *Truth and Lies in Literature* (London: Hamilton, 1986), 227.

18. Goethe himself observed, "[T]he explosion *Werther* caused was so far-reaching because the young people of that era had already undermined themselves; and the shock was so great because everyone could now burst forth with his own exaggerated demands, unsatisfied passions and imaginary sufferings." *The Sorrows of Young Werther* (New York: New American Library, 1962), 149. That is to say, individualism, the essential component of romanticism, already flourished when the book appeared.

19. Ibid., 147. Rougemont also notes that "the publication of *Werther* . . . led to a wave of suicides." Rougemont, *Love in the Western World*, 176.

20. *Werther*, 111, 87, 26, 43.

21. "We long for a love in which we are never reduced or misunderstood. We have a morbid resistance to classification by others, to others placing labels on us." Botton, *On Love*, 108. The concern with being understood is also encouraged by psychotherapy, which considers that the major task of the therapeutic process is the achievement of a better, deeper understanding of the individual and especially his or her motivation.

22. *Werther*, 27.

23. Ibid., 30.

24. Ibid., 58.

25. Ibid.

26. Christina Nehring, *A Vindication of Love: Reclaiming Romance for the Twenty-First Century* (New York: Harper, 2009), 35.

27. *Werther*, 25–26.

28. Ibid., 92, 93.

29. Ethel S. Person has written, "There is a striking overlap between the language of love and that of religion. . . . Some degree of self-surrender in the service of . . . self-transformation is a necessary component of merger . . . intrinsic to passionate love." *Dreams of Love and Fateful Encounters: The Power of Romantic Passion* (New York: Norton, 1988), 137. Anthony Giddens too has noted, "Passionate love has a quality of enchantment which can be religious in its fervor." *The Transformation of Intimacy* (Stanford, Calif.: Stanford University Press, 1992), 38. Botton concurs: "In our more passionate moments, we imagine romantic love to be akin to Christian love, an uncritical, expansive emotion that declares I will love you for everything that you are." Botton, *On Love*, 61.

30. *Werther*, 48, 51.

31. Lasch, *Culture of Narcissism*, 194.

32. Werther wants to be buried in the clothes he wore because Lotte "touched them and made them sacred." *Werther*, 126.

33. François-Rene Chateaubriand, *Atala and Rene* (New York: New American Library, 1962), 122.

34. *Werther*, 108.

35. Ibid., 89, 41.

36. Ibid., 41, 82, 28–29.

37. Walter J. Cobb, foreword to Chateaubriand, *Atala and Rene*, xiv, xi.

38. Chateaubriand, *Atala and Rene*, 66, 22–23, 24, 28, 104, 45, 28, 17, 46, 21, 83, 70, 91, 103, 95, 93, 106, 108–109, 124, 99, 102.

39. Gustave Flaubert, *Madame Bovary* (New York: New American Library, 1964), 55, 62, 111, 97.

40. Ibid., 126, 95, 75, 76, 60, 192, 148–149, 150, 163, 195, 272.

41. Erich Segal, *Love Story* (New York: Harper & Row, 1970).

42. "At a moment of generational strife, the story had balm-like powers. There was something for everyone. . . . *Love Story* worked . . . because 'the American public wanted to see a little romantic story'" (this was John Wayne's opinion). "Week in Review," *New York Times*, January 24, 2010, 3.

43. Waller, *Bridges*, 22–156 passim.

44. Marilyn French, *The Bleeding Heart: A Love Story for and About Adults* (New York: Summit Books, 1980).

45. Ibid., 145, 20, 25, 27, 24, 34, 66, 80, 78, 316, 328.

# Chapter 3:
# Popular Romanticism in America

1. Miller, *Intimate Terrorism*, 78, 74, 95–96, 52.

2. Brigitte Berger, *The Family in the Modern Age: More Than a Lifestyle* (New Brunswick, N.J.: Transaction, 2002), 153.

3. Darrin M. McMahon, *Happiness: A History* (New York: Atlantic Monthly Press, 2006), 283.

4. Nathaniel Branden, *The Psychology of Romantic Love* (New York: Bantam, 1981), 2–3, 139.

5. Fisher, *Why We Love*, 3, 214, 51, 111, 5, 23.

6. William R. Jankowiak and Edward F. Fischer, "A Cross-Cultural Perspective on Romantic Love," *Ethnology*, April 1992, 150, 151.

7. Eva Illouz, *Consuming the Romantic Utopia: Love and the Cultural Contradictions of Capitalism* (Berkeley: University of California Press, 1997), 40.

8. For a feminist analysis of the popularity and reception of this type of fiction, see Janice A. Radway, *Reading the Romance: Women, Patriarchy and Popular Literature* (Chapel Hill: University of North Carolina Press, 1984).

9. Miller, *Intimate Terrorism*, 147, 52.

10. Martin K. Whyte noted that people above working-class status are less inclined to homogamy. See his *Dating, Mating and Marriage*, 122–123.

11. Fisher, *Why We Love*, 103–104.

12. Such strategies are sometimes described in women's magazines, which "advise organizing the search for a soul mate like a job search, offering tips, for example, on places where one is likely to meet men. . . . The romantic conception of love is explicitly replaced by more realistic discussions of socioeconomic and psychological compatibility." Illouz, *Romantic Utopia*, 191.

13. Rougemont, *Love in the Western World*, 193–194.

14. Buss et al., "A Half Century of Mate Preferences," 492.

15. Cherlin, *Marriage Go-Round*, 9.

16. As early as in the last three decades of the nineteenth century, "Breath and body perfumes, talcum powder and toilet water, all were placed in settings redolent of luxuriant sensuality. There was a strikingly overt eroticism about many of these [advertising] images." Jackson Lears, *Rebirth of a Nation: The Making of Modern America, 1877–1929* (New York: HarperCollins, 2009), 149.

17. Illouz, *Romantic Utopia*, 92, 94, 96.

18. Ibid., 189.

19. Ibid., 54, 146, 151.

20. Ibid., 288–289.

21. Norman Mailer, *The Deer Park* (New York: G. P. Putnam, 1955).

22. Ibid., 96, 180, 25, 16, 18, 39, 310, 120, 202, 203, 15, 6, 13.

23. John Bowe, ed., *Us: Americans Talk About Love* (New York: Faber and Faber, 2010).

24. Julie Scalfo, "A Bachelor's Effort to Understand Love," *New York Times*, January 28, 2010.

25. Cited in ibid.

26. Bowe, *Us*, xx; Scalfo, "Bachelor's Effort."

27. Bowe, *Us*, 72, 311, 10–11, 32.

28. Lynne Pearce and Gina Wisker, eds., *Fatal Attractions: Re-scripting Romance in Contemporary Literature and Film* (London: Pluto Press, 1998), 2, 3, 70, 69–70, 73.

29. Quoted in Megan Marshall, *The Cost of Loving: Women and the New Fear of Intimacy* (New York: Putnam, 1984), 33.

30. Nehring, *Vindication of Love*, 29, 7, 271, 13, 29, 236, 275, 102, 28, 70–80, 6, 9, 144, 194.

31. Letter by Henry J. Friedman, *New York Times Book Review*, July 12, 2009.

32. Martha Nussbaum, "The Passion Fashion," *New Republic*, September 23, 2009, 44.

33. Whitehead, *No Good Men Left*, 4, 1, 2.

34. Ibid., 183–184.

35. Ibid., 100, 106.

# Chapter 4:
## Expert Advice on Dating and Mating

1. Dr. Phil McGraw, *Love Smart: Find the One You Want, Fix the One You Got* (New York: Free Press, 2005), 4–5.

2. Ellen Fein and Sherrie Schneider, *The Rules: Time-tested Secrets for Capturing the Heart of Mr. Right* (New York: Warner Books, 1995), 6.

3. Whitehead, *No Good Men Left*, 7, 20.

4. Laura Kipnis, *Against Love: A Polemic* (New York: Pantheon Books, 2003), 67, 33–34.

5. Ibid., 97–98.

6. Whitehead, *No Good Men Left*, 18.

7. Kipnis, *Against Love*, 68.

8. Whitehead, *No Good Men Left*, 18.

9. Glenn and Marquardt, *Hooking Up*, 40, 6.

10. McGraw, *Love Smart*, x, ix, 197, 216, 4, 5, 8, 6, 83, 237, 245, 262, 255, 9, 10, 277–278, 82, 86, 183, 185, 95, 107, 97, 174, 176, 177, 93, 22, 28, 23.

11. John Gray, *Mars and Venus on a Date* (New York: HarperCollins, 1997).

12. Ibid., 354, 342, 329, 12, 91, 159, 16, 42.

13. Joyce Brothers, *What Every Woman Ought to Know About Love and Marriage* (New York: Simon & Schuster, 1984).

14. Ibid., 18, 301–303.

15. Ibid., 21, 22, 35.

16. Ibid., 43, 276, 143, 135.

17. Ibid., 60, 71.

18. Greg Behrendt and Liz Tuccillo, *He's Just Not That Into You* (New York: Simon Spotlight Entertainment, 2006).

19. Ibid., 47, 53.

20. Fein and Schneider, *The Rules*, 6.

21. Ibid., 126, 162, 26, 88, 8, 97–98, 65, 55, 70, 144, 136, 225, 118, 136, 136–137.

22. Ellen Fein and Sherrie Schneider, *The Rules II: More Rules to Live and Love By* (New York: Warner Books, 1997), front matter.

23. Ibid., 55–56, 34, 38, 130, 101.

24. Ellen Fein and Sherrie Schneider, *The Rules for Online Dating: Capturing the Heart of Mr. Right in Cyberspace* (New York: Pocket Books, 2002), xxi.

25. Ibid., 18–19, 56.

26. Gary Chapman, *The Five Love Languages: How to Express Heartfelt Commitment to Your Mate* (Chicago: Northfield, 2004).

27. See *New York Times Book Review*, November 15, 2009, 29.

28. Chapman, *Five Love Languages*, 15, 34, 55.

29. Alan Loy McGinnis, *The Romance Factor* (San Francisco: Harper & Row, 1982), 2.

30. Ibid., 3, 13, 70–71, 75, 161, 177, 85, 8.

31. Judy Kuriansky, *The Complete Idiot's Guide to Dating*, third edition (New York: Alpha Books, 2003).

32. Ibid., xxi, 341, 186–188, xxiv, xxi, 119, 126, 132, 298, 313, 332, 83, 11, 86, 91, 100, 30, 309, 341.

33. Hilary Rich and Helaina Laks Kravitz, *The Complete Idiot's Guide to Perfect Marriage*, third edition (New York: Alpha Books, 2007).

34. Ibid., xxi, 47–48, 5, 13, 259, 50, 125, 74, 284, 307, 293.

35. Barbara De Angelis, *The Real Rules: How to Find the RIGHT Man for the REAL You* (New York: Dell, 1997).

36. Ibid., 1–2, 14–15, 34, 74–75.

37. Denene Millner, *The Sistahs' Rules: Secrets for Meeting, Getting and Keeping a Good Black Man* (New York: Quill, 1997).

38. Ibid., xiii–217 passim.

39. Kenneth J. Appel and Beverly S. Appel, *It Takes Two.Com: A Psychological and Spiritual Guide to Finding Love on the Internet Personals* (Oakland, Calif.: Regent Press, 1999).

40. Ibid., 82, 90–91, 102, 123, 127, 128, 126, 78.

41. Myreah Moore and Jodie Gould, *Date Like a Man: To Get the Man You Want* (New York: HarperCollins, 2000).

42. Ibid., xiii, 29, 30, 132, 150–151.

43. Ben Young and Dr. Samuel Adams, *Ten Commandments of Dating: Time-Tested Laws for Building Successful Relationships* (Nashville, Tenn.: T. Nelson, 1999), xiii–xiv.

44. Ibid., xiii–xiv.

45. Juanita Bynum, *No More Sheets: The Truth About Sex* (Lanham, Md.: Pneuma Life, 1998).

46. Ibid., 61–62, 149, 204, 205, 209.

47. William July II, *Confessions of an Ex-Bachelor* (New York: Broadway Books, 2003), xiii.

48. Wendy L. Walsh, *The Boyfriend Test* (New York: Three Rivers Press, 2001), viii, 82–89, 121, 122–124, 240.

49. Neil Clark Warren, *How to Know If Someone Is Worth Pursuing in Two Dates or Less* (Nashville, Tenn.: T. Nelson, 1999), xi–xii.

50. Thornton Calvo and Laurence Minsky, *25 Words or Less: How to Write Like a Pro to Find That Special Someone through Personal Ads* (Lincolnwood, Ill.: Contemporary Books, 1998), xii, 14.

51. Dawn Eden, *The Thrill of the Chaste* (Nashville, Tenn.: T. Nelson, 2006), 32, 25.

52. Catherine Anne Lewis, *Reborn Virgin Women: If You Wanna Be Happy Keep Your Pants Zipped* ([S.I.]: Replica Books, 2007), 231, 233, 234.

53. Darren Star is the producer of *Sex and the City*.

54. Tara McCarthy, *Been There, Haven't Done That: A Virgin's Memoir* (New York: Warner Books, 1997), 210, 61.

55. Evelyn Millis Duvall, *The Art of Dating* (New York: Association Press, 1958).

56. Ibid., 107, 97, 45–46, 17, 31, 32, 87, 112, 183, 200, 202, 88, 54, 241, 245.

57. She is not the only social critic who has expropriated the word "gulag" for dramatic effect in a search for more effective ways to denigrate American society—by claiming it is morally equivalent to, or worse than, highly repressive countries such as the former Soviet Union. Little reflection is needed to grasp the absurdity of comparing bad marriages in America to the Soviet forced-labor camps.

58. Kipnis, *Against Love*, 18–195 passim.

59. Maureen Dowd, *Are Men Necessary? When Sexes Collide* (New York: G. P. Putnam, 2005), 40–240 passim.

60. This is the central argument of Eva S. Markowitz's *In Therapy We Trust*.

# Chapter 5:
# Self-Presentation and Wish Lists
# in Printed Personals

1. Raymond Shapiro, *Lonely in Baltimore* (New York: Random House, 1983), Preface.

2. Kenneth J. Gergen, *The Saturated Self: Dilemmas of Identity in Contemporary Life* (New York: Basic Books, 1991), 178, 155.

3. *Historical Statistics of the United States: Millennial Edition, Population* (New York: Cambridge University Press, 2006).

4. Coontz, *Marriage*, 276; Rebecca L. Davis, *More Perfect Unions: The American Search for Marital Bliss* (Cambridge, Mass.: Harvard University Press, 2010), 256.

5. Janet Morahan-Martin and Phyllis Schumacher, "Loneliness and the Social Uses of the Internet," *Computers and Human Behavior*, 10 (2002), 668.

6. Sherry Turkle, *Life on the Screen: Identity in the Age of Internet* (New York: Simon & Schuster, 1995), 192, 228.

7. Geoff Dench in Dench, ed., *Rewriting the Sexual Contract* (New Brunswick N.J.: Transaction, 1999), ix.

8. Quoted in John Tierney, "Hitting It Off, Thanks to Algorithms of Love," *New York Times*, Science Section, January 29, 2008. The psychologist quoted was Eli Finkel of Northwestern University.

9. Shapiro, *Lonely*, preface.

10. Gergen, *Saturated Self*, 62, 177.

11. There is a specific if partial explanation of this—at least as far as the *New York Review of Books* is concerned, as will be shown below.

12. Whyte, *Dating, Mating and Marriage*, 12–13.

13. See also my "Counter Culture of the Heart," *Society*, January-February 2004, reprinted in *The Only Super Power*, 2009.

14. "Liberal Liasions," *The Nation*, January 25, 2010.

15. Joseph Epstein thus characterized the *Review*: "For years the *New York Review* remained academia's house organ, the spiritual home of people who pretended they were all out for the powerless without ever for a moment able to envision themselves outside that utopia where good taste and intelligence, intellectual and social power combine. It was the journal of those happy few . . . left-leaning, right-living intellectuals, happily safe atop a cloud of nearly celestial snobbery." *Snobbery: The American Version* (Boston: Houghton Mifflin, 2002), 152.

16. The preceding data and others to follow were kindly provided by Raymond Shapiro, business manager of the *Review* for several decades.

17. According to an article discussing the personals in the *Review*, "as many as three-quarters of the advertisers are women . . . many . . . in their 50s or above." Catherine Keenan, "Love in the Personals," *Sidney Morning Herald*, January 3, 2004. My own reading of these ads supports this estimate.

18. This of course applies to all similar communications, printed as well as electronic.

19. Personals, *New York Review of Books*, April 17, 2008, 86.

20. I grew up in Hungary and have remained fluent in Hungarian, which allows me to read Hungarian publications.

21. Gergen, *Saturated Self*, 111–112, 146.

22. Quoted in Keenan, *Sidney Morning Herald*. "Personals Work! is the name of her ad-writing company, founded in 1992. The majority of her clients are women 35 and up . . . [the] average fee [is] $400–450," which includes consultation with the client and writing the ad. *Woman's Own* website, accessed November 27, 2008. For further confirmation of the ghostwriting by Susan Fox, see Peter Carlson, "Harvard Personals Just Can't Be Matched," *Washington Post*, July 2, 2008; also Ann Harding, "Susan Fox Helps Client to Meet Mr. or Ms. Right," *Boston Globe*, November 26, 2008.

23. David Shaw, "'Rene Russo' Wants Real Harvard Man," *Los Angeles Times*, August 3, 2003.

24. *Yale Alumni Magazine*, July/August 2008, 75.

25. Ibid., September/October 2008, 75.

26. Many social scientists and other intellectuals would disagree because they associate the concept with stereotyping. For an informative examination of the concept, see Alex Inkeles and Daniel Levinson, *National Character: A Psychological Perspective* (New Brunswick, N.J.: Transaction, 1997).

27. Introduction in Rose, *"They Call Me Naughty Lola"*, 2, 7.

28. Ibid., 32, 43, 19, 21, 33, 37, 75, 76, 83, 123, 129, 149.

29. Ibid., 9.

30. All advertisements referred to or quoted appeared in the March 5, 2009, issue of the *Advocate*.

# Chapter 6:
# Looking for Love on
# the Internet: Massachusetts

1. Janet Morahan-Martin and Phyllis Schumacher, "Loneliness and the Social Uses of the Internet," *Computers in Human Behavior*, 10, 662.

2. Gunter J. Hitsch et al., "What Makes You Click: An Empirical Analysis of Online Dating," *Choice Symposium*, Northwestern University, 2004, 30.

3. Monica T. Whitty et al., eds., *Online Matchmaking* (New York: Palgrave Macmillan, 2007), 1.

4. *New York Times*, "Style" section, November 24, 2002; see also *Pew/Internet and American Life Project Report*, Washington D.C., March 5, 2006, ii.

5. Hitsch et al., "What Makes You Click," 2.

6. Fisher, *Why We Love*, 217.

7. Coontz, *Marriage*, 285.

8. Morahan-Martin and Schumacher, "Loneliness," 659.

9. Jessica M. Sauter, Rebecca M. Tippett, and S. Philip Morgan, "The Social Demography of Internet Dating in the United States," paper presented at the Southern Sociological Society meeting, March 25, 2006, 5.

10. Researchers found that "involvement (commitment and seriousness) tended to be lower in cyberspace, whereas misrepresentations tended to be higher." Whitty, et al., *Online Matchmaking*, 24. Two other studies estimated that 18 percent and 48 percent of subscribers to different dating sites were married without disclosing it. Ibid., 83. Yet another study found that 46 percent of women "were more likely to misrepresent their looks . . . by using a photo a few years out of date." Only 6.7 percent of men engaged in this kind of misrepresentation. Ibid., 62.

11. Ibid., 90.

12. Morahan-Martin and Schumacher, "Loneliness," 662.

13. Joe Schwartz, *The Complete Idiot's Guide to Online Dating and Relating* (Indianapolis: Que, 2000), 1.

14. See also Sauter et al., "Social Demography."

15. *Dating Site Advisor* website, accessed December 10, 2008.

16. *Pew/Internet Report*, iii, 7, 11, 6, 9, 10, 12. Other studies found that 8 percent of men and 5 percent of women reported marrying someone they met online. Whitty et al., *Online Matchmaking*, 81.

17. Hitsch et al., "What Makes You Click," 2–10, 20–27, 30.

18. See Tierney, "Hitting It Off." Likewise, Rebecca L. Davis observes, "The science of marital happiness grew to be a major American industry (and remains so to this day with websites like Match.com)." *More Perfect Unions*, 131.

19. Rachel Lehman-Haupt, "Is the Right Chemistry a Click Nearer?" *New York Times*, February 12, 2006.

20. Schwartz, *Online Dating*, 58.

21. The reality of regional cultural difference was confirmed in the longitudinal study of Buss et al., "Mate Preferences," esp. 500.

22. It is a mystery why many correspondents felt compelled to include their favorite color under "favorite things." Did they think that preference for a certain color is relevant for compatibility?

23. Linda Marx, "Vows: Christina Matthews, Benjamin Macfarland III," *New York Times*, April 19, 2009.

24. Whitty et al., *Online Matchmaking*, 44.

25. "Spiritual but not religious" has also been the choice of many celebrities: "Most stars turn their backs on orthodox beliefs and cobble together their own . . . theology, a spiritual Esperanto so unspecific and inclusive that it offends no one." Daniel Harris, "Celebrity Spirituality," *Salmagundi*, Fall-Winter 2008–2009, 103.

# Chapter 8:
# Looking for Love on
# the Internet: California

1. George F. Kennan, *Sketches from a Life* (New York: Pantheon, 1989), 49–50.

2. Recent economic difficulties raise questions about the future of these attitudes and preoccupations since they are closely related to what used to be high levels of affluence.

3. According to 2006–2008 estimates, a total of 17.2 million were not born in the state. This figure includes both persons born abroad and those born elsewhere in the United States. See http://factfindercensus.gov.

4. I have been somewhat puzzled about the supposed attractions of being sarcastic. Perhaps the word is being used in some idiosyncratic way.

5. Stephanie Rosenbloom, "Dating: What's the Big Idea?" *New York Times*, July 4, 2010.

6. Quoted in Daniel J. Boorstin, *The Americans: The National Experience* (New York: Random House, 1965), 330.

7. Alexis de Tocqueville, *Democracy in America* (New York: Vintage, 1957), II, 232–233.

8. At a micro level a similar phenomenon may be observed in movie theaters when, as is often the case, people in the audience respond with (nervous) laughter to something horrible unfolding on the screen.

9. "Results from Our Singles Survey," *AARP Magazine*, November–December 2003.

10. Lori Gottlieb, *Marry Him: The Case for Settling for Mr. Good Enough* (New York: Dutton, 2010), 242.

11. See also Whitty et al., *Online Matchmaking*, 44.

12. Frank Furedi, *Therapy Culture: Cultivating Vulnerability in an Uncertain Age* (New York: Routledge, 2004), 141, 19, 144, 1.

13. Wallerstein and Blakeslee, *The Good Marriage*, 329.

14. David M. Buss and Michael Barnes, "Preferences in Human Mate Selection," *Journal of Personality and Social Psychology*, 50:3 (1986), 562.

15. According to the 2005 Pew study, "roughly half of the singles who had tried online dating had actually gone on a date as a result, and only about one-third of those formed a long-term relationship." Quoted in Gottlieb, *Marry Him*, 117.

16. Nicola Dohring, "Studying Online-Love and Cyber Romance," in B. Batinic et al., eds., *Online Social Sciences* (Seattle, 2002), 5.

17. Aaron Ben-Ze'ev, *Love Online: Emotions on the Internet* (Cambridge: Cambridge University Press, 2004), 247–248.

18. Zygmunt Bauman, *Liquid Love: On the Frailty of Human Bonds* (Cambridge: Polity Press, 2003), x, xiii, 62, 7.

19. Ben-Ze'ev, *Love Online*, 4–6, 86–94.

20. Ibid., 21, 18.

21. Gottlieb, *Marry Him*, 114.

# Chapter 9:
# Conclusion: The Entitlement to Happiness

1. David Hume, *A Treatise on Human Nature* (Oxford: Clarendon, 1896), Book III, Part II, Section II, 484.

2. Elizabeth Gilbert, *Committed: A Skeptic Makes Peace with Marriage* (New York: Viking, 2010), 78–79.

3. Andrew Delbanco, *The Real American Dream: Meditation on Hope* (Cambridge, Mass.: Harvard University Press, 1999), 94, 23.

4. Darrin M. McMahon, *Happiness: A History* (New York: Atlantic Monthly Press, 2006), 290.

5. Delbanco, *American Dream*, 5–6.

6. Miller, *Intimate Terrorism*, 60, 80.

7. Delbanco, *American Dream*, 104.

8. On the celebrity cult, see Daniel Boorstin, *The Image* (New York: Harper & Row, 1961); also Paul Hollander, "Our Society and Its Celebrities" and "Watching

Celebrities," in *The Only Super Power*; and Hollander, "Michael Jackson, the Celebrity Cult and Popular Culture," in *Society*, March–April 2010.

9. Miller, *Intimate Terrorism*, 108.

10. Giddens, *Transformation of Intimacy*, 45.

11. Kipnis, *Against Love*, 61, 72.

12. Person, *Dreams of Love*, 14–15.

13. Ibid., 85, 83, 125.

14. Harville Hendrix, *Getting the Love You Want: A Guide for Couples* (New York: H. Holt, 1988), 66–67.

15. Ibid., 115.

16. Deirdre Bair, "The 40-year Itch," *International Herald Tribune*, June 5–6, 2010.

17. Ibid.

18. "Correspondence," *New York Times*, June 12, 2010.

19. There's also an older, more traditional view of happiness and how not to acquire it: the idea that "shortcuts to happiness are sinful, that happiness is not worth anything unless you have worked for it." Louis Menand, "Head Case," *New Yorker*, March 1, 2010, 74.

20. Sheehy, *Sex and the Seasoned Woman*, 289, 51, 58.

21. David Crary, "Carnal Satisfaction Ebbs for 45-plus Set," *Boston Globe*, May 7, 2010.

22. Gottlieb, *Marry Him*.

23. Ibid., 51, 133, 280, 275, 131, 277, 91.

24. Cherlin, *Marriage Go-Round*, 139.

25. Coontz, *Marriage*, 258, 202.

26. Barbara Ehrenreich, *Bright-sided: How the Relentless Promotion of Positive Thinking Has Undermined America* (New York: Macmillan, 2009), 54, 46, 51, 56.

27. Cited in ibid., 90.

28. Ibid., 205.

29. Elizabeth Long, *The American Dream and the Popular Novel* (Boston: Routledge, 1985), 191–192.

30. Thomas Dumm, *Loneliness as a Way of Life* (Cambridge, Mass.: Harvard University Press, 2008), ix, 21.

31. Miller McPherson et al., "Social Isolation in America: Changes in Core Discussion Networks Over Two Decades," *American Sociological Review*, June 2006.

32. Boorstin, *The Image*, 4.

33. Emile Durkheim, *Suicide* (Glencoe, Ill.: Free Press, 1951), 252–253.

34. Attempts to modernize in an authoritarian political framework, as in the former Communist states, did not lead to a great opening up of individual choices, nor did these experiments endure. Present-day China represents a new and far more successful attempt to modernize under an authoritarian political system that *is* more permissive and therefore likely to experience the emergence of problems related to personal choice and fulfillment, similar to those found in modern Western societies.

35. Gilbert, *Committed*, 45–46.

36. Cherlin, *Marriage Go-Round*, 184, 186.

# Appendix 1

The following questions are similar to those found on dating websites such as match.com (discussed in chapters 6–8). Copyright issues prevent the actual match.com questionnaire from being reproduced here, but these questions and/or options mirror those that were used by match.com.

# Basic information

The following questions will help you find your matches; the more information you give, the better matches we can provide.

**Why are you on this site?**

No answer

**What is your current relationship status?**

Single

**What is your gender?**

Male

**Who are you seeking?**

Women

**How should we search?**

Search within 50 miles

**Where did you grow up?**

USA

**What is your astrological sign?**

Gemini

**What is your height?**

6 feet 3 inches

**What is your eye color?**

Blue

**What is your body type?**

Athletic

**What is your hair color?**

Brown

**What type of sports/exercise do you like?**

- ☐ Baseball
- ☐ Basketball
- ☐ Cycling
- ☐ Football
- ☐ Dancing
- ☐ Hockey
- ☐ Dancing
- ☐ Running
- ☐ Skiing
- ☐ Yoga
- ☐ Other

**What do you like to do during your spare time?**
Share a few of your favorite pastimes.

**What are some of your favorite places?**
These can be travel destinations, restaurants, etc.

**Interests - your ideal match**
What would you enjoy doing with your dates?

- ☐ Exploring new ares
- ☐ Book clubs
- ☐ Dining out
- ☐ Museums

- ☐ Movies
- ☐ Nightclubs
- ☐ Political interests
- ☐ Playing sports
- ☐ Shopping
- ☐ Traveling
- ☐ Volunteering

**What are some of your favorite movies, TV shows, and foods?**
Feel free to add other favorites!

**What was the last book you read?**
You can also include magazines, newspapers, etc.

**How often do you exercise?**

2 - 3 times a week ⬍

**Do you drink?**

Yes, but only socially ⬍

**What is your current job?**

Entertainment/Arts ⬍

**Do you have children?**

No, but I would consider having them. ▲▼

**What is your current income?**

I'd prefer not to say. ▲▼

**How do you feel about pets?**

|  | I have. | I don't have, but like | I don't like. |
|---|---|---|---|
| Cats | ○ | ○ | ○ |
| Dogs | ○ | ○ | ○ |
| Other | ○ | ○ | ○ |

**What is your ethnicity?**

Asian ▲▼

**What is your faith?**

Christian/Catholic ▲▼

**What languages do you speak?**

☐ English
☐ French
☐ German
☐ Japanese
☐ Italian
☐ Russian
☐ Spanish
☐ Other

**What is the highest level of education you have completed?**

Bachelor's degree ▲▼

**What are your political views?**

Choose from this list ▲▼

**Do you have any siblings?**

I'm an only child.

**I would most likely donate to charities that**

help people.

**Which comedian would make you laugh the most?**

Tina Fey

**If you received a big bonus, what would you do with the money?**

Go on a trip.

**Your match- height preference?**
Now we'll begin questions asking about your ideal match.

5 feet 4 inches

**Your match- hair color preference?**

No preference

**Your match - body type preference?**

Slender

**Your match - ethnicity?**

No preference

**Your match - religious views?**

No preference.

**Your match - highest level of education completed?**

Bachelor's degree

**Your match - languages spoken?**

☐ English

☐ French

- [ ] German
- [ ] Japanese
- [ ] Italian
- [ ] Russian
- [ ] Spanish
- [ ] Other

**Your match - current job?**
[ No preference ▲▼ ]

**Your match - salary range?**
[ No preference ▲▼ ]

**Your match - smoking habit?**
[ No preference ▲▼ ]

**Your match - drinking habit?**
[ No preference ▲▼ ]

**Your match - wants kids?**
[ No preference ▲▼ ]

**Your match - has kids?**
[ No preference ▲▼ ]

**Now describe yourself and who you are seeking.**
This will appear on your public profile page.

**Your profile tag line**

This will appear on the top of your profile page and search results.

Submit

# Appendix 2

The sampling was in part determined by match.com. Using criteria of gender, age and location, the website generated five hundred questionnaires for Massachusetts, California, and Alabama and an average of four hundred for Nebraska. To make matters simpler and more manageable, random samples of eighty questionnaires (or 16 percent of these totals) were selected, tabulated, and coded. The sample size in Nebraska averaged approximately three hundred for each category (female, male, younger and older age groups). The same percentage was applied to create a random sample from these lower numbers.

# Index

"comfortable with himself," 114, 143

commercials, 43, 58–59, 86, 115, 131, 184, 217n62

Communist Hungary, 111

comparisons, 30, 57, 130, *151, 156, 166,* 188–89, *190,* 191–98

compassion, 33, 112, 129, 142, 146, 150, 182, 184–85, 188, 195

compatibility/compatible, 14–15, 33, 88, 124, 143, 166, 170, 195, 197; essential, 27, 56, 66; establishing, 139; indicators, 140; perfect, 75; search, 147; socioeconomic, 16

competitiveness/competitive, 7, 14, 20, 22–25, 45, 74, 77, 120, 122, 159, 192, 201, 210; in American society, 194; culture, 120; pressure, 115; rejecting, 148; society, 30, 59, 124, 145, 194

complementarity, 78

*The Complete Idiot's Guide to Dating* (Kuriansky), 83–86

*The Complete Idiot's Guide to Perfect Marriage* (Rich/Kravitz), 86–87

*Confessions of an Ex-Bachelor* (July), 92

connections, 5–8; nature, 33–34; spiritual, 93

conservative, 181, 183, 185, 187; California, 179, 188; culture, 199; disposition, 136; older men, 188; political attitude, 140, 149, 152, 155, 157–58, 160, 162–63, 166–67, 169, 172, 174

consumer, 23, 96, 128, 165, 193; culture, 111, 197–98; society, 16, 60, 93

consumerism, 154

consumption, 42, 44, 58–60, 200, 202, 217n62; centrality of, 24; elaborate, 180; levels, 148; patterns, 20, 114; philosophy, 25; voracious, 48

Coontz, Stephanie, 3, 11, 102, 134

cosmetic surgery, 99

*Cosmopolitan,* 99

counterculture, 105, 130; beliefs, 38, 45; California, 179; critics, 95; impulses, 141; spirituality, 148; values, 179, 207; veterans, 117

coupledom, 70, 95–97

courtship, 10, 14, 19, 70, 197; advertising/advertisements, 6; culture, 71; Internet and, 197; trial period, 9

cuddling, 132, 153–54, 184

cult of celebrity, 201

cult of cheerfulness, 208–9

cultural relativism, 83, 144

*Date Like a Man* (Moore/Gould), 90–91

dating/dates, 25, 56, 60, 83–86; bureaus, 215n35; customs, 191; dangerous sense of entitlement, 206; expert advice, 69–100; liberal online seekers, 136; manuals, 72; misrepresentation, 198; paid coach, 14–15; philosophy, 80; profile, 75; services, 13; as sport, 90. *See also* electronic personals; Internet; online dating; printed personals

Dating Site Reviews Index, 136

Davis, Rebecca, 102

Dean, James, 60

De Angelis, Barbara, 87–88

*The Deer Park* (Mailer), 60–63

Delbanco, Andrew, 200–201

determinism/deterministic, 94, 100

Dickens, Charles, 192

discretion, 127

disenchantment, 18, 202, 203

diversity, 5, 84, 110, 117

divorce, 11–12, 22, 41, 49, 58, 82, 83, 107, 109, 126, 168, 170, 174–75, 199, 206, 212; DWF, 106, 110, 112, 113, 115; DWM, 115; as failure, 203; impact of late, 203–4; as opportunity, 202–3; printed

# A Note on the Author

**Paul Hollander** is professor emeritus of sociology at the University of Massachusetts at Amherst. Born in Budapest, he left Hungary in late 1956, then studied at the London School of Economics, the University of Illinois, and Princeton University, where he received a PhD in sociology. He has been a Ford Foundation fellow, a Guggenheim Foundation fellow, and an associate of the Davis Center for Russian and Eurasian Studies at Harvard University. He lives in Northampton, Massachusetts.